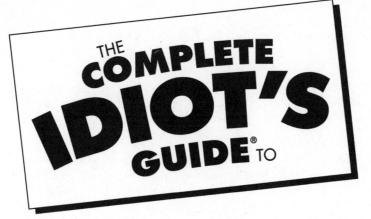

THE
COMPLETE
IDIOT'S
GUIDE® TO

# The Middle Ages

*by Timothy C. Hall, M.A.*

ALPHA

A member of Penguin Group (USA) Inc.

*I dedicate this work to my loving and inspiring wife, Debra, and my handsome son, Thomas.*

## ALPHA BOOKS

Published by the Penguin Group

Penguin Group (USA) Inc., 375 Hudson Street, New York, New York 10014, USA

Penguin Group (Canada), 90 Eglinton Avenue East, Suite 700, Toronto, Ontario M4P 2Y3, Canada (a division of Pearson Penguin Canada Inc.)

Penguin Books Ltd., 80 Strand, London WC2R 0RL, England

Penguin Ireland, 25 St. Stephen's Green, Dublin 2, Ireland (a division of Penguin Books Ltd.)

Penguin Group (Australia), 250 Camberwell Road, Camberwell, Victoria 3124, Australia (a division of Pearson Australia Group Pty. Ltd.)

Penguin Books India Pvt. Ltd., 11 Community Centre, Panchsheel Park, New Delhi—110 017, India

Penguin Group (NZ), 67 Apollo Drive, Rosedale, North Shore, Auckland 1311, New Zealand (a division of Pearson New Zealand Ltd.)

Penguin Books (South Africa) (Pty.) Ltd., 24 Sturdee Avenue, Rosebank, Johannesburg 2196, South Africa

Penguin Books Ltd., Registered Offices: 80 Strand, London WC2R 0RL, England

International Standard Book Number: 978-1-59257-831-3
Library of Congress Catalog Card Number: 2008933148

11   10   09      8   7   6   5   4   3   2   1

Interpretation of the printing code: The rightmost number of the first series of numbers is the year of the book's printing; the rightmost number of the second series of numbers is the number of the book's printing. For example, a printing code of 09-1 shows that the first printing occurred in 2009.

*Printed in the United States of America*

**Note:** This publication contains the opinions and ideas of its author. It is intended to provide helpful and informative material on the subject matter covered. It is sold with the understanding that the author and publisher are not engaged in rendering professional services in the book. If the reader requires personal assistance or advice, a competent professional should be consulted.

The author and publisher specifically disclaim any responsibility for any liability, loss, or risk, personal or otherwise, which is incurred as a consequence, directly or indirectly, of the use and application of any of the contents of this book.

Most Alpha books are available at special quantity discounts for bulk purchases for sales promotions, premiums, fund-raising, or educational use. Special books, or book excerpts, can also be created to fit specific needs.

For details, write: Special Markets, Alpha Books, 375 Hudson Street, New York, NY 10014.

**Publisher:** *Marie Butler-Knight*
**Editorial Director:** *Mike Sanders*
**Senior Managing Editor:** *Billy Fields*
**Executive Editor:** *Randy Ladenheim-Gil*
**Senior Development Editor:** *Phil Kitchel*
**Production Editor:** *Megan Douglass*
**Copy Editor:** *Nancy Wagner*

**Cartoonist:** *Shannon Wheeler*
**Cover Designer:** *Bill Thomas*
**Book Designer:** *Trina Wurst*
**Indexer:** *Tonya Heard*
**Layout:** *Brian Massey*
**Proofreader:** *John Etchison*

# Contents at a Glance

# Contents

# Introduction

People associate the Middle Ages with a period of darkness in Europe. To most, the people of the Middle Ages were barbaric and uncivilized, and modern civilization seems to be far superior in comparison. This belief about the Middle Ages is *wrong*.

If you examine the Middle Ages, you will start to see some uncomfortable similarities to our "superior" modern age, including a gap between the rich and the poor, violent acts done in the name of God, gangs of barbarians threatening the peace, poverty and migration created by war, questions over the authority of church and state, people looking for riches in the wrong places, and diseases without cures. Maybe after you read this book, you will realize that the modern world is not so different.

This history of the Middle Ages begins with the breakup of the Roman Empire and ends at the dawn of the Renaissance. It studies the political, economic, social, and cultural development of the three successor cultures of Rome—Byzantine, Islamic, and Germanic—with an emphasis on the latter. Among the topics to be covered in this book will be: the end of Rome, the rise of Christianity, the era of Germanic migrations, the Germanic West, the Catholic Church in the West, the Carolingian Empire, the ninth-century invasions, feudalism and manorialism, the Byzantine Empire, the rise of Islam, the Crusades, the development of medieval kingdoms and nation-states, class structure in the Middle Ages, the Renaissance of the high Middle Ages, the Mongol invasions, and the beginnings of the Reformation. This book also surveys the impact of these topics on the modern world.

The study of the Middle Ages includes several reoccurring themes:

- The causes and effects of the migration of people
- The creation and expansion of kingdoms and nations
- The development of religion and culture
- The conflict and cooperation between church and state
- The people and their response to the environment
- The growth of trade and commerce

So with the themes in focus, I wrote without placing as much emphasis on every historical detail. Instead I have tried to paint the historical picture with broad-sweeping thematic strokes. If you are interested in the fine details, use the further readings found in Appendix C to select an appropriate volume to find out more.

# How This Book Is Organized

**Part 1, "The Early Middle Ages (550–1000),"** starts with the fall of the Roman Empire and the development of Western civilization from its rubble in Europe. But this development is not immediate. Several factors make it unique. As the Roman Empire reaches its peak, it is converted into a Christian empire. It is the Christian Roman Empire that rules over Europe, Asia, and Africa. Later, as that empire declines and collapses, it leaves three cultures behind that influence the events of the European Middle Ages. These cultures are the Byzantine, Islamic, and Germanic cultures.

Europe, once free of the Roman Empire, is overrun by the primitive and disorganized Germanic tribes. But the institutions of the Christian religion of the Roman Empire continue during this time and become the glue that holds Europe together. After a short period of stability during the reign of Charlemagne, Germanic tribes of Europe are transformed in kingdoms as they create new political and economic systems based on both Germanic and Roman structures.

**Part 2, "The High Middle Ages (1000–1300),"** begins with Europe seeing improvements from darker days of the early Middle Ages. There was a new optimism in Europe. In politics, the kingdoms of Europe were becoming more effective. Part of this was because the threat of invasions from the Vikings, Magyars, and Muslims was declining. In addition, the climate of the continent got warmer. A warmer climate coupled with new inventions allowed the manors of Europe to produce surplus crops. With the surplus, population and economic activity increased. With more people and trades, the older cities of Europe expanded and new cities appeared. Also with economic prosperity came an intellectual and cultural flowering. The church developed Christian theology more in depth than it had since the time of late antiquity and the early church. Universities like Oxford and the University of Paris were founded to educate a new professional and intellectual class made of nobles and a new middle class. From these universities came new ideas of self-awareness, reason, and logic.

**Part 3, "The Late Middle Ages (1300–1500),"** begins with the beginning of a decline in Europe caused by several events. In politics, two wars distracted the major kingdoms of Europe from nation building, the Hundred Years' War between the England and France, followed by the English Civil War, called the War of the Roses, which diverted resources from England's nation building. In the early Middle Ages, the church pitched in when kingdoms faltered but this time the church had its own set of problems. Religiosity grew oppressive as people sought stability in daily life. Controversy also surrounded the popes with the Babylonian Captivity and the Great Schism. These controversies brought up questions about the spiritual and earthly authority of the church. Things went from bad to worse with the Great Famine and the Black Death. The Great Famine weakened the constitution of the population and the Black Death finished them off. Between the two events over a third of the population of Europe was wiped out. People started to look to a "glorious" past, that of Rome and Greece, for relief and inspiration. As a result, the Renaissance or "rebirth" started in Italy and spread to northern Europe. This event ushered in the modern age of Europe.

## Extras

 **Age-Makers**

These sidebars will inform you of key historians and their work relating to the Middle Ages.

**Middle Age Myths**

These sidebars will dispel misconceptions perpetuated about the Middle Ages today.

**def•i•ni•tion**

These sidebars will give you definitions of terms that will make you medieval smart.

 **Notable Quote**

These sidebars will give you an interesting or important quote from the Middle Ages that is related to the topic in which you are reading.

**Illuminations**

This feature will inform you of really interesting facts and key points relating the Middle Ages to the present and also making you a hit at most any party.

## Acknowledgments

This volume would not have been possible without the help of some important people in my life. First, I would like to thank my beautiful wife, Debra; wonderful son, Thomas; and supportive family for their understanding and patience with the long hours I put in on this text.

Other thanks go to Jackie Sach for getting me this work. Thanks to the faculty and staff at Franklin Academy for their support, especially my colleagues Mrs. Wyman and Mrs. Nation-Gaddy, who put up with my odd musings and rants patiently. Finally, thanks to Dr. Michael Enright of East Carolina University, whose words of encouragement, example, and resources kept me focused.

## Trademarks

# Part 1

# The Early Middle Ages (550–1000)

This section begins with the end of the Roman Empire and the emergence of a new civilization in Europe. But that change was not as abrupt as many think. Christianity transformed the Roman Empire; then Roman authority over Europe, Asia, and Africa gradually declined and collapsed, leaving three unique cultures to influence the events of the European Middle Ages.

Free from Roman imperial control, Europe was overcome with invasions and political and economic turmoil that left the region underpopulated and in ruins. But the institutions of the Roman Empire and Christian religion continued during this period and became the glue that held Europe together. After a short period of stability followed by another wave of invasions, Europeans developed new political and economic systems based on local control. By the end of Part 1, we see the maturing of a new civilization in Europe, distinct from the Roman Empire, but still its child.

# The Roman World

## In This Chapter

- ◆ The beginning of the Roman Empire
- ◆ *Pax Romana:* Roman Peace
- ◆ Roman state religion
- ◆ Jesus and Christianity
- ◆ The beginning of Rome's decline

The Roman Empire began on the Italian peninsula, which most people recognize from its bootlike shape. The location of this boot, which extends into the Mediterranean Sea in southern Europe, gives the peninsula a very mild and sometimes damp climate that, coincidentally, is great for farming. Of course, the peninsula's nutrient-rich soil doesn't hurt, either. The peninsula is also protected by some natural barriers, which prevented migrations and invasions. Finally, the Italian Peninsula juts out into the center of the Mediterranean Sea, which makes it a central point for sea trade in the Mediterranean Sea basin. All these geographic advantages combined to make the Italian peninsula an excellent foundation for an empire.

The Roman Empire was one of the largest the world had seen. It occupied and dominated the Mediterranean Sea basin and straddled three different continents: Europe, Africa, and Asia. It also extended northward into Europe, deep into present-day France, Germany, and England, ruling these territories by a combination of strong armies, efficient administration, loyal conquered elites, and the Latin language. Later, as the Roman Empire declined, three unique cultures—Barbarian, Byzantine, and Islamic—filled the power vacuum that was left, each having a dramatic impact on the course of the European Middle Ages.

# The End of the Roman Republic

The end of the Roman Republic began with revenge and ended with an emperor. Octavian, grandnephew and adopted son of Julius Caesar (r. 49–44 B.C.E.), wanted revenge for the murder of his granduncle, so he formed the Second Triumvirate with Marc Anthony and Lepidus to exact revenge on Caesar's enemies. Once they accomplished this, these three men divided the large Roman Republic into three parts.

Of course, that didn't last long. Octavian wanted more power and worked to that end, reaching his goal of total control of the republic/empire in 31 B.C.E., with the defeat of Marc Anthony in Egypt. Octavian took the name Augustus Caesar, by which most people remember him, and ruled the Roman Empire from 27 B.C.E. to 14 C.E.

During his reign, Augustus systemically took power away from the Senate and became the sole lawmaker and law executor, ending the representative government of the old Roman Republic. Although most would consider the end of representative government a tragedy for Rome, it did provide stability for an expanded empire to which the republican form of government was unsuited. In fact, this stability began a 200-year period of peace in Roman history called the *Pax Romana* or Roman Peace.

However, the new Roman Empire that Augustus established couldn't be all roses. The first four emperors who ruled from 14 to 68 C.E., called the Julian emperors because they were all related to Julius Caesar, brought some interesting episodes of intrigue.

Tiberius Caesar was paranoid of treachery within his administration (one could hardly blame him, considering the recent events!) and accused innocent people of treason. The emperor Caligula was mentally disturbed, and it showed. (He wanted to raise his horse to a position as consul; the only thing that prevented it was his assassination.) Claudius was old and could not focus on affairs of the state. And, finally, Nero was cruel and also mentally disturbed. It was rumored that in order to have a palace built in a populated section of Rome, Nero set fire to it and "while Rome burned, Nero fiddled."

# The Good Emperors

After Nero, the Senate put things back on track and in 96 C.E. began to elect emperors. What followed were the aptly named "Five Good Emperors." Nerva, the first, ruled with justice and temperance. Trajan, who followed Nerva, increased the empire to its greatest size. Then Hadrian strengthened the empire's frontier defenses with fortresses and walls, one of which, found in northern England, is named Hadrian's Wall after him. Next, Antoninus Pius maintained a steady hand on the rudder of prosperity that the empire produced. And finally, Marcus Aurelius, Stoic philosopher, maintained order and stability, bringing even more wealth to the empire.

> **Illuminations**
>
> Marcus Aurelius was not only an emperor but also a learned and prolific writer who advanced the philosophy of stoicism, which taught that duty and reason should have precedence over emotions. Heavily influenced by stoicism, Aurelius wrote a series of emperor's maxims in *Mediations,* thoughtful and useful ideas about political life still used by rulers today. The *Star Trek* character Mr. Spock brought stoic beliefs to American television audiences. Live long and prosper!

# Pax Romana

The early Roman Empire and *Pax Romana* saw several significant improvements in Roman rule. First, the emperors learned to choose their provincial governors very carefully, which kept the provinces under control. They also ended the office of *Pontifex Maximus* and became chief priests of the Roman state religion themselves. In fact, starting with Augustus, emperors were considered divine gods on Earth and as such, worthy of worship. These rulers also made conquered peoples citizens of Rome, with the same rights and privileges, which spread loyalty in the provinces. Conquered peoples were even allowed into the Roman legions.

The Roman Empire enjoyed unprecedented prosperity and wealth, most of which came from trade, including imports and exports from England to China. This prosperity allowed the Roman people to have over 130 holidays in which to enjoy festivals, races at the Circus Maximus, or gladiatorial contests at the Coliseum.

Roman architecture produced many impressive projects, such as the Pantheon, finished in 128. In addition, the Romans built one of the first major roadways—the Appian Way—portions of which still survive to this day in several locations around

Rome. Interestingly enough, in the province of Velletri just outside of Rome, a part of the Appian Way is actually being used for transport.

Roman education advanced as well. The Romans did borrow a great deal of knowledge from the conquered Greeks, but unlike the Greeks, who generally focused on theory, the Romans looked to the practical. For example, they systemized the theories of the Greek physician Galen, which formed the basis of Roman medical science. And Roman astronomy was based on the perfected work of the Egyptian astronomer Ptolemy. With Latin as the standard and official language of the Roman Empire, literature improved. *The Aeneid*, written by the Roman poet Virgil, compares to Homer's *Iliad* in beauty, style, form, and epic dimensions. Other Romans wrote accurate (by the day's standards) histories of Rome—most notably Livy and Tacitus.

> **Notable Quote**
>
> The study of history is the best medicine for a sick mind; for in history you have a record of the infinite variety of human experience plainly set out for all to see; and in that record you can find yourself.
>
> —*History of Rome,* Livy

# Roman Religion and Christianity

During the *Pax Romana*, a new religion was established that would eventually conquer the empire, following the roads and trading networks established and protected with Roman legions. This new religious force, Christianity, changed the face of Rome and Western civilization.

## Roman State Religion

The Roman state religion focused on the worship of the empire and the Roman pantheon of various gods and goddesses. Romans believed that observation of rituals made them right with the gods and that it was a Roman citizen's duty to perform the appropriate rituals to ensure the peace and tranquility of the empire. That fact did not make Romans intolerant of other religions, and other religions from Persia, Greece, and Africa flooded Rome after the conquests of the empire. To be accepted by the Romans, people of those religions needed only to perform the prescribed rituals at the appropriate times. Belief in the Roman rituals was not a requirement.

# The Setting for Early Christianity

One group of people inhabiting conquered territories of the Roman Empire had very different religious beliefs from the Romans. The Hebrews, or Jewish people of the Middle Eastern region of Palestine, believed that there was only one god, Yahweh, and he had made a covenant with the Jewish people. Unlike the other peoples of the Middle East or the Roman Empire, the Jewish people held firmly to their monotheism.

The Jews' religious beliefs were closely tied to their history. Palestine was conquered several times by different powers that rose and fell in the Middle East, including the Babylonians, who destroyed Jerusalem and enslaved many Jews in Babylon. Later, in 536 B.C.E., Cyrus, the Persian emperor, allowed the Jews who had been taken to Babylon in captivity to return to Jerusalem. The Jews rebuilt their temple to God in Jerusalem and set up their own kingdom, which enjoyed some independence from their Persian overlord.

By the fourth century B.C.E., Alexander the Great had conquered Palestine. After his death, it was ruled by the Greek Ptolemies and later by the Syrian Seleucid kings, both successors of Alexander's empire. During this time Hellenistic culture was a great influence on the Jews. Many started to use the Greek language rather than their own language, Hebrew. As a result, in 200 B.C.E., Jewish scholars translated their holy writings into Greek. This work, known as the *Septuagint*, was completed by over 70 Hebrew scholars.

During the second century B.C.E., the Seleucid king Antiochus IV (175–163 B.C.E.) tried to force-convert the Jewish people to accept the many other forms of Hellenistic worship. He stopped the observance of their Sabbath and practice of the rite of circumcision. In addition, he took the wealth of the Temple of Jerusalem and set up an alternative statue of Jupiter in the inner sanctum. Of course, the Jewish people were outraged by this infringement of their religious belief.

In 168 B.C.E., the Jews revolted against the Syrians. Judas Maccabeus was the leader of this revolt, which succeeded in driving the Syrians out of Jerusalem by 165 B.C.E. The Jews purified the temple and rededicated it to God. This event is still celebrated by Jews each December as the Feast of Dedication, or Hanukkah.

In 161 B.C.E., Judas was killed, but his brothers continued to struggle for the freedom of the Hebrew kingdom. Eventually they were able to establish an independent kingdom that lasted until the Romans under Ptolemy the Great conquered it in 63 B.C.E.

# Rival Jewish Sects

During the second and first centuries B.C.E., the Jewish people were divided into several political and religious factions or sects. All believed in the one God, but they differed over how to interpret God's law and religious practice. The four main sects were the Sadducees, Pharisees, Essenes, and Zealots.

The Sadducees were a wealthy and well-educated group. Most were priests, landowners, and merchants. As a result of their powerful standing in Jewish society, they controlled the Sanhedrin, the Jewish religious council that dealt with the violations of criminal, civil, and religious law. Despite this, the Sadducees had little real influence with the common people. While they believed that the Torah, the Jewish scripture, was the only source of authority for the Jewish people, they still took on Hellenistic culture and compromised with the Roman occupiers of Palestine.

The Pharisees were middle-class Jews who were very scholarly and followed very closely the rituals of worship and living that set the Jewish culture apart from Hellenistic culture. They wanted to live in accordance with God's law set forth in the Torah and tradition. Pharisees believed that if they devoted themselves to the study of the Torah and observed its laws, they would obtain life after death.

The Essenes were an especially pious group who devoted themselves to the study of scripture, prayer, and fasting to help them prepare for the end of the world, which to them was imminent. They looked for a Messiah or anointed one to be sent by God to save the Jewish people.

Little was known about the Essenes until 1947, when a shepherd boy was searching for a lost goat and saw a small cave opening in a hill near the Dead Sea. Scared to explore alone, the shepherd left the site to find a friend. Together, they climbed into the opening and found several clay jars containing scrolls. At first, the scholars who looked at the Dead Sea Scrolls thought that they were worthless. But in 1951, archaeologists explored the region and discovered the foundations of a building that they believed to be an Essene monastery. In addition, they found fragments of other scrolls dating from the third century B.C.E.

Some of the scrolls referred to a Teacher of Righteousness whom the Essenes honored, but no one has been able to identify this figure. Scholars do think that the Essene group may have had over 4,000 members by the time of Jesus' birth. The Essenes were known as Followers of the Way. They lived under strict discipline laid out in a manual. The Essenes also believed that a prophet would come to help them defeat the Romans and start a new age for the Hebrew kingdom. Finally, they loved

Jewish law and observed Hebrew rites and traditions, including one sacred meal that served just bread and wine.

The influence of the Essenes on early Christianity is open to debate. Some scholars have suggested that John the Baptist and early followers of Jesus were members of the Essenes.

The last group of Jews was known as the Zealots, or people of action. They were mainly a splinter group of the Pharisees who interpreted several prophetic writings of a Messiah as a great military leader. This leader would restore the Jews' political power and independence that they had under King David. Due to the success of the Maccabean revolt of 168 B.C.E., the Zealots organized into local groups that met in northern Palestine planning the overthrow of Roman rule. Later, when Jesus emerged, they became interested in his ability to inspire and motivate the Jewish people, but Jesus rebuked the Zealots and their political stance, after which they discounted him.

# King of the Jews

Under Roman rule, the Jewish people of Israel were given some freedoms, including a degree of religious freedom and self-rule. By 6 B.C.E., the Romans revoked that self-rule and sent a Roman procurator to rule the nation of Israel. This action caused widespread unrest, and the four groups reacted in very different ways. The Sadducees and Pharisees favored cooperation with the Romans; the Essenes preferred to wait on a Messiah or savior to save them from Rome; and the Zealots thought, "Why wait?" They wanted a violent overthrow of Roman rule.

During this period of Roman rule and unrest, Jesus of Nazareth was born. Although we can find little of Jesus in the historical record, his disciples provided many details of his life and teachings in the four gospels that make up the first four books of the New Testament of the Bible.

**Notable Quote**

"Render therefore to Caesar the things that are Caesar's, and to God the things that are God's."

—Matthew 22:21 RSV

## The Gospels

Historians, religious scholars, and theologians have relied on the New Testament of the Bible to find out about the life of Jesus. The first four books of the New Testament provide the most information. They are Matthew, Mark, Luke, and John, and are thought to have been written shortly after the death of Jesus by several of his disciples or followers. These books are often called the Gospels or good news. They include many of the teachings of Jesus but are themselves the subject of debate, because no one actually recorded what Jesus said while he was alive. In addition, the original manuscripts to the Gospels have been lost and the reports of the disciples often contradict each other. The first three books, Matthew, Mark, and Luke, are known as the synoptic gospels, because their information is similar. The other gospel, John, says little about the life of Jesus but details many of his teachings.

Regardless of this lack of historical sources, historians have determined the outline of Jesus' life. So we begin in 4 B.C.E., when, according to most modern scholarship, Jesus was born. The name Jesus is the Greek version of the Hebrew name *Joshua*. Jesus was born Jewish and was educated in the ways of traditional Jewish culture. While some Jewish people would accept his teachings, most rejected them because they differed greatly from the orthodox Jewish norm. The few who did accept his teachings found their lives so different that they spent their lives saying to the Hellenistic world of the Roman Empire that they had seen the Messiah.

## The Life of Jesus

When Jesus was born, Palestine was ruled by Herod, a Roman-backed ruler. Herod adopted the Jewish traditional practices, married the daughter of the last Maccabean king, and helped to fund the Temple. Still, he was not popular with the Jewish leaders and people. One reason was that Herod promoted Hellenistic culture and was seen as a Roman puppet. At the time of Jesus' birth, he ordered the slaughter of thousands of Jewish infant boys. This has been connected by the Gospels to Herod hearing rumors that a Messiah had been born.

The Gospels give scholars little information about Jesus' early childhood except that his family was from Nazareth in Galilee and he was accepted into the Jewish faith at the age of 12 in the Temple of Jerusalem. All of the Gospels pick up the life of Jesus at the age of about 30 years when he appears at the Jordan River to be baptized by his cousin, a preacher named John the Baptist.

## John the Baptist

John the Baptist was a man who preached against sin and introduced the rite of baptism to the Judeo-Christian tradition as an act of purification. This has led some to think that John was a member of the Essenes. People from across Palestine came to hear

John preach repentance. Many believed his radical view and submitted to baptism by immersion in the Jordan River. This was an act that symbolically washed away sin. As the result of his success with the people, Herod had John the Baptist arrested and executed by beheading.

## The Teachings of Jesus

According to the Gospels, after Jesus was baptized by John the Baptist, he had a vision in which the Holy Spirit spoke to him and as a result, he began to preach. Jesus traveled through Palestine teaching and healing the people who came to him. When in public, he attracted crowds of people.

Jesus preached a simple message. First, because all people are children of God, they should help each other. Also, people should love God, repent of their sins, and accept God's forgiveness. Lastly, people should forgive others and care for the poor. A central point of the message of Jesus was the idea that a new age was at hand, the kingdom of heaven. That kingdom would be brought to the world through a Messiah, the son of God. Jesus' exact meaning on this point has been debated. Some have questioned whether Jesus saw himself as the Messiah.

The popularity of Jesus and his teachings made him very unpopular with the various Jewish sects. To add insult to injury, Jesus also hung around unscrupulous types, including Gentiles (non-Jews), tax collectors, and prostitutes. The Sadducees disliked him because his teachings on the Messiah and the new kingdom would disrupt the status quo with Rome. Additionally, they resented his criticism of the operation of the Temple. Jesus said it was a "robber's cave." The Pharisees hated Jesus because he taught that God was more concerned with love than Jewish law.

## The Death of Jesus

When Jesus started his preaching, he picked 12 men known as the apostles to help him. The Gospels relate how Jesus and his apostles traveled to Jerusalem to observe the Passover. This was a celebration that commemorated the deliverance of the Jewish people from slavery in Egypt. When Jesus arrived, he was welcomed by the crowds of people as king or Messiah. The Jewish authorities grew scared that this outcry might be interpreted by the Romans as a sign of revolt. They arrested Jesus and turned him over to the Roman authorities. Pontius Pilate, the Roman procurator of the region, ordered Jesus to be put to death by crucifixion, a traditional Roman form of execution. The date of Jesus' death has been placed around 30 C.E. by historians.

Although Jesus' story is compelling, it doesn't seem to be extraordinary. But his teachings will become a religion that will change the Roman Empire and Europe.

# The Spread of Christianity

The death of Jesus did not stop his teachings from spreading; many of his followers believed he rose from the dead and was their Messiah, the Savior of Israel. Inspired by this belief, now called Christianity, Jesus' followers spread his teachings across the Mediterranean rim along Roman roads and trade routes.

Two leaders emerged during this early Christian movement to facilitate its takeover of the hearts and minds of the Roman Empire: Simon Peter or Peter, who became the first bishop of Rome, and Paul of Tarsus.

## Peter

After the death of Jesus, Peter, one of the original 12, became the first leader of the Christians. At first, the Christians continued to worship as Jews in synagogues and the Temple. They also continued to follow Jewish custom. Under the leadership of Peter, they often met in private homes to pray, read scriptures, and discuss the life of Jesus. Also, Christians began to share a simple meal, introduced by Jesus the night before his arrest, when he gave his followers bread and wine, saying that they were his body and blood.

Peter did not want to confine the teachings of Jesus to only Jews, and at the Council of Jerusalem he helped to enact the decision to preach to Gentiles. Peter, recognized by contemporaries as the leading apostle, founded a Christian church in Rome with him as its first bishop. Sadly, the message of the early Christian church was not accepted by Roman authorities, and Peter was put to death in Rome around 64 C.E. during the reign of Emperor Nero.

## Paul

Another key figure of the Christian movement was Paul of Tarsus. Tarsus was a Greek city-state in the region of Asia Minor. His original Hebrew name was Saul. He was a smart man who was educated as a rabbi and Pharisee. As such, Saul hated the Christians and even approved of the stoning of Stephen, the first known Christian martyr. Saul never actually met or even saw Jesus but while he was traveling along the road to Damascus, Saul was confronted by a vision of Jesus. The experience so moved

Saul that he changed his name to Paul and dedicated his life to preaching the message of Jesus throughout the Roman Empire.

Shortly after his conversion, Paul went to Antioch, which was the capital of the Roman province of Syria. From there, he tirelessly preached the teachings of Jesus to Jews and Gentiles. He then traveled from Antioch carrying the words of Jesus throughout the Roman Empire including the city of Rome itself. As Paul moved, he established small groups that accepted the Christian teachings. The groups met in the home of one of their members to pray and share in the meal that commemorated Jesus' last supper. These groups eventually formed churches. By creating these churches along the trade routes of the Roman Empire, Paul built the foundations for the Christian church in Europe.

## The Letters of Paul

Because Paul was on the move and the Christian groups were very diverse, questions came up about Christian beliefs and worship. To answer these questions, Paul wrote letters or epistles that interpreted the teachings of Jesus and resolved disputes. These letters became the basis for several of the books of the New Testament.

A question that kept coming up was how to deal with the Gentiles who wanted to be Christians. Did they need to accept Judaism first? Paul met with Peter and Jesus' other disciples at the Council of Jerusalem to resolve this issue. Like Peter, he urged them to allow Gentiles to be brought into the Christian faith without adopting Judaism. This policy opened up many converts to the Christian movement.

In 58 C.E., Paul traveled to Jerusalem, where he was quickly arrested by the Romans as a rabble-rouser. As a Roman citizen, Paul had the right to appeal his case to the emperor. He used this right and was transported to Rome. Like Peter, Paul had carried the gospel around the Mediterranean world and to Rome, where he was arrested and executed probably at the same time as Peter.

Despite the persecutions, the new religion spread underground. The Romans viewed Christianity as a threat to the state religion, mostly because Christians refused to perform the Roman state religious rituals. Because the Romans mistrusted this new religion, they persecuted early Christians who often suffered death by crucifixion or sport—throwing Christians to the lions in the Coliseum was once a favorite Roman pastime. These persecutions reached their peak under the emperors Nero and Diocletian. But the Christian church grew despite this violent opposition. In fact, it

## def•i•ni•tion

Martyrs are people who are willing to suffer and die for their religion or cause. During the Middle Ages, dying as a martyr virtually assured sainthood in the Church.

has been said that the Christian church grew because it was watered by the blood of Christian *martyrs*. Why was Christianity so popular? It gave some Romans meaning and purpose in their lives. In addition, Christianity fulfilled the need to belong, which was sometimes hard to find in the vastness and the cosmopolitan nature of the empire. And finally, the teachings of Jesus were attractive to the poor and powerless.

## The Early Church

The early Christians expected Jesus to reappear within a few years after his death and resurrection. But this did not happen and the number of Christians continued to expand. So some realized that there was a need to set down their beliefs and establish an organized church. In the first century, the earliest writings of the New Testament were collected, which included the four Gospels and the letters of Paul. Later, other books were added to and accepted as part of the New Testament.

At first, the Christians met together in small groups in private homes. There really was little distinction in rank among the members. Some groups were even led by women (of which Paul disapproved). Groups followed ceremonies similar to those in the synagogues, including readings from the scriptures, prayers, and the singing of psalms. Eventually, Christians added two rites to these ceremonies. They were baptism for new converts and the ceremony of eating the bread and drinking the wine to commemorate the last supper of Jesus with his apostles.

As Christianity grew, many beliefs and practices were questioned. To address these questions, Christians developed a standard hierarchy. A community of Christians included a bishop, a board of elders, priests, and deacons. The bishop was the highest authority on questions of faith and practice. He also helped priests and deacons administrate the religious business of the church. By the end of the first century, these church leaders became known as the clergy, who were different from the laity, or members of the congregation of the church.

By the second century, the government of the church closely paralleled the Roman administration. Each priest led a parish. A bishop oversaw a diocese or region containing several parishes. Each city usually had its own bishop and a number of priests. Several dioceses were combined to create a province, which was governed by an archbishop.

At first, the bishops of Rome, Constantinople, Antioch, and Alexandria had a measure of equal status. Later, the bishop of Rome assumed the title of pope and claimed supremacy over the rest. This assumption was sometimes disputed, and as a result the other bishops were given a title, albeit of a little lesser status, called patriarchs. With the hierarchy, there were struggles for power and jurisdiction that plagued the early Christian church.

# Roman Decline

By the fourth century, a majority of the empire had converted to Christianity. This was very apparent in 313, when pagan Emperor Constantine issued the Edict of Milan, granting official tolerance for the religion. Constantine himself later converted to Christianity. Once given official tolerance, the Christian religion became an unstoppable force in the empire, and in 395 Emperor Theodosius the Great adopted Christianity as its official religion, putting an end to the pagan traditions that had endured for 800 years. Some historians have pointed to this historical moment, the Roman conversion to Christianity, as the beginning of the decline of the empire.

Two emperors, Diocletian and Constantine, tried to stop this decline. Diocletian, who ruled the empire from 285 to 305, quite a long time in comparison to the previous 22 emperors, made his rule more efficient by dividing the empire into four administrative units. He also worked on economic reforms to fight the inflation of prices, including using price and wage freezes. His successor, Emperor Constantine, enjoyed a long rule as well. He consolidated his rule over the empire, constructed a new capital city in the east, named Constantinople, after himself, and was able to make both economic and military reforms to help slow the empire's decline. But neither Diocletian nor Constantine was able to do more than slow the decline. Their administrative reforms were only a quick and temporary patch.

## Middle Age Myths

Most religious historians of the past believed that Christianity swept the Roman Empire in mass conversions in cities and the country. In reality, current research indicates that the spread of Christianity was very slow and generational. Women in urban centers converted first, then raised Christian kids who carried on the Christian tradition.

In reality, the decline of the Roman Empire can never be attributed to one factor, as many possible factors influenced the decline, which began around 180. Between 235 and 284 there was a great deal of political upheaval, as evidenced by the 22 emperors who ruled during that period. Also, after the third century, Germanic tribes, which had remained outside the borders of the empire, pushed for entry inside Roman territory. The Germanic problem caused taxes to be raised higher and higher to fund and equip a large army to protect the borders. Also, trade and small industry declined. The empire's well of wealth started to run dry.

## The Least You Need to Know

♦ With expansion into Europe, Asia, and Africa, an empire ruled by an emperor replaced the Roman Republic.

♦ The followers of Jesus of Nazareth founded the Christian religion during the period of *Pax Romana*.

♦ Christianity spread throughout the Roman Empire and became its official religion in 395.

♦ The Roman Empire fell into political and cultural decline during the fifth century.

# The Barbarian World

## In This Chapter

Outside the boundaries of the Roman world were lions, tigers, bears—and, more importantly, *barbarians.* Although the Romans originally saw them as uncivilized, these barbarians eventually became part of the Roman world, adding their own twist as they helped continue the Roman legacy into the modern world.

## The Celtic World

During the period of the Roman Republic and early empire, a group of people known today as the Celts populated Europe. They had migrated to Europe during the Bronze Age, and by the second millennium B.C.E.

**def•i•ni•tion**

The term **barbarian** simply meant foreigner to the Greeks and the Romans. A barbarian was someone who did not speak Greek or Latin but gibberish sounding like "ba-ba-ba"; hence the name.

inhabited most of Europe. The name "Celt" is vague, but if language is culture, then their Celtic language made them distinct from the Germanic and Slavic tribes that also populated portions of Europe at the time. The Celts had exceptional talents in music, poetry, metalwork, and cloth making, which was not always appreciated. The Romans were amused that the Celts wore pants called breeches (a Celtic word) instead of tunics.

The Celts were not a very organized people. They lived as farmers in small villages surrounded by cultivated fields, although some of the more adventurous traded across Europe with the Romans and others. Their low-key culture lent itself to the creation of hundreds of independent tribes spread all over Europe. These tribes occasionally fought each other, but the wars were short and localized. No single ruler truly tried to unite them all into an empire to rival the Romans.

So the Romans took advantage of the Celts' inability to unite and pushed into Europe during the last century B.C.E. and first century C.E. Eventually they conquered most of the Celtic people or pushed them beyond the fringes of the empire into modern-day Ireland, Scotland, and Wales. The Roman Empire's European borders were soon firmly established at the Rhine and Danube rivers.

Roman culture transformed the Celtic culture as their villages turned into provincial estates. Celtic landholders became part of the Roman aristocracy through intermarriage, producing a Gallo-Roman aristocracy in France and England. But descendents of free Celtic farmers who did not own land became serfs or slaves to the new Gallo-Roman aristocracy. Then, just as everything got settled in this Gallo-Roman world, a new world came crashing in.

# The Germanic Barbarians

During the first century, a new group of barbarians from the region of central Europe called Germania, began to confront the Roman world, although they had met briefly in the days of the Roman Republic. These Germanic tribes saw the Roman territory across the Rhine and Danube rivers as the place to be. Because the empire had roads, a warmer climate, indoor toilets, and hot baths, the tribes continually sought to gain a foothold in the Roman world.

Most of what we know about the early Germanic tribes comes from the Roman historian Tacitus, who wrote a descriptive volume on these peoples titled *Germania* around 98 C.E. His true intent was to criticize the Roman people for their shortcomings by comparing them to the simple, noble virtues of the Germanic people, so he sought to idealize them. For this reason, we need to view most of *Germania* with a critical eye, but several things Tacitus described were on the mark. First, the Germanic people tended to be tall, blue-eyed people with blonde or reddish hair. They worshipped many different Germanic gods, who bore a close resemblance to the Roman gods.

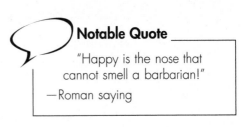

**Notable Quote**

"Happy is the nose that cannot smell a barbarian!"

—Roman saying

In addition, Tacitus detailed their belief in the king or *rex* as a descendent of the gods who was sacred, as was his blood. Sounds good to be a king, right? Wrong! Sometimes if the lands did not prove to be fertile, they believed the king's blood would help. So killing the king and ceremonially spilling his sacred blood was sort of a pastime. The idea of the sacredness of the king was sometimes aided by the creation of myths that incorporated the king's divine origins. These myths also helped develop the idea of ethnic origins.

**Notable Quote**

"If they get not rain, they blame me; if they get not sunshine, they do likewise. If hard times befall them—whether hunger, or pestilence, or whatever it may be—I always have to take the blame for it. It is as if they do not realize that I am a human being, and no god."

—Gustav I Vasa, founder of the Swedish royal house of Vasa (1523–1660)

# The Start of Bigger Tribes

Like the Celts, hundreds of Germanic tribes formed around successful war leaders and kings. As these tribes warred and mythologized from Tacitus' time to the third century, they coalesced into several different tribal kingdoms, including the Franks, Vandals, Angles, Saxons, Jutes, Ostrogoths, Visigoths, and the Goths. A *rex* still led these kingdoms but, due to his sacred nature, did not fight in battle. The war leader, or *dux*, sometimes became powerful enough to split from the tribal kingdom and become a *rex* of his own tribe, then had to create his own mythic origins for his kingship and tribe. So the tribal kingdoms became larger but also occasionally splintered. This made instability the rule and the tracking of tribes a chore for any historian.

## The Three Germanic Components

The social and political organization of the Germanic tribal kingdom rested on three key cultural components: kinship, the *comitatus*, and tradition. Kinship in the Germanic tribes was traced through both parents, creating large and elaborate kinship networks. The importance of kin was the protection it provided. If someone wronged or physically harmed a member of a Germanic kinship network, everyone banded together to take out retribution on the offender. The offender's kin then responded in kind, and the cycle of violence snowballed out of control in the classic pattern of human aggression. Of course this type of activity was very destructive, so most of the tribes created a *wergild*, a system of payment, instead of vengeance. The size of the wergild depended largely on the victim's age, sex, and social status.

The *comitatus* or warband was also part of the tribal political organization. This *comitatus* was a group of warriors bound together by loyalty and an oath of allegiance to a war leader or warlord. In this brotherhood, the warriors treasured honor, fidelity, and courage as the highest virtues.

Using tradition or custom, the third key component, each tribe tried to maintain the peace. This was enforced by the general agreement of the tribe and as such was only applicable to those within a specific tribe. So each tribe had its own traditions and also its own law codes. But in general, most barbarian law codes mainly tried to limit violence within the tribe. It sought to provide peaceful resolutions to disagreements that might otherwise end in bloodshed and death. Of course, intertribal disputes were another issue because not all tribal law codes coincided.

## Oath-Helpers and the Ordeal

Two unique concepts developed in Germanic tribal law appear to us especially backward and barbaric. The first was the use of *compurgation*. In this, judgment of a disputed case was determined by the number of "oath-helpers" who were willing to swear on behalf of the parties involved. If a party didn't have enough oath-helpers, or there was perjury by any of the oath-helpers, guilt was easily and quickly determined.

The second method used to determine guilt was the use of the ordeal, which worked as follows: the accused party or parties was handed a red-hot iron or stone from a boiling cauldron. Of course, this would severely burn the accused. If the burn healed quickly and properly, then the accused was innocent because the gods clearly favored him. If the party was guilty, the wound would not heal properly.

> **def•i•ni•tion**
>
> **Compurgation** is the proof of innocence provided by oath-swearing.

Of course, this sounds like nonsense from our perspective, but within the Germanic tribes these actions built community consensus and reunited a tribe torn by dispute.

# Roman Accommodations

The first four centuries of contact between the Roman and Germanic worlds were remarkably peaceful and accommodating. The Romans engaged in trade with the Germanic tribes across the border and recruited many Germanic warriors into the Roman legions as special auxiliary units. So by the mid-fourth century, most of the Germanic tribes appreciated and enjoyed the Roman Empire and had no real desire to plunder and destroy it. But in the end they did just that.

## The Coming of the Huns

Trouble began in 370. The Huns, a nomadic people from the steppes of Asia who excelled as mounted warriors, migrated into eastern Europe, pushing the Germanic tribes off their established lands and westward into the borders of the empire. The Visigoths were the first Germanic tribe that sought permission to settle in lands within the protective Roman borders. They appealed to the eastern Emperor Valens (r. 364–378), who let them enter in 376. But by 378, the Visigoths were causing all sorts of trouble. Emperor Valens led an army to teach them a lesson but was soundly defeated and killed at the Battle of Adrianople. Emperor Theodosius (r. 378–395), who succeeded Valens, quickly pacified the Visigoths by giving them lands in the Balkans.

Theodosius' response was the beginning of the pattern established during the late fourth and early fifth centuries between the Romans and Germanic tribes. The Huns or another Germanic tribe from the north or east would put pressure on a certain tribe. The Romans would allow the tribe to immigrate into the Roman Empire. Then some type of conflict would occur between the Romans and Germans, resulting in eventual accommodation and settlement.

### Age-Makers

Saint Augustine of Hippo (354–430) was a bishop of Hippo in North Africa and a father of the church who exercised enormous influence over Western theology, philosophy, and history. In his most important book, *The City of God*, he responded to the sack of Rome, which some blamed on the Christians' soft religion, by stating that the virtues of the pagan past can only be fulfilled through Christ. Augustine also noted that history is not cyclical but has a beginning and an end through God: *I am the Alpha and Omega; beginning and end.*

## Retreat!

But the Visigoths were not completely satisfied with their situation in the Balkans, so by the early 400s their king, Alaric, started massing an army for an assault on the Italian peninsula and Rome itself. The Roman emperor Constantine III recalled all the Roman legions from the Rhine and Britain, but that didn't help, and in 410 the Visigoths sacked Rome and established a kingdom in former Roman territories in Gaul and Iberia.

As soon as the other Germanic tribes saw Rome's defenses down, they migrated across the Rhine River and took over. Without the Roman legions, Britain was soon overrun by the Angles, Saxons, and Jutes. The Vandals destroyed and pillaged down through Gaul, Iberia, and into Africa in the 420s and 430s. (We get the term vandalism from their destructive actions.) By 430, they conquered the city of Hippo, home of the great Christian thinker, Saint Augustine, who died as they besieged the city.

### Middle Age Myths

The legend of King Arthur came from the period when the Angles, Saxons, and Jutes were invading Britain. Ambrosius Aurelianus, a British chieftain, resisted the advances of the Germanic tribes until his final defeat at the Battle of Mount Badon. Later, medieval historians and writers including Geoffry of Monmouth and Chrétien de Troyes picked up on this valiant struggle and expanded on the story, which took on a life of its own and became the Arthurian tradition.

## Attila, the Scourge of God

The Huns, who started the Germanic migrations into the Roman Empire, were not far behind. Led by Attila (r. 433–453), they had conquered most of central Europe and gained tribute payments from the Eastern Roman Empire. In 450, when the much stronger eastern empire refused payment, Attila decided to take it out on the western half. Luckily, a combined Roman and Visigoth army defeated Attila in 451.

But Attila was not to be stopped that easily. Shortly thereafter, he invaded the Italian peninsula again and succeeded in gaining all the territory up to the city of Rome. Fearful of Attila and the Huns, the Roman emperor at the time fled the poorly defended city, leaving Pope Leo I to deal with the invaders. According to some, Pope Leo I walked out to meet Attila and discuss the terms of Rome's possible surrender flanked by Saints Peter and Paul. Considering they'd been dead for over 400 years, Attila was suitably impressed and turned his troops around.

The story is great, but, truth be told, Attila and the Huns were probably not strong enough to conquer, much less hold, the city of Rome and would have turned around regardless. After Attila's death in 453, a majority of the Huns were absorbed into the different Germanic and Slavic populations of central Europe.

# The Church During the Decline

The Christian church continued to grow as the Roman Empire declined. But as discussed before, Jesus did not establish an organization to carry on his teachings, nor did he write his teachings down. As long as the apostles lived, they could tell people about Jesus and his message. After some time, questions arose that Jesus did not address directly. As a result, the church was created and evolved. The clergy of the new Christian church were in charge of conducting services, administering the church, and clarifying questions of Christian doctrine.

The early leaders of the church were faced with many different controversies. They tried to resolve these controversies by meeting in councils to establish an orthodoxy, or right opinion. If Christians ignored the decisions of the church councils, they were guilty of heresy. The punishment for heresy was excommunication, or being cut off from the church. It was during the second and third centuries that most of the church controversies sprang up. They involved issues such as the nature of Jesus, the role of the church, and the means by which to obtain salvation. Two heresies, in particular, were a thorn in the side of the church: Gnosticism and Arianism.

## Gnosticism

Gnostics were dualists. They believed that the world was made up of two forces, good and evil, that are constantly at war with each other. Gnostics also taught that the physical world was evil while only the world of the spirit was good. They thought that the

God of the Old Testament was evil because he had created the physical world. Jesus, on the other hand, was a messenger sent by the good, all-knowing God to reveal to the people the knowledge of good and evil.

But Gnostics denied that Jesus was fully human when he walked the earth. Instead, they emphasized the mystical and miraculous nature of Jesus. All of these Gnostic beliefs were a threat to the church. They denied the humanity of Jesus and favored a mystical faith closer to Hellenistic mystery religions than Christianity.

## Arianism

Another major controversy for the church came from the teachings of a priest named Arius (256–336) of Alexandria. His teachings focused on the nature of Jesus. Arius thought and taught that God existed before Jesus. So Jesus could not have been eternal or equal to God. As a result of Arius' teachings, other church leaders led by Athanasius, the bishop of Alexandria, taught that Jesus was the true God and the same substance with God. The Arian controversy spread quickly over the Christian Roman Empire. Clergy and laity both debated various points in the controversy. Finally in 325, Emperor Constantine called a council of bishops to meet at Nicea in Asia Minor to settle the issue. The Council of Nicea, as it was called, declared Arius and his teachings heretical and composed the Nicene Creed as a statement of the church's orthodox belief.

After the council, Emperor Constantine ordered that the writings of Arius be burned and Arius sent into exile. But that did not end Arianism. Arian missionaries had traveled to the Germanic tribes living north of the Danube River converting the Visigoths. They spread Arianism to the Ostrogoths and the Vandals, who brought it to Western Europe.

## The Bishop of Rome and the Authority

During the early centuries of the church, the bishops of the larger provinces met in councils, like the Council of Nicea, to decide issues of heresy and faith. Later, in addition to the councils, the church adopted the concept of apostolic succession. This concept was based on the belief that Jesus had directed his apostles to carry his teachings throughout the world and his apostles passed this authority on to the bishops of the church. Since the chief apostle Peter went to Rome to be martyred, the bishops of Rome believed that Jesus had chosen Rome as a special site of his church. With that status, the bishop and Church of Rome claimed authority over the other clergy of the church.

Also to help in the fight against heresy, the church established an authoritative body of Christian literature. Over time, church leaders and scholars examined the writings about Jesus and the early church, deciding which were accurate testimonies of the faith. As a result, 27 accepted writings were combined into the New Testament, while the Jewish writings of the Torah and Septuagint were placed in the Old Testament. Both the Old and New Testament became the Christian Bible that was undisputed for the course of the Middle Ages.

## The Church Fathers

During the fourth and fifth centuries, several key individuals helped to shape church doctrine and orthodoxy. These men, including Saint Ambrose, Saint Jerome, and Saint Augustine, became known as the church fathers. They worked to develop a universal or catholic set of beliefs and doctrines for the emerging church.

Ambrose (339–397) was one of the most influential spiritual leaders of the Roman Empire during his time. Born in Gaul, he was raised in a Catholic family (the Arian heresy was competing with the Catholic Church in Gaul) and received a traditional classical education that included Greek and Latin in order to prepare him for a legal career. He also learned about the principles of the church under the well-known priest Simplicianus. Around 370, he became a provincial governor residing in Milan. Ambrose did not intend to enter the church but when he went to oversee the election of a new bishop, the people proclaimed the popular governor Ambrose as bishop.

As bishop of Milan from 373 to 397, Ambrose protected the church against Roman civil authorities and saw that rulers were following Christian moral law. His most famous display as moral authority took place when he ordered the Eastern Roman Emperor Theodosius to do public penance in Milan for ordering a massacre of Christians in one of the Greek city-states. Later, after the emperor died, Ambrose preached his funeral sermon praising him for seeking to unite the Eastern and Western Roman Empires.

It was Ambrose's preaching that made him stand out. His preaching helped to convert Saint Augustine and many other powerful Romans. As such, he demonstrated the power of the church's influence in politics and society for centuries to come.

Jerome (342–420 C.E.) was one of the most controversial and colorful of the church fathers. He was also one of early Christianity's greatest scholars. Born in the Balkan Peninsula, Jerome went to Rome to become a student of classical learning. It was in Rome that he was baptized in the church and pursued an ascetic life. But even after his baptism, Jerome favored the pagan philosophers and writers of antiquity. Eventually his passion for pagan philosophy got him into trouble. According to Jerome, God came to him in a dream and said "you are a Ciceronian, not a Christian." After Jerome woke up, he pursued Christian philosophy and writings exclusively.

Jerome eventually left Rome to become a hermit in the Syrian Desert for five years. In the hot desert, he learned Hebrew. Later in 379 C.E., Jerome was ordained a priest in Antioch and attended the First Council of Constantinople, which was deciding on doctrinal issues of the early church. He then went back to Rome with Pope Damasus I. The pope, impressed with Jerome's scholarship, commissioned him to translate a new Bible from the original language of Hebrew and Greek to Latin. This project took Jerome 15 years to complete. The result of his labor was the Latin Vulgate Bible, which was to be the authorized Bible of the church for over a thousand years.

In addition to his work on the Bible, Jerome was the spiritual director for some of the wealthier women of Rome, including the widow of a Roman senator, named Paula. But controversy surrounded his work with the group, so he returned to the Middle East in 386, settling in the town of Bethlehem. Paula came with him and they remained life-long platonic friends. This friendship was criticized by many of Jerome's critics who suspected improprieties between the two, although the rumors were untrue. So in the town of Jesus' birth, he spent the last 30 years of his life studying and writing. To this day, his cell in which he lived is preserved in the Church of the Nativity in Bethlehem.

During his years in Bethlehem, Jerome completed the Bible translation and authored biblical commentaries, essays, and letters against the various heresies of the day. He was feared by most because of his remarkable scholarship and sharp criticism. To Jerome, any enemy of the church was his enemy. So he refuted the heresies of Helvidius (who denied the virginity of Mary), Arius, and Pelagius. Through his quill the church began to develop a strong orthodox backbone.

## The City of God

One of the most important and influential of the church fathers to Europe and Western Civilization was Saint Augustine (354–430) of Hippo. He was born in North Africa to a devout Christian mother named Monica and a pagan father. Augustine followed his father's religious path and became pagan. He studied in Carthage to become a professor of rhetoric and philosophy. At Carthage, Augustine lived a wild and decadent life but eventually became interested in Manichaeism, a heresy similar to Gnosticism. Later he was offered a position to teach rhetoric in Milan. It was there that he heard the bishop Ambrose preach. Ambrose's sermons about Jesus, sin, and forgiveness moved Augustine. He was overwhelmed by sadness for his past life and discontinued his old lifestyle.

Augustine discussed his conversion experience in his autobiography titled *Confessions*. He told how he was thinking in a garden when he heard the voice of a child say, "Take up and read!" At that point, Augustine picked up a Bible and opened it up randomly to a Bible verse on accepting Jesus as your savior and protector. He decided immediately to convert. Ambrose baptized Augustine into the church and he returned to his home in North Africa. By 391, Augustine was ordained as a priest and shortly thereafter became bishop of Hippo.

With his new position as bishop of Hippo, Augustine combated heresy through his writing. But when the Visigoths sacked Rome, some Romans blamed the rise of the church in the empire. Augustine then felt it was his duty to respond in defense of the church. His response was *The City of God*.

In this long volume, he developed a Christian philosophy of history as the revelation of God's will. God had let the Romans acquire an empire but it was a temporal empire or city of man. The only city worth acquiring was the heavenly city or the city of God. Augustine also detailed some other thoughts. One was the concept of original sin. This doctrine developed by Augustine was based on the idea that sin was the result of the disobedience of Adam and Eve. All humans are sinners at birth and are destined for eternal punishment unless they repent through the grace of God. But if God is aware of all of history, then he is also aware of who will repent. In this, Augustine helped to formulate the doctrine of predestination.

## Augustine vs. Pelagius

Not every church leader was an Ambrose, Jerome, or Augustine. Pelagius, a British monk, disagreed vehemently with Augustine's concept of original sin. He thought that each human had free will in which each individual had the ability to choose between good and evil. Also Pelagius taught that God gives grace, love, and forgiveness to all that repent of their sins. Although Pelagius developed a following, Augustine wrote against his teachings and was able to suppress him as a result. Pelagius was declared a heretic by the church and sent into exile.

Augustine died in 430 with the Vandals besieging the city of Hippo. Like Hippo, the Roman Empire would fall to barbarians. But the legacy and influence of the church fathers were assured as the church filled the authoritative and administrative void that the Roman Empire left as it declined.

# The Real End of Rome

The only part that remained of the mighty Western Roman Empire was the territory of the Italian peninsula. But smaller did not mean better. Emperors sat on the Roman throne, but Germanic kings ruled. Finally in 476, the Visigoth king Odovocar (r. 476–493) put an end to the charade and deposed the last of the Western Roman emperors, a boy named Romulus Augustulus or "little Augustus" (r. 474–476). Odovocar then sent the imperial insignia and word to the Eastern Roman emperor that he wished to rule on behalf of the empire. The Eastern emperor Zeno (r. 474–491) responded by sending an army of Ostrogoths led by King Theodoric to invade the peninsula. After a prolonged war and a peace settlement, Theodoric invited Odovocar to have a drink with him. After a few drinks, Theodoric murdered Odovocar and claimed rule of the Italian peninsula for himself—not the Eastern Empire—which made him the first true medieval king of Europe.

# King Theodoric and a Brief Revival

Theodoric ruled the peninsula well and respected Roman culture and administrative expertise. He used the Romans to run the civil administration of the government while his warriors provided the sinews and muscle of the administration. Using that pairing, he was able to repair some of the old infrastructure of the peninsula. All of this improved the declining political and economic climate of the Italian peninsula, allowing for a small, short, yet very influential intellectual revival.

## Boethius

Boethius (c. 480–524) was a part of this intellectual revival, producing a series of works that created the framework for a new medieval intellectual tradition. Boethius based his teachings on seven liberal arts, divided into the *quadrivium* and *trivium*. The *quadrivium* consisted of arithmetic, geometry, astronomy, and music; the subjects of grammar, rhetoric, and logic made up the *trivium*.

To aid in the education of the liberal arts, Boethius translated many works of Plato and Aristotle, which became the fundamental texts for scholars and pupils for the next 500 years. In 524, Boethius fell out of favor with Theodoric over the issue of religion. Theodoric had accepted the tenets of Arian Christianity; Boethius did not. Theodoric had Boethius imprisoned over this little matter of religion and later had him executed.

---

While in prison, Boethius wrote one of the masterworks of the Middle Ages, *The Consolation of Philosophy*. In it, he argued that spiritual development and the search for truth is more important than worldly successes or fortunes. Boethius' arguments on the relationship between humans and the world later influenced countless others.

---

## Cassiodorus

The intellectual revival did not end with Boethius. A scholar of merit and distinction, Cassiodorus (c. 490–583) served Theodoric as a high counselor. After the king died, Cassiodorus retired to his family estate to found a monastery where he assembled an essential reading list titled *On Divine and Human Readings*, which balanced both pagan and Christian works. After assembling his list, which became essential for scholars and students for centuries, Cassiodorus encouraged the monks at the monastery to copy those texts from the list as their holy duty. Thus he preserved many of the literary works of pagan and Christian antiquity.

# The Passing of Rome

Despite the brief period of economic, political, and intellectual revival during the reign of Theodoric, there was no doubt that the Roman Empire had passed into the mists of history. Ever since, historians have asked a simple question: why did Rome fall?

We can be certain of no true cause for the fall, but several factors contributed to it. Some historians have suggested that the conversion of the empire to Christianity led the Romans to spend more time thinking about the afterlife than the here and now of the empire. In addition, the cohesive power of the Roman state religion was lost. Other historians believe that a decline in traditional Roman values associated with the simple, humble, agrarian lifestyle of the Roman Republic was the reason for the fall.

Other factors include successive plagues, which weakened the empire; slavery, which made the Romans lazy and unemployed; and even lead poisoning from their indoor plumbing. Finally, one factor has carried a lot of credence with historians: the fact that the Romans struggled to find a workable political system to control such a vast empire for an extended period.

Whether it was because of one of these factors or all of them, when the Roman Empire fell it left a void in Western Europe, but its legacy lasted.

The Romans left several different things for the Germanic tribes to use in the creation of a new European civilization, including Roman law, administrative structures, and the Latin language. Additionally the Romans left the dream of the glory of Rome, which Europeans through the ages, from Charlemagne to Napoleon to Mussolini, continued to nourish and be haunted by, making it one of the most enduring legacies of any civilization to date.

## The Least You Need to Know

♦ Beginning in the first century B.C.E., the expanding Roman Empire conquered the Celtic tribes of Europe.

♦ The Germanic tribes stayed outside the Empire's borders but were slowly Romanized by trade and military service.

♦ When the Huns invaded Eastern Europe, the Germanic tribes sought entry into the Roman Empire.

♦ The church combated controversy with the help of the church fathers, councils, and popes.

♦ The Roman Empire fell in 476, leaving Germanic kingdoms in control of Europe.

# The Byzantine and Islamic Cultures

## In This Chapter

- ◆ The origins of the Byzantine Empire
- ◆ The Byzantine emperors
- ◆ The Byzantine culture
- ◆ The Arabian peninsula
- ◆ Muhammad and the origin of Islam
- ◆ Islamic empires and culture

Two other cultures influenced the course of events during the European Middle Ages: the Byzantine and the Islamic. Although their effect was less direct than the Germanic culture's, it was no less important. Both helped preserve Greek learning and Roman traditions, and the conflict between the two cultures and with the Germanic culture served as a catalyst for Europeans throughout the Middle Ages.

# The Byzantine Empire or the Old Roman Empire

The Byzantine Empire, or Byzantium, as it is sometimes called, was the eastern half of the Roman Empire, which had been divided administratively in 395 C.E. Constantinople (modern-day Istanbul), its capital and cultural center, was built up by the Roman Emperor Constantine, who favored the site and the eastern territories of the Roman Empire. The city itself is located on the narrow Bosporus Strait overlooking the Black Sea, making it a natural crossroads for trade between Europe and Asia. Geographically located in Europe, Constantinople is only twelve miles away from the continent of Asia and the culture of the "East" across the Bosporus Strait. This unique geographic situation gives the city a unique position of almost being of two worlds, the West and the East.

Maybe this unique position enabled Byzantium to survive long after the barbarian invaders killed the last emperor of the Western Roman Empire. Or maybe it was because of the combination of Latin and Greek heritage that it took on. The emperors still spoke Latin, but the people of Byzantium spoke Greek. The emperors did look to their Western Roman past but also stressed the Greek heritage of the territories of Byzantium. Regardless of its dualistic nature—West and East, Latin and Greek—after the fall of the Roman Empire in 476, most people of the classical period considered the Byzantine Empire the New Rome. So to most, Rome did not fall but rather continued in another location.

# The Geography of an Empire

The Byzantine territory consisted of more than just the city of Constantinople and its immediate area. During various times the empire held territory in Asia Minor, North Africa, the Balkans, and Italy, including the city of Rome itself. But as Islam expanded and the Germanic barbarians consolidated power and developed kingship, the empire lost its territory in North Africa and in Italy. Although the walls of Constantinople were besieged several times, the empire retained its possessions in Asia Minor and the Balkans for most of its existence.

## The Emperors

During the Byzantine reign many different dynasties and interesting characters served as emperors. While spending much time evaluating the merits of each dynasty and subsequent emperors would be pointless in this text, we can make some generalizations about the imperial office of Byzantium.

First, there were many periods of political peace and prosperity but also many times of instability caused by issues of imperial succession. Oddly, during these periods the bureaucracy saved the day by continuing with the daily business of the empire. Some dynasties did stand out as exceptional, including the dynasties of Justin (518–610) and Heraclius (610–717), the Syrian dynasty (717–820), and the Macedonian dynasty (867–1059). Similarly, some emperors are today recognized as exceptional rulers who put their stamp on the imperial office. These emperors include Justinian the Great, Heraclius, and Leo III.

**Notable Quote**

"Justice is the constant and perpetual wish to render every one his due. The maxims of law are these: to live honestly, to hurt no one and to give every man his due."

—*Corpus Juris Civilis*

## Justinian the Great

Justinian the Great ruled during the dynasty of Justin from 527 to 565 and was sometimes called the "Emperor that never sleeps" because of the long hours he dedicated to the empire at the height of its power. Militarily, Justinian was able to defeat the Persians and secure the empire's eastern borders. In addition, he tried with some success to expand their borders to include the former territories of the Western Roman Empire, including territories in Italy, Sicily, and the city of Rome itself.

Domestically, Justinian reinitiated the Roman legal tradition by compiling the laws of the empire into the *Corpus Juris Civilis* or *The Body of Civil Law* that remained a standard legal work in Europe well into the nineteenth century. He also spent time revitalizing Constantinople, including overseeing the additions to the Hagia Sophia, a large and beautiful Christian church that became a central point of the city and inspired many people with its magnificent art and architecture. In one instance, during the tenth century a mission of pagan Russians came to the Hagia Sophia to see the Orthodox Christian religion and were so impressed that one member of the delegation reportedly said, "There God dwells among men."

**Age-Makers**

Jerome (c. 342–420) was one of the most controversial and colorful scholars of church history. He made numerous contributions to literature, but his most important by far was his translation of the Bible from Hebrew into Latin. This translation was essential to the production of the Latin Vulgate Bible, which would remain *the* Bible for the next 1,000 years.

## Heraclius and Leo III

Heraclius and Leo III were two other outstanding emperors of the empire. Heraclius ruled from 610 to 641, beginning the dynasty of Heraclius, and while he ruled, the empire took a more eastern direction. Unlike previous emperors, Heraclius spoke Greek rather than Latin. During his entire reign he was preoccupied with resisting several Islamic and Persian invasions. Although he was unable to completely stop the Islamic expansion into the Levant and Egypt, he did break Persian power and influence in Asia Minor.

Leo III or Leo the Isaurian, who ruled from 717 to 740, was the first emperor of the Syrian dynasty. Unlike his predecessor Heraclius, he was able to defeat the Islamic armies and reclaim much of the territory of the Levant. He also added more territory from Asia Minor. Interestingly, Leo III pursued a controversial *iconoclastic* policy that offended the western Christians and started the slow division in the Christian church that still exists to this day, although now for reasons other than the theology of icons. It has been speculated that Leo III, despite being a devout enemy of Islam, was heavily influenced by Islam's theology, which resulted in his policy of iconoclasm.

## def•i•ni•tion

**Iconoclasm** or iconoclastic refers to policies or people who oppose the religious use of images and advocate the destruction of such images.

# Byzantine Religion and State

Byzantine culture and religion were almost entirely inseparable, just as the empire and the Christian church were. There was no separation of church and state. Christianity, culture, and empire intertwined to produce the grandeur and ceremony that was the Byzantine Empire because the emperors led the Christian church, the empire, and the people. This authoritative stance did not make relations with the Christian church in the West and its leader, the bishop of Rome, or pope, easy. Also, despite the unifying force of church and state, the Byzantine Empire was often torn by theological controversy.

## Theological Controversy

One theological controversy that did come up in the Byzantine Empire centered on the nature of Jesus. Monophysites believed and taught that Jesus had only a single divine nature. This idea had spread to many Christians in Egypt, Syria, and parts of

Asia Minor. But this ran counter to the orthodox church teaching that said Jesus was one person with two natures: divine and human. When the church sought to fight this heresy, disputes erupted throughout the empire. As a result, Christians in Egypt renounced the authority of the patriarch of Constantinople and bishop of Rome, becoming the Coptic Church.

Another controversy came about during the eighth century over the use of icons or sacred religious images. Many saw the icons as images to be worshipped and not a representation of holy scenes and people. Some prayed directly to the icons. Church leaders and some Byzantine emperors were uncomfortable with this practice, believing that it might be idolatry or the worship of images. This was forbidden many times in the Bible but especially in the Ten Commandments.

In 725, Emperor Leo III had enough and issued an edict that forbade the worship of icons and removed all religious paintings and statues from churches and public places. Some have suggested that he was influenced by the Islamic view of icons filtering through Constantinople. Islam also rebuked the use of any religious images. The edict led to widespread riots in Constantinople and other regions of the empire. Riots turned into armed conflicts between iconoclasts or image-breakers and people who thought the reverence for icons was a justifiable form of worship. Of course, during the conflicts, churches and icons were destroyed.

Pope Gregory II (715–731) soon had to take a stand on the issue that was dividing the Byzantine Empire. He declared that icons could be used to help the people who were illiterate to understand the Christian faith but not worshipped. Iconoclasts were declared to be heretics and outside the church.

This declaration did not end the controversy, which raged on into the ninth century. Some emperors supported the use of icons while other banned them. The conflict was eventually resolved and icons were restored to the churches in the Byzantine Empire. But this controversy added to the strains between the western and eastern churches.

## Breaking Up

Other issues emerged between the eastern and western churches or Byzantine Church and Roman Catholic Church. Since the beginning of the church, leaders in the eastern and western churches had been rivals for power. In addition, during the ninth century, the popes felt neglected. The Byzantine emperors did not seem to want to help them in their struggles against the Lombards and Muslims on the Italian Peninsula. Finally, there was a fierce competition between Latin- and Greek-speaking missionaries for the hearts and minds of the Slavs of eastern Europe.

Old arguments between the eastern and western churches returned and helped to create more of a divide. One of the arguments was over the Nicene Creed, which a church council had issued in 325. The Roman Church and the Eastern Church had not agreed on the exact wording of the creed. By the eleventh century, this issue combined with the conflicting claims over the authority of the church in southern Italy led to a final divorce. In 1054, Pope Leo IX (1049–1054) sent a delegation to Constantinople to meet with the patriarch. The meeting did not go well, and the patriarch and the papal delegation excommunicated each other, starting the schism or division between the eastern and western church that has continued to the twenty-first century.

> **Notable Quote**
>
> "Great stir and bustle prevails at Constantinople in consequence of the great conflux of merchants who resort thither from all parts of the world."
>
> —*Itinerary*, Benjamin of Tudela

The church in the West was headed by the pope and used Latin in services. The church in the East was headed by the patriarch of Constantinople and used Greek in services. Later the church in the West will be called the Roman Catholic Church while the church in the East will be called the Eastern Orthodox Church.

## The Economy of Byzantium

The Byzantine Empire lasted for almost a millennium because of the strength of its economy. The base of this economy was agriculture, which the emperors continually protected by enforcing various governmental polices. Maybe learning from the decline of the Western Roman Empire, the emperors recognized the importance of an agricultural base.

In addition, because of the geographic location of the empire, commerce and trade fueled the economy. Using the well-developed Silk Road, goods from China and India poured into Constantinople before making their way into Europe. This made Byzantium, and more specifically, Constantinople, one of the richest cities and civilizations of the late antiquity. Also, silk weaving developed as an industry in the empire as early as 550, again adding fuel to the massive economy.

## Byzantine Art and Learning

Supported by the strength of the economy, the arts and learning flourished within the borders of the empire. In art, the subject of the Christian religion dominated. Despite the iconoclastic tendencies of the empire, icons and mosaics depicting Jesus, Mary, the

Apostles, and a variety of saints and martyrs were created. Intricate illuminated manuscripts of the Bible were also made.

And just as art was heavily influenced by religion, so was education and learning. The Eastern Orthodox Church provided schools for parishes to train priests and the laity. Medicine, law, philosophy, math, geometry, astronomy, grammar, and music were all taught in these schools. Of course, all the subjects were taught with a decidedly religious perspective. Higher education was also available at the University of Constantinople, founded in 850, which trained scholars and lawyers for service in the bureaucracy of the empire. Some of those scholars spent their time copying the classical writing of the Greeks and Romans for libraries.

Christianity once again dominated literary achievements as literature focused on the salvation of the soul and obedience to God's will. Hymns and poems were written in honor of Jesus Christ and his mother, Mary. Books most commonly detailed the lives of the various saints for the people's instruction. All these products of Byzantine art, architecture, and scholarship were heavily studied and imitated in Europe by the Germanic and Slavic people. Byzantine culture even influenced the culture of Islam to the east.

## The Spread of Eastern Orthodox Christianity

With the amazing amount of energy spent pursuing religious ends, it seems only fitting that the empire sought to spread the message of Christianity. During the 300s and 400s, many monasteries and religious communities were founded. Later these monasteries sent missionaries to the northern lands to convert the pagan Slavs and Germanic tribes.

The missionaries Saint Cyril and Methodius were the most successful at this type of dangerous missionary work. Around 863 Cyril developed an alphabet loosely based on the Greek alphabet to help in his conversion of pagan tribes. Later this alphabet, known as Cyrillic, formed the basis for the Russian and other Slavic languages. This missionary work and subsequent spread of Christianity is arguably the most enduring legacy of the Byzantine Empire. As it declined, the once pagan, now converted Christian Slavs carried on its traditions.

# Out of the Sands of the Arabian Peninsula

Islam rose out of the hot sands of the Arabian peninsula and, like Byzantine culture, influenced events directly and indirectly in Europe during the Middle Ages. It also held a body of Greek knowledge lost at the end of the Roman Empire.

## Arabian Peninsula and the Bedouin

The Arabian peninsula is one million square miles of scarcely populated hot plains and arid desert between the Red Sea on the west and the Persian Gulf on the east. The people who chose to live in this hostile climate, the Bedouin, were typically nomadic and herded sheep, camels, and goats from vegetated area to area. Like most nomadic cultures, the Bedouin lived in tribes of related families, and a sheikh or chief led each tribe. Their culture was simple in most respects, but eventually it developed its own written language, Arabic, and a trade network that spanned the peninsula.

## Mecca

As the commerce network developed, connecting all points of the peninsula, it became a crossroads for the trade of luxury goods between the west and the east trading settlements. As a result, Bedouin towns grew in population and strength. Mecca (sometimes spelled Makkah) was such a town, which developed quickly in the 500s C.E. because it was a commercial crossroad. It also was a place of religious pilgrimage for the Bedouins and Arabs.

The Bedouin religion during this time had grown into an eclectic mix of polytheism and *animism*, and at Mecca, a shrine had been constructed to house the mysterious stone of Kaaba and statues of other Arabic gods. As trade connections increased in Mecca, so did contacts with the monotheistic religions of Judaism and Christianity. This interreligious contact would arguably have a major influence on the Bedouin and Arabic religion.

### def•i•ni•tion

**Animism** is the conviction that life is produced by a spiritual force separate from matter. This belief sometimes includes the belief in the existence of spirits and demons which inhabit particular objects. The tradition of "knocking on wood" to avoid bad luck comes from European animist beliefs, in which knocking on wood scared the evil spirit of the tree away.

# Muhammad

Muhammad was born into this cultural background in Mecca around 570 C.E. His parents died early in his life, and his closest relative, an uncle, raised him. Muhammad was involved in the practice that made Mecca what it was: commerce. After practicing the trade for several years, he married a wealthy older widow and consequently, at the age of 25, was financially set.

But the life of luxury did not suit Muhammad. In his spare time he walked the city of Mecca and saw many problems. He worried about the greed of people and the mistreatment of the poor. His sense of concern and disillusionment drove him to spend many hours alone in the desert pondering the meaning of life and suffering. Around 610 he heard a voice in his head instructing him to recite and warn the people. Muhammad came to the conclusion that it was Allah, the Arab word for God, speaking to him. And so beginning in 613, he shared with others what Allah told him, after reassurances from a relative that he wasn't crazy.

## Muhammad's Message

In general, Muhammad's message was simple, very much like the Bedouin culture. His message was that there was only one God, Allah, and everyone was equal in his eyes so everyone should be treated equally (not a bad message, at any rate). The merchants of Mecca did not receive this message well because they perceived the economic inequalities as a natural condition. In addition, Muhammad's new religion, now called Islam, meaning "submit," was a threat to the economic livelihood of the city, a good portion of which came from the pilgrims who visited the Shrine of Kaaba. From the merchants' viewpoint, if the population of Arabia accepted Islam, the revenues received from pilgrims visiting the Shrine of Kaaba might dry up. After all, according to Muhammad, the stone was part of the pagan past. So in response, the merchants persecuted Muhammad and his first followers, called Muslims.

> **Notable Quote** ____
>
> "They stirred up against him [Muhammad] foolish men who called him a liar, insulted him, and accused him …. However, the Messenger, continued to proclaim what God ordered him to proclaim."
>
> —*The Life of Muhammad*, Ibn Ishaq

## Exile and Return

These persecutions did not stop Muhammad but inspired him to form a separate Islamic community. In 622 he left Mecca to travel to Yathrib, a nearby city that appeared to be more sympathetic to his message. His journey to this city is known as the *Hijrah* and now marks the first year of the Muslim calendar. In Yathrib, Muhammad formed an Islamic state named Medina (sometimes spelled Madinah). By 630 he returned to Mecca with an army of followers to conquer the city for Islam. When he arrived at Mecca, the city gates swung open to him, and he was accepted as the city's rightful ruler. Then very rapidly, Muhammad took his forces and his appeal to the Arabic people of the peninsula and consolidated the whole Arabian peninsula under the rule of an Islamic state.

# Islamic Teachings

During this period the practices of Islam solidified into what they are today. At the foundation of Islam is the *Quran* (sometimes spelled Koran). The story has it that the angel Gabriel revealed the content of the Quran to Muhammad over 22 years. The text was written in Arabic and, according to tradition, should only be read as such if one is to understand the truth of its revelation. In the end, that revelation became the holy book of Islam and the final authority in matters of faith and lifestyle for the Islamic people.

## The Five Pillars of Islam

The Five Pillars of Islam found in the Quran represent the core of the practices of Islam. According to the Quran, a member of the Islamic faith must practice these five pillars. The first pillar is faith, which is professed in the recited creed, "There is no God but Allah, Muhammad is His prophet." The second pillar is prayer five times daily, announced or called by the *muezzin* or reciter. The third pillar is almsgiving or *zakat* which means simply giving to the poor. The fourth pillar is the required fasting during the holy month of Ramadan. The fifth and final pillar is the undertaking of a pilgrimage to Mecca or *hajj* once during one's lifetime.

In addition to the practices found in the Quran, Islamic social teachings can be found in the *Hadith*, a collection of sayings and acts of Muhammad. Also *Sharia*, or Islamic law, is derived from both the Quran and Hadith.

## The "People of the Book" and the "Seal of the Prophets"

Another fundamental belief of Islam is that Allah sent many other prophets, including Moses, found in the Old Testament, and Jesus, found in the New Testament of the Bible, to instruct the people. Because of that belief, Muslims accept Christians and Jews as people who worship the same God, and they are sometimes referred to as

"People of the Book." However, in the Islamic view, Muhammad was the last prophet. Through him, Allah revealed the full and perfect religion; in other words, Muhammad was the "Seal of the Prophets." So although Islam establishes some kinship with the People of the Book, there is also friction because Jews and Christians have not accepted the Seal of the Prophets.

# After Muhammad

In 632, after Muhammad died, the Islamic state he forged was passed on to men called caliphs, meaning successors, who were elected for life. The first of these men was Abu Bakr, Mohammad's close friend and associate. He was followed by Umar and Uthman. These men were named "The Rightly Guided Caliphs" because of their exceptional leadership abilities and religious devotion. During their rule, the Islamic state expanded to the rest of the Middle East including North Africa, Egypt, Persia, and Levant (area of Palestine). But after the "Rightly Guided Caliphs," questions about the succession of caliphs caused a major rift in the unity of Islam.

## Division

When Uthman died in 656, a dispute over who would succeed him led to civil war between members of Muhammad's family, including Muhammad's son-in-law and wife. Finally, after several years of struggle, another leader—not related to Muhammad's family—named Muawiyah announced that he was the new caliph and established his rule of the expanded Islamic state. A majority of Muslims accepted his rule, which marked the beginning of the Umayyad Dynasty. These Muslims refer to themselves as Sunni or the "People of Tradition and Community," and today this group makes up about 80 percent of the Islamic community.

But some members of the Islamic community did not accept Muawiyah's rule because he was not related to Muhammad. This group is known as the Shiites, from Shi'at Ali or "Party of Ali," a title that references the Shiite belief that Ali was Muhammad's rightful successor.

## The Umayyad Dynasty

The Umayyad dynasty founded by Muawiyah did not retain power long, but it did spread the Islamic faith through conquest. The first major change the dynasty initiated was to move the capital from Mecca to Damascus in present-day Syria. From the strategic vantage point of Damascus, the Umayyad dynasty was able to add even more territory to the Islamic state, including all of North Africa and the Middle East. More importantly, Islamic faith spread to the continent of Europe through the conquest of Spain. Islamic forces were only stopped from entering and conquering the region of France by the Merovingian ruler Charles Martel at the Battle of Tours. The Umayyad dynasty also harassed the borders of the Byzantine Empire. Only the high and thick walls of Constantinople protected eastern Europe from falling to Islamic rule.

But the underlying political philosophy of the Umayyad dynasty spelled its defeat. Unlike the "Rightly Guided Caliphs," the dynasty's government was politically rather than religiously based, and this political orientation did not sit well with many Muslims. To some, Muhammad's original intent was to spread Islam through conversion. The Umayyads preferred to be religiously tolerant and accepting of other religions. They allowed nonconverts in conquered territories to keep their legal systems and worship as they pleased. This policy made ruling conquered territories much easier for the Umayyads, but, oddly enough, converts to Islam were actually taxed in an effort to maintain the old Islamic aristocracy. A change in rule was in the works.

## The Rise of the Abbasids

By 747, Muslims had become disenchanted with the Umayyad rule. This group, numbering 50,000, had started to settle in eastern Iran. The Abbasid family, whose ancestors had been a cousin of Muhammad, allied themselves with this group to overthrow the Umayyad dynasty in 750. From there, they moved the capital of the Islamic state to Baghdad, once the site of Babylon and a major cultural center of the old Persian Empire. This gave the Abbasid dynasty a distinctly cosmopolitan outlook. During the Abbasid reign, which lasted until 1258, and specifically during the rule of Harun al-Rashid (786–809), Islamic culture experienced its Golden Age as the empire became a truly global civilization, incorporating a variety of religions and cultures within its large borders.

# Islamic Culture

It almost goes without saying that the teachings of Islam heavily influenced the culture of both the Umayyad and Abbasid empires. But oddly, the Islamic culture retained much of its male-dominated culture despite the teachings of the Quran on the equality of women. Muslim men could have up to four wives and many slave women with which to form a harem. In addition, women were "kept," meaning they stayed at home not seen or heard. Of course, this also meant women received little education.

Muslim males, on the other hand, entered school at the age of seven. After completing their required education, some continued their studies at *madrasas,* or theological schools, where they learned to become political or religious leaders in Islamic society.

# Art

Despite the inequalities, Islamic culture did flourish in the areas of art, literature, and philosophy. Calligraphy, the art of elegant handwriting, developed in response to the need for religious decoration that did not involve human images. (The Islamic people were extreme iconoclasts whose influence could be felt in the Christian Byzantine Empire!) So, too, developed the art of arabesque, in which intricate geometric designs were created for religious decoration.

> **Notable Quote**
>
> "How beautiful is that which [Aristotle] said in this matter! We ought not to be ashamed of appreciating the truth and of acquiring it wherever it comes from, even if it comes from races distant and nations different from us."
>
> —*On First Philosophy,* Al-Kindi

# Philosophy and Literature

During the Abbasid period, in which Islamic culture reached its zenith, many libraries were created and stocked across the empire. This expansion can be compared with the spread of libraries and learning during the Greek Hellenistic period. Because of this expansion, there were advancements in the areas of philosophy and literature.

Muslim philosophers, most notably Ibn-Rushd, Ibn Sina, Al-Kindi, and Moses Maimonides, tried to combine the teaching of the Quran with those of Greek philosophy, the teachings of Aristotle in particular. Others, like Tabari, Ibn al-Athir, and Ibn Khaldun, wrote histories in which events were arranged in the order they occurred. Ibn Khaldun even went so far as to scientifically examine history by looking for cause-and-effect relationships in events. Finally, in literature, Muslim writers produced many influential works, including the *Rubaiyat* by Omar Khayyam and *A Thousand and One Arabian Nights*.

**Age-Makers** _____

Ibn Khaldun (1332–1406) was an Islamic historian/philosopher who studied the lifespan of civilizations. In his book *Muqaddimah*, or *Introduction*, he developed the concept that civilizations or dynasties had a cycle of three generations typically strong, weak, and dissolute.

## The Least You Need to Know

♦ The eastern Roman territories kept Roman imperial tradition alive as the Byzantine Empire.

♦ The Byzantine Empire was a crossroads of trade and a center of cultural diffusion between the East and the West.

♦ Byzantine scholars and culture produced classical and Christian learning which was transmitted to Europe.

♦ Muhammad and his followers, Muslims, established the beliefs and practices of the Islamic faith.

♦ At its height, the Islamic Empire encompassed all of the Middle East, North Africa, and modern-day Spain.

# Chapter 4

# The New Medieval World

## In This Chapter

- ◆ Early medieval society
- ◆ Local kings and bishops
- ◆ Franks and Visigoths
- ◆ The monastic movement
- ◆ Pope Gregory the Great

Roman rule was no more. Many lands of Europe had been abandoned. Local Germanic kings and Gallo-Roman aristocrats dominated the European political landscape. To many, this time period during the sixth and seventh centuries marked the true "Dark Ages." But this view is very limiting. The Catholic Church worked as a unifier of the old Roman and Germanic worlds to create an early medieval world that was the start of European Christendom.

## Early Medieval Society

At first three elements formed the glue that held early medieval society together: ethnicity, militarism, and marriage, all of which were the foundations of stability in Europe.

## Let's Work Together

Ethnicity, simply defined as a grouping of people of similar race, language, or culture, was one of the important components of the early medieval world, especially as a political tool. After the Roman Empire ended, Gallo-Romans and the Germanic tribes merged over several generations. As a result, the ethnic lines of the Germanic tribes blurred greatly, and the Germanic kings were forced to give their people ethnic identities to create a sense of togetherness and stability, politically and socially. So the "Franks" became "Franks" only because the king of the time identified them as such. Many in the Frankish Kingdom probably did not feel any more Frankish than before, but after several successive generations of Frankness, the ethnicity of a people called the Franks was created.

## You're in the Army Now

The Germanic tribes that inherited the Roman Empire definitely had aggressive tendencies as warfare was a way of life and culture. We can find the poster child for this culture of war in the epic poem *Beowulf*. This poem of 3,000 or so poetic lines, often dated to the eighth century, tells the story of Beowulf, who engages in three epic battles with various monsters. The ideals of kingship, loyalty, service, and kinship in the Germanic warrior culture are brought to life for all to see and imitate.

These warrior elites soon replaced the more civilized Gallo-Roman aristocratic society, but sadly, these elite warriors were generally not as noble acting as Beowulf. In fact, they were more like armed thugs who happened to be in charge of Europe. As such they were up to all sorts of devious and bloody deeds in order to maintain political control. But control they maintained, and with it stability.

## Let's Get Married

Marriage practices were the final component that helped create togetherness. Polygamy, or multiple marriages, was the standard practice, but, of course, multiple marriages were only allowed for men. Women were mostly treated as possessions, and it would be some time before they received at least some due in the medieval world.

Marriages or unions were arranged in three different ways, and a king or nobleman could have many variations of these arrangements for his multiple unions. The first was the formal marriage, which required the father of the bride to transfer authority over his daughter and daughter's property. Another was the informal marriage, which did not require any transfer of property or authority, making it more easily dissolved. Finally there was the much more informal state of concubinage, where the woman could be out of favor and kicked from the harem at the king or noble's whim. (Again, the women's rights movement is far, far off).

These cultural attributes, by today's standards, are not very fashionable. But after the Roman Empire, they served as stabilizers for medieval Europe.

# The Early Medieval Political Arena

At the end of the Roman Empire, several Germanic tribes formed kingdoms that became the foundations of the European nations; these were the Ostrogoths, Visigoths, Franks, Anglo-Saxons, and Vandals. All these kingdoms faced difficulties because there was little gold to mint, it was difficult to collect taxes, and violence was the rule of the day. Overcoming these problems required unique solutions.

## Localism and Kingship

Because the Germanic kings claimed authority but seldom had the power to wield it, personal loyalty meant everything to a king. That personal loyalty hopefully came from aristocratic families that governed the lands surrounding their estates. These families or lords provided local control over the people in the form of taxes, protection, and justice in lieu of the king. This type of local control was mostly effective for the people, but at times stressful for the king because he had to prevent his lords from gaining too much power.

In the cities, the situation was a little different because the bishops of the Catholic Church held the power. The bishop's cathedral became the headquarters of an episcopal government that helped administrate the city. As a result, the church got into the business of collecting taxes, dispensing justice, and keeping up the infrastructure.

## A Holy Relic with Your Drink?

With the decline of trade during the early medieval period, the bishops had a difficult time maintaining a balance in the treasuries, a problem they overcame with the power of the saints. The Christian saints and martyrs were believed to transmit God's power, wisdom, and love in both life and death. So the relics of the saints were something to see and touch. (One person even ground up a saint's bones and added it to his drink.)

Christians made pilgrimages to the various shrines of the saints in major churches and cathedrals scattered across Europe. The most famous pilgrimage destination was Tours, where the bones of Saint Martin of Tours (372–397) lay.

## Saint Martin of Tours

Martin of Tours was born in France, the son of a Roman soldier. Like his father, he entered the Roman imperial army, but had a change of heart and felt compelled to do charity for others. During one of these moments of charity, he believed that Christ came to him in a vision and told him to leave the military and pursue a spiritual life. As a result, he deserted the army and journeyed to northern Italy and the Balkans.

By 360, Martin had become a friend of a holy monk, Hilary of Poitiers, who with Martin's help founded the first monastery in Gaul (France). As a result of his labors, Martin was appointed bishop of Tours in 371. But even in his new position, he did not stop working to promote monasticism in Gaul. In addition, Martin was responsible for the conversion of many of the people of Gaul to Christianity. During his lifetime, he was revered for many possible miracles and was one of the few holy men who was popular without dying a martyr for the church. Later, Martin of Tours was declared to be the patron saint of France.

To view a relic like that of St. Martin of Tours, a pilgrim only needed to pay a small fee, which made the bishop of Tours a very powerful man. Additionally, pilgrims paid for lodging and food in the city of the relic. So the city's economy got a boost, and money wasn't a problem for many bishops.

## Gone

With localism dominating the political landscape, survival was difficult for some of the Germanic kings and kingdoms. From the sixth to seventh century, the Ostrogoths and Vandals disappeared, conquered by the expanding Byzantine Empire and the Lombards. Two exceptions were the Merovingian Franks and the Visigoths in Iberia.

## Merovingian Gaul

The Franks, who migrated to Gaul during the fourth and fifth centuries, were by far the largest of the Germanic tribes that migrated the least, which gave them a measure of stability. Their earliest known historic king was Childeric, who ruled during the late fifth century. His grave was discovered in the seventeenth century at Tournai. Relatively unimportant, he was the father of Clovis, who put the Franks on the map.

King Clovis (482–511) ruled the Franks with a combination of ruthlessness and compromise. Ruthlessly, he murdered any relative who might have a claim to the throne. But Clovis was not all violence. He compromised a great deal with the land-holding aristocracy and worked for unity within the aristocracy by joining Frankish and Gallo-Roman interests.

Clovis's queen, Clotilda, was a convert to Catholic Christianity, and he himself saw the need to convert to Christianity to help unify his kingdom, although stories of his wife's influence or divine providence did abound. Clovis had a choice between Catholic and Arian Christianity but chose Catholic, most likely for political reasons. The Gallo-Roman aristocracy was mostly Catholic and also more politically stable. After his conversion, Clovis nurtured the church, again more for political than spiritual reasons, and it became a unifying force for his kingdom.

Thus began the rule of the Merovingian line of the Franks, sometimes referred to as the long-haired kings. Dagobert I (r. 629–638) and several more able Merovingian rulers followed Clovis, establishing a base for the creation of the Frankish Empire.

> **Notable Quote**
>
> "Oh woe, for I travel among strangers with none of my kinfolk to help me!" Clovis did not refer to their absence out of grief, but craftily, to see if he could bring to light some new relative to kill.
>
> —*The History of the Franks,* Gregory of Tours

## Gregory of Tours

A substantial amount of information that scholars have on the early Franks comes from the quill of Gregory of Tours (539–594). Gregory was born of Gallo-Roman aristocracy and became bishop of Tours in 573. As bishop, he had a great deal of success in dealing with the Germanic Merovingian rulers of Gaul. Gregory had particular success with King Childebert I, from whom he acquired spiritual and political protection for the church. Thus he had considerable spiritual and political influence in the newly established Frankish Empire.

Besides church and state, Gregory was also a scholar and historian. He wrote all of his works in Latin in the tradition of classical

> **Age-Makers**
>
> Gregory of Tours (539–594) was a bishop of Tours and one of the most respected historians of the Middle Ages. He wrote *The History of the Franks,* an indispensable source that traces the history of the world from creation to the end of the sixth century and the rise of the Franks.

antiquity. His most famous work is the *Historia Francorum* or *History of the Franks*, the primary source of sixth-century French history to this day. It was compiled by Gregory using eyewitness accounts and firsthand documents. In it, Gregory covers history from the creation to 591, focusing on the end of the fourth century and the rise of the Franks. He also authored a number of works on the saints, including the *Lives of the Fathers* and *The Glorious Martyrs*, a study of the miracles of the New Testament. Thus Gregory of Tours is indispensible to an understanding of the Franks of the early Middle Ages.

## The Visigoths

When the Visigoths swept into the Iberian peninsula during the early sixth century, they had to overcome many challenges to create a lasting kingdom, most of which revolved around the Catholic or Arian question. The Visigoth kings were initially Arian Christian. But the Visigoths needed to retain the old Roman administration and its methods of tax assessment and collection, and that aristocracy tended to be Catholic Christian, which created a problem for the Visigoth kings.

As a result, King Reccared converted from Arian to Catholic Christianity in 587, which caused a virtual holy stampede as Visigoth nobles and priests saw the proverbial writing on the wall and converted. To remain in a Visigoth king's good favor, being a Catholic Christian appeared to be best, and in 589, that unspoken policy became official when the Council of Toledo ended Arianism in the kingdom.

But the Council of Toledo did not bring religious peace to these lands. There may have been Christian harmony, but there was Christian and Jewish discord. The Iberian peninsula's flourishing Jewish population was occasionally subjected to forced conversions instituted by the Visigoth kings as a way to unite the kingdom. Oddly, the Visigoth nobles used those times to undermine the king's power by offering political protection to Jews. Eventually the undermining of the kings worked, and during the eighth century, Muslim forces from North Africa conquered the kingdom.

# The Early Medieval Church

The church replaced the Roman Empire in the everyday lives of the people. This was done partly through the local bishops but also through the growth of monasticism and one very energetic pope.

## Got Monk?

To many Christians of the early medieval world, chaste *asceticism* described in the Bible was the perfect form of life. If one could not control himself and be chaste, marriage was the second best option. But chastity was seen as the best way of a holy life. In response to this need, communities of men and women—or monasteries—were created.

**def•i•ni•tion**

**Asceticism** is a life of extreme self-restraint and self-denial, which usually involves the denial of all human appetites, including hunger, sex, and sleep.

## Holy Hermits

Saint Anthony (250–355) was the pioneer of this monastery movement. Anthony was a very devout Christian who wanted to live a solitary, ascetic life and sought that life in the Egyptian desert. Strangely, he could not maintain his life of solitude long because other Christians flocked to his desert site in an effort to lead a religious and holy life. So Anthony responded by creating a community of hermits who lived together but did not communicate with each other.

Other holy hermits followed Anthony's ascetic ideals but in different fashions. For example, Simeon the Stylite (390–459) spent most of his life on top of a 60-foot pillar in the desert. From atop his pillar, he spouted divine favor, protection, wisdom, and advice. Rulers as well as just plain folk came from all around to hear his religious take on life.

## Monk Light

But the monasticism and asceticism of the desert was harsh, so Pachomius (287–346) and Basil the Great (330–379) brought the solitary life of the desert monks to a wider audience. They created companionship monasteries, less ascetic monasteries based on companionship, not solitude. The men in these communities shared their spiritual journey with each other as a form of encouragement. Later John Cassian (360–435) took this form of monasticism to Europe, where many people readily accepted it, including women (nuns) seeking a religious life.

By the time monasticism arrived in Ireland, the country had already been uniquely Christian since the fifth century with the help of Saint Patrick (389–461).

# Saint Patrick

Patrick was not from Ireland but a native of Britain and the son of a Roman citizen. Although raised a Christian, Patrick was not especially religious. When he was 16, he was captured by Irish pirates and sold into slavery. For six years Patrick worked as a shepherd in Ireland. During this time, he underwent a spiritual conversion. By 407, Patrick made his escape from slavery.

Patrick reached the southeastern coast of Ireland and managed to convince a sailboat captain to allow him to accompany them. Tradition has it that Patrick's path then led him to the continent of Europe where he spent time wandering. Eventually, Patrick found his way home back in Britain, a very different person than who he once was.

Patrick was absolutely convinced that God had called him to be a minister to his former oppressors, the Irish. As a result, he started the course of study to become a priest. But his course of study was very basic since he entered the priesthood so late in life. Nevertheless, he mastered the principles of the church and was very familiar with the Bible. Some historians have suggested that Patrick may have spent some time in Gaul with a famous scholar of the early Middle Ages named Germanus of Auxerre. But in general most of his training for the church occurred in Britain. Sometime after 431, Patrick was appointed to be bishop of Ireland, a position that he had wanted for some time since he thought that God wanted him to return to Ireland. He spent the rest of his life among the Irish, preaching and establishing the Christian Church there. Patrick helped to unite the Christian faith with Celtic culture. To some, he came to embody the Irish and, through his simple and conservative style, Patrick won the hearts and the minds of the people of Ireland.

Many accounts of Patrick's life are embellished with wild stories and legends, so there are many unanswered questions about his life. In general, most historians have used Patrick's spiritual book, *Confession*, and his *Letter to Coroticus* admonishing an Irish chieftain for being involved in the slave trade to piece together the details of his life. Nevertheless, he is one of the most popular saints in the world and a symbol of Ireland.

After Patrick's death, Christianity continued to spread throughout Ireland. But since the island of Ireland lacked large urban centers and accompanying churches and cathedrals, Irish monasteries assumed many of the functions of the bishops of Europe. All these Irish monasteries combined a life of solitude with community by creating compounds with separate cells. Additionally, the Irish added double monasteries that combined monks and nuns and also family monasteries founded by aristocratic Irish families.

Eventually Irish monks were even so bold as to reach out to the rest of Europe with missionaries and pilgrimages. Two of these adventurous monks were Columba and Columbanus.

## Saint Columba (521–597) and Saint Columbanus (540–615)

Columba was born to a noble Irish family. He entered monastic school in Ireland at Neville and later joined the monastery of Clonard. In 551, he was ordained as a priest and traveled Ireland, founding several churches. But by 563, he left Ireland to do missionary work in Britain. Columba and a group of his followers settled on the island of Iona on the southeast coast of Scotland, where he founded a church and monastery that would serve as a base of operations for missionary work in the region of Scotland. Columba spent the rest of the years of his life trying to Christianize the pagan tribes of Scotland. As a result, he earned a wide reputation for being a saintly man and Iona became a center for learning and culture during the early Middle Ages.

Columbanus was also born in Ireland, in the province of Leinster. He was educated for the priesthood at the monastery of Bangor in County Down. Around 590, Columbanus left Ireland for the European continent. He ended up in Gaul and began to establish monasteries at Luxeuil and Annegray. But not everyone took kindly to his presence in Gaul.

In 603, he had to defend the monasteries he founded at a synod. This was largely due to the fact that they were based on Celtic traditions that he had brought from Ireland. Seven years later, he was expelled from the region of Burgundy. Columbanus then traveled to Switzerland and preached in the region of Alamanni. But soon he was forced to move on when the Burgundians took over the region in 612. Fleeing to Italy, he founded the monastery of Bobbio in 613, where he remained until his death.

During his life, Columbanus was thought to be a miracle worker by many of the people he encountered. He was also seen as a scholar of considerable depth since most of his sermons, poems, and letters are steeped in classical literary influences. Columbanus also developed a monastic rule that was known for its strict authority and severity. It was used throughout Europe until it was replaced by the Rule of St. Benedict.

## Saint Benedict

Saint Benedict of Nursa (480–550) provided the most lasting contribution to monasticism in Europe and has even been called the father of Western monasticism. Benedict was a superb organizer who in his monastery sought a moderate asceticism with gentle discipline and flexible orderliness. His work *Rule of St. Benedict* became a written model for the monasteries of Europe, combining prayer, devotional reading, work, and a pledge of poverty, chastity, and obedience to resist money, sex, and ambition. To prove his asceticism worked, Benedict founded a great monastery on top of Monte Cassino in Italy, which became one of the chief centers for religious life in Europe.

The monastic movement's impact cannot be overemphasized. Linked by the common objective of spreading Christianity, these autonomous institutions spread throughout Europe. As part of this objective, they developed repositories of learning, missionary activity, administrative procedures, agricultural organization, and technological innovation. And although the monks were not individually wealthy, the monasteries became among the richest autonomous institutions in Europe. All this made the monasteries a large civilizing influence in the early medieval world.

## Pope Gregory the Great (590–604)

If monasticism helped fill some of the cultural and spiritual void in Europe during the early Middle Ages, Pope Gregory the Great, the last of the church fathers, helped fill much of the rest.

Gregory was the son of a Roman senator and a member of a noble family. At first Gregory pursued a career in politics and was appointed prefect of the city of Rome in 573. But he wasn't satisfied and renounced his political life. Gregory used his large inheritance to establish seven monasteries, one of them on his own estate, which he joined as a monk in 574. But his reputation was so good among the clergy of the church that in 578 Pope Benedict I appointed him a deacon.

The following year, the pope sent Gregory to Constantinople as an ambassador to secure the help of the Byzantine Empire against the Lombards. In Constantinople, Gregory gained experience dealing with the Byzantine Empire, but knew that acquiring aid from them was a lost cause. As a result, Gregory returned to Rome and his monastery. When the pope died in 590, Gregory was quickly and unanimously elected pope. He tried to avoid this, not feeling worthy of the title, but was consecrated nonetheless.

As pope, Gregory found the situation of Italy and Rome to be precarious. The Italian peninsula was in a state of ruin. The Lombards were a constant threat and the Byzantine Empire was unreliable as an ally. So Gregory threw himself into solving the problems that faced the church. Because of the void of government authority, he assumed many civil powers, which advanced the growing temporal position of the papacy. He fed the poor in Rome and reorganized the territories of the papal states.

Gregory also saved Rome from an attack by the Lombards by concluding a peace agreement with their leader in 593.

Pope Gregory also introduced reforms into the church. He created guidelines for religious practice in the *Book of Pastoral Rules*. Gregory helped to convert the Anglo-Saxons by sending Augustine of Canterbury on a missionary trip to the British Isles in 596. A monk before he was pope, Gregory favored the monasteries and tried to appoint abbots and monks to powerful positions within the papacy and granted special privileges to monasteries. He is also given credit for the creation of the form of musical worship that came to be called the Gregorian chant.

In addition to administration and reform, Gregory was a prolific writer. He first authored the *Dialogues,* which is an account of the lives of early Christian saints. Gregory also wrote many sermons, several Biblical commentaries, and over 800 letters.

By the time of his death, Gregory's popularity was at an all-time high, making him responsible for the wide acceptance by Christians of Europe of the authority of the pope over the church. He also solidified the idea that the pope was a major political player in both Italy and Europe. Thus, in the end, his abilities founded the medieval papacy.

## Spreading the Word

As discussed earlier, Pope Gregory sent the monk Augustine (d. 604) to England to help convert the Anglo-Saxon kingdoms. In 597, he converted the politically strong kingdom of Kent and its king, Ethelbert, with some help from the queen. Augustine then became the first bishop of Canterbury, the traditional seat of the church in England.

Some initial problems arose between Irish and Roman Christianity as they coexisted in England, mostly involving the dating of Easter. The Synod of Whitby in 664, guided by the famous Abbess Hilda (614–680), resolved the issue, and as a result, the Anglo-Saxons experienced a unified religious revival that created a vigorous Christian society on the island.

## The Flowering Intellectual Life

Despite what most people in the modern world think, the early Middle Ages were not "dark" at all. Christianity and the church helped to develop intellectual and cultural life. In Ireland, the monasteries taught both Latin and Greek and developed a rich artistic tradition evidenced in the creation of the *Book of the Kells,* an illuminated manuscript of the Bible. In the Anglo-Saxon kingdom of Northumbria, there was a renaissance of learning. Illuminated manuscripts, vernacular poetry, and architecture were created that exhibited an astounding complexity for the period.

The scholar Bede the Venerable (673–735) was part of this Renaissance. Most of what historians know about Bede comes from Bede himself in the later chapter of his *Ecclesiastical History of the English People*. Bede was born in the Anglo-Saxon kingdom of Northumbria. At the age of seven, he was sent to the abbot of the monastery of Wearmouth, Benedict Biscop, to be raised as a monk. Later around 681, Bede was transferred to the monastery of St. Paul in Jarrow. There, he was ordained a deacon at 19 and a priest at 30 years of age.

Bede hardly ever traveled outside of his monastery walls, let alone the kingdom of Northumbria, with the exception of one trip to the monastery of Lindisfarne and the town of York. He died at the monastery of Jarrow and was buried there until the eleventh century, when his remains were moved to the Durham Cathedral.

Within the sheltered life of the monastery, Bede produced numerous important works on grammar, scripture, and history. His commentaries on the Bible included ones on all four gospels, the Acts of the Apostles, and other books of the Old and New Testaments. Bede did not limit himself to Biblical commentary. He also produced a study on Pliny the Younger and Suetonius, two very influential Roman writers. Bede authored grammars and treatises, including two on time: *On Time* and *On the Reckoning of Time*. In addition, he wrote several biographies, including ones on St. Cuthbert and the abbots of Wearmouth and Jarrow. Bede was also the first to use the term *Anno Domini* (A.D.) or "Year of the Lord" in his dating. This convention is the basis of our dating to this day, although the term has changed to Common Era (C.E.).

Bede's chief and most important work was the *Historia Ecclesiastica* or *Ecclesiastical History of the English People*, which chronicles the history of England from just prior to the birth of Jesus to the turn of the sixth century. It was written with a great deal of skill and scholarship. Bede took care to use objective sources for his history. Although it details some questionable miracles, the history remains a primary source for historians of Anglo-Saxon England to this day.

## A Dimming of the Lights

After the period of the Irish monastic missionary efforts and the Northumbrian Renaissance, the intellectual life of Ireland and England began to dim, but Anglo-Saxon missionaries were still being sent to Europe. Saint Boniface (675–754) went to Gaul and helped reform the church of the Franks using Benedictine idealism and organization. His efforts established closer ties between the church of the Franks and the papacy. Following Boniface, Alcuin (735–804), a student of Bede, traveled to the court of the Holy Roman Emperor Charlemagne (742–814) and there helped affect the Carolingian Renaissance in central Europe.

As the early medieval world emerged, three things became apparent. First, the Catholic Church developed into a very important aspect of the culture of Europe. In addition, the interests of church and state merged, creating an uneasy partnership in the establishment of stability over Europe. And, for the most part, the cultural leadership of Europe was in the hands of the church and politically strong kings.

## The Least You Need to Know

- The early medieval world depended on the elements of ethnicity, militarism, and marriage to create stability.

- Strong kings, local aristocrats, and bishops dominated the politics of the early Middle Ages.

- The monastic movement was born in the deserts of Egypt but changed when it reached Europe and became a cultural catalyst.

- Pope Gregory the Great helped to stabilize the church administratively and spread Christianity throughout Europe.

- The Northumbrian Renaissance in Anglo-Saxon England represented one of the cultural high watermarks of the early Middle Ages.

# Chapter 5

# Charlemagne and the Carolingian Empire

## In This Chapter

- ◆ The do-nothing kings
- ◆ Charles the Hammer
- ◆ Pepin the Short
- ◆ Charlemagne and the Carolingian Empire
- ◆ The Carolingian Renaissance

After the fall of the Roman Empire, local kings, bishops, and aristocrats ruled Europe. King Clovis of the Franks provided enough political power to begin the creation of an empire. Although this Frankish and later Carolingian Empire was a shadow of the Roman Empire, it did give Europe a stability comparable to that provided by old Rome.

# The End of the Merovingians

When King Clovis died in 511, the Frankish kingdom was divided among his four sons, as was the Germanic custom. This division of power quickly created weaknesses and prevented any single king from establishing effective control. As a result, Clovis's sons were politically feeble and frequently fought among themselves for control over the Frankish kingdom. With the exception of Dagobert I, the heirs of Clovis's sons were incompetent; the longhaired kings became synonymous with "do-nothing" kings.

**Notable Quote** _____

"Nothing was left to the king. He had to content himself with his royal title, his flowing locks, and long beard."

—*Life of Charlemagne*, Einhard on the Merovingian kings

## The Do-Nothing Kings

Under the do-nothing kings, the local nobles or aristocrats took control of many of the lands and ignored most of the commands of the kings. As a result, during the seventh and eighth centuries, the weakened Merovingian kings turned over more of their political powers to officials called the mayors of the palace. These officials traced their title and position back to nobles who once were honored by caring for the horses and stables of the Merovingian kings.

## The Mayors of the Palace

After some time, the mayor of the palace became the power behind the throne, and by the eighth century one family, the Carolingians, had that position locked up. The family passed the position of mayor of the palace from father to son but always kept the Merovingian king on the throne because old Germanic customs and beliefs in the sacredness of the king still ran deep. For the Carolingians, to end the Merovingian line could spell doom for the Frankish lands; at least that is what the people thought, and that counted to the Carolingians.

## The Hammer

One of the most successful mayors of the palace was Charles Martel (714–741), also known as Charles "the Hammer." Charles consolidated Frankish political power over new territories. Although officially only a mayor of the palace, he granted church and political offices at will and ruled effectively without having to establish a puppet long-haired Merovingian king.

Charles drew on the treasury of the church to equip a new Frankish army to help consolidate his power. Of course, this act did not make him any friends with the church. He also sowed the seeds of feudalism in the development of his new army. To pay his warriors, Charles gave out land titles conditional upon the loyalty of the warrior. The end result of Charles's labors was an efficient and reliable mounted army. It was the precursor of the armies of mounted knights of the Middle Ages.

With his new and improved army, Charles defeated a superior invasion force of Muslims at the Battle of Tours in 732. This battle, also called the Battle of Poitiers, was with an Islamic Moorish invasion force led by the governor of Cordoba. Historians are not actually sure where the battle took place, but it has been suggested that there were probably several large skirmishes, after which the Moors retreated back to Spain.

Traditionally, the Battle of Tours has been seen as Christendom's greatest victory, sparing Europe an Islamic invasion and takeover, but this has been overblown. The Moors probably retreated because of internal problems such as the Berbers in North Africa. Regardless, the battle ended most of the Muslim incursions into Gaul, or France, from that point forward. Like any smart politician, Charles Martel claimed the title as Savior of Christendom and set up his son to be the first Carolingian king of the Franks.

# Pepin the Short?

Charles Martel's heirs crafted a new course for the Frankish kingdom, creating the Carolingian Empire, which generated greater stability for Europe and shaped many of the events of the Middle Ages.

In 741, after the death of Charles, Pepin III or the Short (r. 751–768) became the mayor of the palace for King Childeric III (r. 743–751). Like most of the mayors of the palace, Pepin thought the do-nothing king was incompetent. But unlike his forebears, Pepin plotted to become king himself. Around 750, he requested that the respected abbot of the monastery of Saint Denis travel to Rome to ask Pope Zacharias (r. 741–752) if it was possible that, since Pepin acted as the king of the Franks, perhaps he should in fact *be* king of the Franks.

Because the pope needed protection against the Lombards who were continually threatening papal lands, he responded quite positively to the abbot's inquiry. With church approval, in 751, Pepin convinced the Frankish nobles to back his claim as king. Bishop Boniface then anointed Pepin with holy oil and made him *the* king of the Franks, and the former King Childeric III was unceremoniously shorn of his long hair and shipped off to a monastery to become a reluctant monk.

### Middle Age Myths

In 755, shortly after Pepin concluded a military campaign against the Lombards in Italy, a document was found in which Emperor Constantine (r. 306–337) granted supreme authority of the Italian peninsula to Pope Sylvester I (r. 314–335) and the church. This document, called the Donation of Constantine, was used throughout the Middle Ages in support of papal claims to temporal authority in Italy. The Renaissance scholar Lorenzo Valla later showed it to be a forgery in 1440.

Apparently, there had not yet been enough anointing. A few short years after Bishop Boniface proclaimed Pepin the King of the Franks, Pope Stephen II (r. 752–757) traveled the route to Paris and again anointed Pepin. In exchange for a papal anointing, Pepin assembled a Frankish army and defeated the Lombards for the pope. He then forced the Lombards to give up territory in central Italy, which he gave as a gift to Pope Stephen known as the Donation of Pepin. The donation changed the nature of the papacy, giving the pope *temporal* as well as spiritual power over land. Those lands remained under papal rule until the ninth-century Italian unification.

## def•i•ni•tion

Temporal authority refers to authority that is worldly, not spiritual or religious, in nature.

# Charlemagne

Pepin's son Charles succeeded him in 768, and Charles impressed so many by his actions that he was called Charles the Great or Charlemagne (r. 768–814). During his rule, which lasted almost a half of century (very long even by today's standards!), Charlemagne created an empire that stretched from the Iberian peninsula in the west to present-day Germany in the east.

## Charlemagne the Warrior

Charlemagne was a man's man—tall, athletic, and charismatic. Although he was never able to read and write himself, Charlemagne was well spoken. (The story goes that he slept with a book under his pillow in the hopes of acquiring the ability to read!) He married five times and refused to allow his daughters to marry lest it create problems of succession to the throne.

Charlemagne's goal as king was to unite all the small Germanic kingdoms into the Frankish Empire, now called the Carolingian Empire, and he embarked on over 50 military campaigns. Starting in 774, when the Lombards reneged on their treaty with Pepin the Short and attacked the papal territories, Charlemagne invaded the Italian peninsula, soundly defeated them, and declared himself their king. Shortly afterward, Charlemagne crossed the Pyrenees Mountains to fight the Muslims for control of northern Spain. With their defeat, he created a border kingdom called the Spanish March.

Charlemagne also moved the Frankish Empire into northern and central Europe. He campaigned several times against the Saxon tribes that lived between the Rhine and the Elbe rivers, conquered them, and forced them to convert to Christianity. He also invaded Bavaria and drove out the Slavic tribes and Avars from the upper Danube River. When the smoke cleared, Charlemagne controlled the area of present-day France, Belgium, the Netherlands, Germany, Austria, Switzerland, and northern Italy. Quite an accomplishment for one ruler's lifetime!

## Charlemagne the Churchman

Like many rulers of the early medieval world, Charlemagne allied himself very closely with the church. In 799 when a mob drove Pope Leo III (r. 795–816) from Rome, he came to the court of Charlemagne, who quickly assembled a force that went to Rome and restored the pope. As a result, Pope Leo III crowned Charlemagne "Holy Roman Emperor" on Christmas Day in 800 in Rome.

Charlemagne probably looked at the title as a mixed bag. Although the title seemed to carry the old prestige of Rome, it also was given by the church and pope, implying that the church had authority over

> **Notable Quote**
>
> "It was at the time he received the title of emperor and Augustus, to which at first he was so averse that he remarked that had he known the intention of the pope, he would not have entered the church on that day."
>
> —*Life of Charlemagne*, Einhard

kings. In response to this threat, Charlemagne named his own son as his successor, without the pope presiding over the ceremony. But the coronation of Charlemagne demonstrated that the idea of Rome and a Christian empire lingered in the minds of the European people.

## Charlemagne the Administrator

Beyond his military achievements, Charlemagne was a highly efficient administrator who chose able people to help him run his empire. When Charlemagne delegated authority, he demanded results. As part of his administrative plan, he divided the Carolingian Empire into 300 districts or counties. In each county, a count administered the secular business; a duke directed military affairs; and a bishop took care of spiritual matters. In counties on the frontiers, he created special commanders to administer both civil and military affairs.

Charlemagne closely monitored all the counties through messengers who acted as royal inspectors. They supervised the administration of the counties and punished those who did not follow orders. The inspectors were changed often and rotated frequently to prevent over-familiarity between inspectors and administrators. To seal the deal, all administrators and inspectors were required to take an oath of allegiance to Charlemagne.

The laws of Charlemagne were based on the principles of Germanic law, but since the Franks were Christian rather than pagan, they extracted many of the pagan elements. The laws dealt with both secular and religious affairs, helping to unify the empire and also merge the interests of church and state.

# The Carolingian Renaissance

Charlemagne was not only concerned with the creation of a strong and efficient empire but also with the learning and culture of his lands and the lack of education among the clergy, many of whom did not know Greek or even Latin, the language of the church mass. So Charlemagne established schools to train the clergy.

## Carolingian Schools

The schools that Charlemagne established were a very important component of the Carolingian Renaissance. The groundwork for the schools was laid in 787 with a law that Charlemagne enacted that was sent to the abbot of the monastery at Fulda to execute. The law instructed the abbot to establish places in monasteries and bishops' houses in the Frankish lands where learning could take place to train the clergy. Sometimes referred to as the first charter of modern education, the decree was followed by several others that augmented education in the Frankish Empire.

Although primitive in comparison to the standards of the universities of the High Middle Ages, the Carolingian schools were a bold and innovative step forward in education. The seven liberal arts were taught at the schools as well as theology, which resulted in the further development of the Latin Vulgate Bible originally translated by Jerome. In addition, Latin was returned as the language of education and the educated, which had not been the case since the fall of the Roman Empire. Also the Carolingian schools displayed a remarkable amount of equality educating both nobles and people from the other classes.

The chief school was the Palace School in Aachen. But many of the other schools associated mostly with cathedrals and monasteries became leading centers of education in Europe during this period. Although the quality of the education did not last past the end of the Carolingian dynasty, they were important in the establishment of an educational system that would endure throughout the Middle Ages and associate the church with learning and intellectual achievement.

The establishment of schools by Charlemagne stimulated a renaissance of scholarship and learning in the Carolingian Empire. Famous scholars came to Charlemagne's court at Aachen at his invitation to participate in the establishment of schools and learning. The Anglo-Saxon scholar Alcuin set up a palace school for Charlemagne's sons and daughters and children of the Frankish nobles at the court. Additionally, Charlemagne encouraged monasteries to establish schools for boys of all social classes, which he visited to check for progress.

As part of his education imitative, Charlemagne founded monasteries for the purpose of employing monks in the important process of copying the works of classical Greece and Rome, Saint Jerome's Latin Vulgate Bible, and the works of other early church leaders. The monks or scribes illuminated the first letter of each paragraph with colorful and complex designs and filled the margins with painted scenes from the text. These scribes also developed a form of writing called *Caroline minuscule*.

**def•i•ni•tion**

Caroline minuscule, a form of script developed by the monks of the Carolingian Renaissance, was a combination of lower-case letters with the capital letters taken from the Latin Roman script. We still use this form of script today.

# Alcuin

Alcuin of York (735–804) was one of the central figures in the early Carolingian Renaissance. He was a native of the Anglo-Saxon kingdom of Northumbria receiving his education at the cathedral school in York. By 766, he was a teacher at the York Cathedral, and in 768 Alcuin was promoted to headmaster.

While visiting France in 781, Alcuin met Charlemagne. The ruler was so impressed with Alcuin that he was offered a position as head instructor of the palace school at Aachen. Later, Charlemagne took him into his confidence and Alcuin became a prominent advisor to the court.

From there, Alcuin helped to guide and shape the Carolingian Renaissance. He wrote manuals of education and created the course of study focusing on the dialogues, the *trivium* and elements of the *quadrivium* laid out by Boethius, and the works of Saint Augustine. Alcuin also attracted to the palace school at Aachen some of the sharpest minds of the time, including Peter of Pisa and Paul the Deacon. Alcuin himself taught Amalarius of Metz and Rabanus Maurus, who would both become prominent theologians of the early Middle Ages.

Of course, Alcuin advised Charlemagne on important spiritual and theological matters, including the Adoptionist heresy. This belief, which had come by the way of Spain, held that Jesus was the Son of God through adoption only—not by divine birth. Alcuin was very effective in ending this heresy by vigorous verbal and written defenses of the doctrine of the church. Later Alcuin retired to the famous monastery of St. Martin in Tours to become the spiritual guide for the monks there until his death in 804.

### Age-Makers

Alcuin (735–804) was an Anglo-Saxon scholar. Working for Charlemagne, Alcuin's scholarship increased dramatically. His writing on rhetoric, logic, and dialectic became the basis of many of Europe's cathedral schools. But most importantly, Alcuin carefully revised the Saint Jerome's Latin Vulgate, ensuring its accuracy.

# John Scotus Erigena (800–880)

Another one of the more important scholars during the later years of the Carolingian Renaissance was John Scotus Erigena. Erigena, a name meaning "born in Ireland," was born ... in Ireland ... in 800. He later left Ireland to move to France in 845 where he took over one the Carolingian schools, the Palatine Academy, at the invitation of King Charles the Bald. He stayed in France for at least 30 years. Later at the request of the Byzantine Emperor John, Erigena translated into Latin from Greek some of the works of Greek philosophy while adding his own commentary. He was thus one of the first to introduce the ideas of Plato from the Greek into the Western tradition. That action would have a deep impact on Christian theology.

Erigena was a free-thinking philosopher and theologian who remained the subject of controversy for most of the Middle Ages. His theology was filled with rational speculations that completely ignored the orthodox theology of the church. His best work of theology was *On the Division of Nature*, which was written during the period of 865 to 870. This work was accepted more than his others and became very influential. In it, Erigena classified nature into four parts:

◆ God

◆ The Word or *Logos*

◆ The material world

◆ God as supreme end

Behind God, Erigena regarded man as the master of the universe, because he has senses and reason to determine causes and mechanisms. He also regarded man to be both divine and animal. He thought that sin was derived from the animal nature, but through the divine within him, man could return to God. In addition, he tried to explain sin as misdirected will. Erigena thought that being and knowing were the same, so God must have known about sin firsthand.

Erigena saw the need for the use of reason in explaining the universe. Much like the later medieval scholastic movement, he tried to combine faith and reason. His basic philosophy determined the tone of Christian theology for most of the Middle Ages. It was further developed by many later thinkers, making Erigena more influential than was ever officially acknowledged.

Since Erigena failed to submit his work for church approval, he fell out of favor with the church and most of his works were condemned as heretical. Tradition has it that he returned to Britain at the end of his life to become a teacher and Abbot of Malmesbury in southern England. There his students stabbed him to death with their pens for "trying to get them to think." Though he was a mysterious figure, historians have widely accepted that John Scotus Erigena possessed one of the finest minds of the early Middle Ages.

# The Decline of the Carolingian Empire

When Charlemagne's health started to fail, he desperately tried to teach his only surviving son, Louis, how to rule the vast Carolingian Empire effectively. But sadly, leadership can sometimes be neither inherited nor taught.

## Louis the Pious

Louis the Pious (r. 815–840), Charlemagne's son, inherited a very large empire. But as his nickname implied, Louis was more interested in worshipping God than ruling an empire. After a few years on the throne, he lost the support of both the Frankish nobles and the clergy. As Louis became politically weak, the nobles began taking more and more political power for themselves.

Louis spent the last years of his reign watching his sons fight over the territories of the empire. Still, when he died, Louis left the Carolingian Empire to his three sons as was the custom. He divided the empire into three regions, spelled out shortly beforehand in the Treaty of Verdun in 843. Charles the Bald (yes, he was bald) received the western region, which later turned into France. Louis the German (yes, he spoke German) got the eastern portion, which became Germany. Finally, Lothair (no, he didn't have a nickname) acquired the strip of land between the two other brothers. The Germans and the French have fought over this narrow corridor, known as *Lotharii Regnum*, Lotharginia, and the Lorraine, ever since.

As the saying goes, "United we stand, divided we fall." With the division of the Carolingian Empire, its political and military power weakened. Lothair's central kingdom soon fragmented into nothing. Descendents of Charlemagne ruled the eastern kingdom until 911, when the last Carolingian king died. The western kingdom held on the longest, maintaining a Carolingian king until 987. French nobles then elected Hugh Capet, count of Paris, as king, and the Capetian dynasty ruled France for the next 300 years.

## Carolingian Legacy

Charlemagne and the Carolingian Empire made a lasting impact on the history and culture of Europe. First, it provided a brief period of peace and stability for much of Europe, initiating an intellectual and cultural renaissance whose influence spanned the rest of the Middle Ages. In addition, Charlemagne provided a contemporary Germanic model of a ruler and an empire. Many of the kings of the Middle Ages looked to Charlemagne and the Carolingian Empire as a standard to match.

## The Least You Need to Know

- By the late sixth century, the Merovingian kings of the Franks were ineffectual and were known as the do-nothing kings.

- The Carolingian mayors of the palace became the de facto rulers of the Frankish Empire.

- Pepin the Short dethroned the last Merovingian king and founded the Carolingian Empire.

- Charlemagne expanded the Carolingian Empire, stabilized Europe, and produced a cultural renaissance.

- After the death of Charlemagne, the Carolingian Empire broke up and fell into decline.

# Chapter 6

# Ninth- and Tenth-Century Invasions

## In This Chapter

◆ The origins of the Vikings

◆ Viking invasions

◆ Viking culture

◆ Islamic raids

◆ Magyar incursions

The end of the Carolingian Empire was due only in part to the divisions among Charlemagne's grandsons as a new storm of invaders swept in from the north, south, and east, harassing the small and weak kingdoms of Europe. These invaders were the Muslims, the Magyars, and the Vikings.

Muslim pirates captured the island of Sicily and raided the coast of Italy. Nomadic tribes called the Magyars, like the Huns before them, swept out of the steppes of central Asia and terrorized Eastern Europe. And finally, the Vikings, forgotten Germanic kinsmen of the Europeans, raided northern Europe.

# The Vikings

Scholars are uncertain of the origin of the word Viking, which was used to describe the raiders from present-day Scandinavia who sailed the sea to attack the coasts of England and northern France starting around the year 800. Many believe the word comes from the fish, the *vik*, which they caught off their shores. Others believe the word comes from *vig*, meaning battle and war. The Vikings were also called the Northmen and the Norse. Regardless, the Europeans of the time probably just thought "terror" when they saw them, as evidenced in the prayer: "O Lord deliver us from the fury of the Northmen."

## Middle Age Myths

To this day, one of the most notable images of Vikings is that of fierce warriors in horned helmets running about raping and pillaging. In historical reality, Vikings did not wear horned helmets. That image was incorrectly created during the resurgence of interest in the Vikings during the late-nineteenth-century nationalist period.

## Origins

These Vikings came from the Scandinavian nations of Denmark, Sweden, and Norway. Once part of the Germanic tribes, they had settled in those regions during the migration period of the fourth and fifth centuries. Many in the past have debated the reason for their vicious raids that started during the late eighth century and lasted through the tenth century. However, most historians think overpopulation and the practice of *primogeniture* was part of the reason.

The sea greatly influenced the Viking way of life and culture. Scandinavian land was rocky, difficult to farm, and unsuitable for pasture, but the sea provided an easy solution. By the eighth century, the Vikings were building advanced sailing ships that could travel long distances very quickly. Propelled by both sails and oars, the ships could reach a speed of 10 knots (a knot being one nautical mile per hour). Many of their ships could hold over 100 men but could be sailed with as few as 15. They could also sail in shallow water, making it easy for Vikings to follow rivers far inland. These ships were strong enough to withstand a stormy sea and light enough to be carried over land if needed.

## def•i•ni•tion

**Primogeniture** is the practice in which the eldest son inherited his father's estate, leaving the younger sons out in the cold.

## The First Raids

In the eighth century, Norwegian Vikings occupied the islands north and west of Scotland. Other Vikings made settlements on the coast of Ireland, building the ports of Dublin, Waterford, and Limerick. By the end of the eighth century, they started to attack Anglo-Saxon England, and in 793, Vikings raided the monastery of Lindisfarne, one of the major cultural centers of Christianity on the island. But the worst was yet to come.

**Notable Quote** _____

"Lo, it is some 350 years that we and our forefathers have inhabited this most lovely land, and never before has such a terror appeared in Britain as we have now suffered from a pagan race, nor was it thought possible that such an inroad from the sea could be made."

— *The Anglo-Saxon Chronicle*

At the start of the ninth century, Vikings from modern Denmark called Danes raided the northern and eastern shores of England. In 886, Alfred the Great (r. 871–899), the Anglo-Saxon king of Wessex, made a treaty with these Danes, allowing them to have control of northeastern England in order to end the raids. The kingdom that was carved out was called Danelaw. But this action did not end the Viking attacks. For the next 100 years, continuous fighting occurred between the Anglo-Saxons and the Danes. By the eleventh century, new waves of Danes invaded the shores of England and, as a result, the Danish King Canute became king of England.

The Vikings also raided the coast of France during the eighth and ninth centuries. For example, in 885, a Viking fleet of over 700 ships sailed up the Seine River and besieged the city of Paris. The siege was not successful, partially due to the leadership of Count Odo of Paris, but still the threat of Viking raids was continuous. They looted and destroyed the monasteries and convents that developed during the sixth and seventh century. In desperation, the Carolingian king, Charles the Simple (bad nickname!), gave land to a threatening group of Vikings led by a chief named Rollo. One of the conditions of the land exchange was that Rollo be baptized Christian and swear to defend France against other Vikings. This land became known as the land of the Northmen, later Normandy.

Vikings from Sweden also sailed the seas of northern Europe looking for lands to raid and plunder. They picked their way down the rivers of present-day Russia until they reached the Volga River. Sailing down the Volga, the Vikings reached the Caspian Sea. They also sailed south on the Dnieper River into the Black Sea and eventually reached Constantinople. By the late 800s, the Vikings not only raided but also came to rule the Slavic people of the region of Russia. The Viking rulers of the Slavs were called *Rus,* from which the name Russia comes. One of those Viking leaders, a man named Oleg, settled in the area of Kiev at the beginning of the tenth century, and the principality of Kiev soon took control of the region, which included territory between the Baltic and Black seas and the Danube and Volga rivers.

> **Notable Quote**
>
> "[In the year 882] Oleg set himself up as a prince in Kiev and declared: 'May this be the mother of Russian cities.'"
> — *The Primary Chronicle*

## The Byzantine Empire?

From Kiev during the ninth and tenth centuries, the Vikings attacked the Byzantine Empire and even besieged the well-fortified city of Constantinople itself. The siege failed because Constantinople had several years of reserve water and food. But the Viking war tenacity impressed the Byzantine emperors.

Eventually, the emperors employed some of the Vikings as an elite corps in the Byzantine army called Varangians. And as trade down the Volga and Dnieper rivers increased between the two civilizations, the Viking attacks tapered off. The Vikings traded slaves, furs, honey, and amber to the Byzantines for silk and luxury goods.

## Iceland, Greenland, and Vinland

But the Viking thirst for raiding and plundering could not be quenched. During the mid-ninth century, Vikings sailed into the Mediterranean Sea and attacked the present-day Spanish coast, invaded North Africa, and raided as far as Egypt.

Other Vikings sailed west from Norway and discovered Iceland. From Iceland, Eric the Red led a group of Vikings to the newly discovered Greenland. Viking settlements in Greenland lasted until the sixteenth century, but the climate was too harsh even for the Vikings' blood.

During the late tenth century, the Vikings of Greenland, led by Leif Erikson, went even further west and reached the coast of North America, establishing a settlement called Vinland or land of the grapes. Archaeologists have discovered evidence of that settlement in northern Newfoundland. At the site, they discovered a Viking long-house, weapons, and tools. But the settlement in North America did not last long. The Vikings fought with the local Native American population they called *skraelings*, and as a result, within a few years, they abandoned Vinland.

# The Viking Culture

To most people, the Vikings appear to have been savage barbarians intent on chaos and destruction. Most historical accounts support this view, but we should realize these accounts were written by people who suffered because of them. Actually, the Viking culture was rich and vibrant.

In their Scandinavian homeland, the Viking economy was based on agriculture, hunting, and fishing. Artisans produced carvings for the prows of their able sailing ships to resemble dragons and other fierce monsters. They also decorated their weapons and jewelry with intricate and abstract designs of horses, boars, and serpents.

The Vikings developed a rich tradition of literature in their long narrative poems, called sagas. They mixed fact and fantasy to produce a tale to be sung to audiences by a fire at night. These sagas were not written down, but wandering bards who traveled from petty kingdom to kingdom memorized them. Not until the thirteenth and four-teenth centuries did Snorri Sturluson (1179–1241) write down some of these sagas.

**Age-Makers**

Snorri Sturluson was born in Norway in 1179 but spent his active political and literary life in Iceland. His greatest works include the *Prose Edda*, which provides us with the stories of the Viking mythology, and *Heimskringla*, which sets out a history of the kings of Norway. Both works are invaluable to an understanding of Viking culture and history.

The Vikings also developed a unique alphabet they called the *futhark* after its first six letters. It consisted of 16 stick-like characters called *runes*. These letters contained no horizontal lines because they might be easily mistaken with the grain of the wood on which they were carved. In Viking mythology, Odin, the leader of the gods, had acquired knowledge of the runes only after being hung on a tree for nine days and nights and then wounded by a spear. Viking

**def•i•ni•tion**

**Runes** were the simple alphabetic script of the Germanic and Viking peoples that were used on wood, rock, and metal.

laws, myths, and customs were all passed through bards. So writing was limited, and runes were only carved on items like bone, wood, stone, and metal.

Women often appeared in the runic inscriptions of the Vikings, indicating that women played a very important role in their culture. Viking women could own property, consent to marriage, and divorce. In an account of the Vikings in North America, the Native Americans surprised a group of Vikings in the woods and had them on the run until the lone woman of the Viking party stopped, turned around with sword in hand, slapped her chest, and basically said to the natives, "Bring it on!" The Native Americans were so shocked they beat a hasty retreat.

# Viking Religion

The Viking religion, which featured a host of gods, has captured the imagination of fantasy writers. Some of their gods are household names even to this day although most people do not realize it.

The one-eyed Odin was also known as Wodin. He was the father of the gods as well as the god of war and wisdom and rode an eight-legged horse named Slepnir. On each shoulder, Odin had a raven that he sent out daily into the world to bring him news. The Vikings worshipped him on Wodin's Day—which later became Wednesday.

Thor was the Viking god of thunder and also the strongest of the gods. He wore a strength-giving belt, carried a magic hammer named Mjollnir, and rode around the heavens in a chariot pulled by two goats. The goats could be eaten at the conclusion of the day and would return good as new in the morning. The Vikings worshipped Thor on Thor's day—later known as Thursday.

The Viking god Frey was a fertility god and as such had power over rain and sunshine. He had a magic sword that fought by itself. If that was not enough, Frey had a ship that could sail both on land and sea carrying all the gods, but could also be folded up to fit in his pocket. Finally he rode on a boar (a symbol of fertility) that had golden bristles. The goddess of love and beauty was Freyja, sister of Frey. She rode a chariot pulled by a pair of cats. When she missed her dead husband, Odur, she cried tears of gold. Yes, they worshipped Frey on Friday.

Loki was the brat of the gods. He caused the death of the god Balder, son of Odin, by trickery, and as punishment for his dastardly deed, Loki was chained to a rock and had a poison-dripping snake hung above him. The drip of the poison into Loki's eyes continued until the end of time, or Ragnorok.

Valkyries were demi-goddesses and warrior women who searched the battlefields for Viking men who had died heroic deaths. These men were carried to Valhalla where they fought battles gloriously and celebrated at the end of the day with feasts of pork and mead (honey ale). So dying heroically in battle was the thing to do in the world of the Vikings. (No wonder they were tough to beat!)

Most Viking kings were buried in a ship in a burial mound with everything they needed in the afterlife, such as weapons, armor, food, and furniture. Although it's still debated, there were several reasons for this burial. For some historians, the kings were simply displaying their wealth and power at a burial ceremony. Others (this writer included) believe the kings were buried in the ground because of the idea of the sacred king found in Germanic tribal culture; kings buried in the ground gave fertility to the kingdom.

## The End of the World

For the Viking culture, the world's end was called Ragnarok, or the Doom, or Destiny of the Gods because it was destined since the beginning of the world. According to Viking myth, death awaited everyone and everything, including the gods. The gods were deeply flawed and neither Odin's wisdom nor Thor's valor would be able to save them from Ragnarok.

The beginning of the end starts with the death of Balder and Loki's banishment from the company of the gods. On Earth, there will be an age of faithlessness and depravity. Ties between kinsfolk will vanish. There will be a long winter lasting three years, followed by three years of war. The sun and the moon will be devoured by wolves. The Earth will start to break up. Mountains will start to fall. The giant wolf, Fenrir, breaks his fetters to hunt for the gods. A giant snake spewing poison will rise from the sea to hunt for men and gods alike. Fire giants will invade the Earth also to hunt. And finally, Loki breaks free from his chains and banishment to settle a score with Odin and the gods of Asgard.

As the signs of the end occur, the gods of Asgard prepare themselves for the final battle. The chosen warriors of Valhalla join the gods for the final scene. Both gods and the warriors know the end is in sight; they know the end is not good, that they will die. So Odin leads the gods and chosen warriors into the field against Loki, the fire giants, Fenrir, and the giant snake. Odin takes on Fenrir the wolf, Thor the giant snake, and Frey the fire giants. Thor kills the giant serpent, but when he walks nine steps falls dead from the snake's venom. Fenrir swallows Odin whole, but Vidar, Odin's son, takes vengeance and stabs the wolf in the heart, killing it. The rest of the gods are killed in the battle along with Loki and the fire giants. The sun grows dark; the stars fall from the sky; the sea washes over the land; and fire engulfs the world. The fire consumes the Earth and then the universe, all sinking into a sea of darkness.

Of course, it's not all gloom and doom! From the ashes of the old order, another world emerges from the sea of darkness with green grass and corn. Two of Odin's sons survive Ragnarok, as well as two of Thor's sons. They build a city for the gods. Two humans also survive, who rebuild and replenish the civilizations of the new earth. The circle of life begins anew.

## The Real End

The Vikings' pagan beliefs slowly faded from their culture once they were converted to Christianity and blended with the rest of Europe. Probably as a result, after the eleventh century, the Viking raids ended and Europeans could breathe easier, at least with regard to threats from the north.

# Muslim Raiders

Although the Viking invasions of northern Europe were the most destructive of the invasions of the eighth through tenth centuries, the Muslim attacks in southern Europe were equally debilitating. During the seventh and eighth centuries, Islamic forces had conquered the Middle East, the coast of North Africa, and much of the Iberian peninsula, but in 732 Charles Martel and his Frankish army stopped the Muslim advance further into Europe at the Battle of Tours.

## Saracen Incursions

Muslim forces gradually gained control of the islands in the western Mediterranean, including Sicily, Corsica, and Sardinia. From their fortresses in Sicily and the Iberian peninsula, the Muslims raided western Italy and the coast of southern France. Europeans called these raiders Saracens, from the Byzantine word meaning "easterners." On several occasions, the Saracen incursions originated in European politics. For example, a rivalry between the Lombards and the Byzantine emperor led Naples to ask for Muslim help in 838. The Saracens did help—and then took the opportunity to make some new conquests in Italy.

And it got much worse before it got better. Muslim forces attacked and destroyed the religious center founded by Saint Benedict at Monte Cassino. They also besieged Rome in 846, and although they did not sack the city, the Islamic forces did plunder the cathedrals of St. Peter and Paul, which were outside the walls. Saracens also raided other parts of Europe and built fortresses in southern France to use as a base for more raids. From there they attacked merchant caravans carrying goods across the Alps. In 972, Muslim forces captured the abbot of the famous monastery at Cluny in southern France. They held him for ransom, which French nobles dutifully paid because the abbot was such an influential Church leader.

Finally in the late ninth century, the forces in Italy started to fight back and destroy Muslim bases in the Italian peninsula. Although the Muslims were expelled from Italy, they held on to bases in Sicily until the mid-eleventh century and forced their cultural standards on the local population. The Islamic capital of Palermo became a bustling commercial center comparable to Cordoba in Spain or Cairo in Egypt. And even after the Europeans expelled the Saracens from the island, their influence remained.

## The Normans Come

In 1060 and 1091, Norman forces from northern France came to Sicily on a mission of conquest looking for new lands. From Sicily these Normans expanded their power and influence over the Mediterranean Sea. This brought them into conflict not only with Muslims but also with Byzantium. In 1071, the Normans captured Palermo, and by 1091 had ended Muslim control of the island.

Count Roger, who ruled the conquering Normans, left much of the Islamic culture in place, and for the next 200 years Christian and Islamic culture blended together in a unique manner. Roger appointed Muslims to high positions in his government. He also respected the learning of Muslim physicians and philosophers. And his son, Roger II, followed his father's example. He established a court that included the Muslim geographer al-Idrisi, who wrote excellent geographies based on reports from travelers. But it did not end with Roger II. Frederick II, the grandson of Roger, continued official patronage of Islamic learning. His continued trade with the Islamic world helped to introduce the world of the east to Western Europe.

# The Huns—No, the Magyars

The third group of invaders to devastate Europe during the late eighth through tenth centuries was the nomadic Magyars. This group originated from the region of the Ural Mountains and the Volga River in modern Russia. They migrated southwest onto the steppes of Russia and by the late eighth century were raiding the Slavic people of Eastern Europe. Like the Huns before them, who also came from the steppes of Russia, the Magyars were excellent horsemen. They had learned to use the stirrup, an innovation that was making its way across Asia into Europe from China. The stirrup allowed a rider to shoot arrows and fight more effectively in the saddle.

By the tenth century, the Magyars had pushed into central Europe at the base of the Alps, leaving a path of destruction. Their raids continued until 955, when Otto the Great, King of Germany, and his armies defeated them at the Battle of Lechfeld in southern Germany. After the battle, the surviving Magyars moved east in retreat and finally settled on the Danube River in present-day Hungary.

# The Results of the Invasions

The invasions of the Vikings, Muslims, and Magyars during the eighth through the tenth centuries caused Europe many problems. The disruption to trade, commerce, learning, culture, and infrastructure was, no doubt, huge. But the people of Europe developed their own set of coping techniques, including the development of the mounted knight, feudalism, and manorialism. This was added to the already existing localism that developed during the sixth and seventh centuries after the fall of the Roman Empire, making Europe an interesting political mess to say the least.

## The Least You Need to Know

- Coming from the region of Scandinavia, the Vikings invaded England, France, and Russia from the eighth through the tenth centuries.

- The Vikings also explored westward to Iceland, Greenland, and North America.

- Viking culture was vibrant and unique, inspiring the imaginations of many years later.

- Muslim forces based in Sicily raided the southern coast of France and Italy during the eighth through tenth centuries until Norman forces conquered the island.

- The Magyars swept into central Europe disrupting the region until King Otto the Great defeated them at the Battle of Lechfeld in the late tenth century.

# Europe's Coping Strategies: Feudalism and Manorialism

## In This Chapter

- ◆ The origins of feudalism
- ◆ The feudal pyramid
- ◆ Knights and castles
- ◆ The origins of manorialism
- ◆ Lords and serfs

With the various invasions of the eighth through tenth centuries, the people of Europe developed new strategies to gain stability, including the systems of feudalism and manorialism.

## Feudalism

Europe already had a tradition of localism that developed during the sixth and seventh centuries after the fall of the Roman Empire. So it was only logical that a localized political and economic system developed during the period of invasions.

Feudalism, from the Latin word *feudum* meaning "estate," became a way of life for many people of Europe during the Middle Ages. At its center were ties of loyalty to local lords and kings. But to say that this system was consistent across Europe would be inaccurate. Building on German customs and law, feudalism began in France, took a strong root, and later spread to other parts of Europe with varying degrees of success.

In the beginning, local nobles acquired large tracts of land from kings for loyal service during war. In return, these nobles granted land to individuals in exchange for military service. But feudalism acquired baggage as it grew. By Germanic custom, individual warriors swore an oath of loyalty to a chieftain or king. In return, the chief supplied the warriors with weapons, horses, and armor. So the ties of feudalism went beyond the exchange of land. With the advent of the stirrup in the late eighth century, the warriors became mounted and carried larger weapons and heavier protection.

## The Feudal Pyramid

Feudalism was based on a system of unwritten rules between lords and vassals. (The word vassal comes from the Celtic word *vassus*, meaning "servant.") The feudal order was like a pyramid. In theory, everyone in the medieval society was indebted to a lord above him; except, of course, the king (who actually did have someone above him: God). Beneath him were nobles who held large tracts of lands, and those nobles had vassals or lesser nobles who, in turn, had vassals or knights who were also granted land. The lord who granted the land was the liege lord.

## Feudal Titles

As feudalism developed through the late first millennium, it became a complex inter-relationship of privileges and responsibilities between lords and vassals, and a hierarchy of titles gradually evolved. The great nobles became dukes, from the Latin word *dux*, meaning "leader." Other noble titles included count, viscount, and baron.

| Illuminations |
| --- |
| The Christian custom of placing the two hands together in prayer comes from the feudal oath of allegiance ceremony. While the vassal was paying homage to the lord, Christians placing their hands together give homage to God. |

## Feudal Ceremonies

The mutual exchange of promises between a lord and his vassal were made actual by a ceremony known as investiture. In this ceremony, the vassal knelt before the lord, placed his hands together between the lord's hands, and then pledged an oath of allegiance and obedience. In return, the lord provided his vassal with a *fief*. The lord also worked to protect his vassal and to ensure justice for him by hearing his and his dependents' cases in court. Additionally, the lord usually gave the vassal a charter or deed and some symbol of the estate, such as a clump of dirt.

**def•i•ni•tion**

A **fief** was a gift of land a lord gave to a vassal in return for military service. At first the fiefs were given only for the life of the vassal, but later they became hereditary.

## The Fief

Fiefs varied in size, and a vassal had complete control over all the people, houses, and villages that came with it. In addition, if he had enough power, he could wage war, mint coins, collect taxes, and make alliances. The only thing he was required to do was give his lord military assistance when asked. The power of the vassal's fief passed to his children, although, in theory, the lord was still technically the owner of the land.

## Your Mission Is ...

The obligations required by the vassal to his lord varied greatly across Europe. For example, in France, a vassal was expected to serve at least 40 days each year in military service to the king. If there was no war at the time, he helped with the courts and the dispensation of justice. Sometimes the vassal was needed for a longer time, in which case he was compensated accordingly. During the late Middle Ages, vassals were allowed to pay money to defer their time in service to their lord. Of course, those payments became a great source of revenue to the lords and allowed them to hire armies rather than depend on vassals.

A vassal was obliged to pay other expenses to the lord, including such expenses as the wedding feast of the lord's daughter and the ransom an enemy who captured the lord might demand. If the vassal did not fulfill his obligations or died without heirs, a lord could seize his estate. But if the lord tried to kill or enslave the vassal or steal his property, including his wife, the vassal was absolved of his obligations.

# Knights in Shining Armor

Feudalism developed in part as a way of providing quick protection and security. Of course, the power and wealth of the nobles was linked to the ownership of estates. So after the invasions of the eighth through the tenth centuries abated, the nobles began to fight among themselves over land, rights, and kin. As a result, small little wars became a recreational activity with the feudal nobles of the Middle Ages.

## The Origins of Knights

In the early medieval period, warriors and later knights wore only padded leather coats and metal helmets, but as the stirrup developed, they needed better protection. As a result, small iron rings were sewn into the padding to give more protection. Eventually, rings were linked together to create chain mail, which provided even better protection. By the millennium, all knights wore armor and even used armor on their horses. As weapons became heavy and more destructive, the armor again changed.

By the high Middle Ages, armor was made of sheets of steel joined together for mobility and protection. Although the knight was covered from head to toe with steel, he could still fight, walk, run, and ride a horse. (He did have to be placed on the horse with a sort of crane.) Once the knight's face was covered, the shield, which had traditionally been round and light, became large, heavy, and painted with a symbol or design known as a "coat of arms" to identify the knight. A coat of arms was handed down from generation to generation, and these coats of arms and their use became known as heraldry.

By the twelfth century, the medieval knight had some standard equipment. Each knight had a lance he used to unhorse enemy knights. He also carried a two-edged sword and dagger on a waist belt. Sometimes for added protection, a knight carried a heavy club, mace, or battle axe. All together the armor and weapons could weigh as much as 100 pounds.

Of course, the sole purpose of the knight was to fight wars, and much of his life was spent doing just that. In the early history of knighthood, a man on horseback charging was more than effective in dispersing men on foot. But new weapons were developed that lessened the shock value of a knight's attack. One weapon developed in the thirteenth century that lessened this shock value was the crossbow. Invented in China and migrating to the West, the crossbow fired a metal bolt that any foot soldier could use to penetrate a knight's armor. But this weapon had limitations, including its awkwardness and short range. The longbow was another useful weapon against knights; it could not penetrate a knight's armor, but when fired in large numbers, it broke up horseback charges. In general, anything that got the knight to fall off his horse was good. Once on the ground, with the weight of the armor, knights were slow to maneuver and fight.

During the early years of feudalism, to become a knight was one way to improve one's position in life. Eventually this opportunity was closed off. Members of the upper classes believed it was lineage, not wartime service, that fixed a person's status in society.

## From Boy to Knight

As the importance of the knight increased in medieval society, the education that only nobles received, which was skimpy at best, became centered on training for knighthood. Nobles expected their sons to become knights or priests, and most boys opted for the life of a knight. So at the age of seven, they were sent to another lord's castle for training. There the noble boy would serve as a page, where the lady of the house taught him how to be a gentlemen with Christian values and culture. She might even teach him to read and write. By the age of 14, the page became a squire to the lord. This involved more warlike duties including caring for the arms and armor and guarding prisoners. During this time the squire learned to use the weapons of a knight.

After completing the stage of a squire by the age of 21, the young man became a full-fledged knight. There was a religious bent to everything in the Middle Ages, and knighthood was no exception. Before the knighting ceremony, the would-be knight had to spend a night in the chapel praying for guidance. The next day, after a holy mass, the young man was knighted by his lord. The ceremony usually involved the touching of the knight with the broadside of a sword. Afterward, there was always lots of celebrating, feasting, and probably hangovers.

As feudalism progressed, the process of becoming a knight became much more ritualistic. Most boys from the upper classes were automatically given the page status at the age of 7, squire status at 14 or 15, and then went through the ritual of becoming a knight at 21 with little training. Fewer boys of ability from poor backgrounds became knights as a result.

> **Notable Quote**
>
> "War is not an evil thing, but good and virtuous; for war, by its nature, seeks nothing other than to set wrong right and turn dissension to peace."
>
> — *Tree of Battles*, Honoré Bonet

## Let the Games Begin!

Knights trained for battle in mock battles called jousts and tournaments, which were just shy of the real thing. Jousts were more formal, with two knights in armor riding toward each other at full speed with lances raised. The purpose of this apparent suicide run was to unhorse the other knight. Tournaments involved teams of knights who fought mock battles with the intent not of killing each other but making each other submit to a ransom. As you can imagine, knights were injured, maimed, and killed, but it was all in good fun.

The tournament became one of the characteristic institutions of the code of chivalry, which we'll discuss shortly. It was disapproved of by the church but was very popular regardless, especially during the twelfth and thirteenth centuries. Men at the tournaments called heralds also became important and influential with their role in regulating the tournaments. For all of the dangers of these tournaments, the secular feudal society accepted them as a training ground for young knights and a great entertainment where valor could be displayed heroically.

## Can't We All Just Get Along?

The Catholic Church tried to reduce the fighting among the knights when the pope issued two pronouncements: the Peace of God and the Truce of God. This movement started during the late tenth century. It was an attempt to curb the violence of the Middle Ages and also to make roads and towns safer for pilgrims and merchants.

The Peace of God was first declared by the pope in 989 in Charroux. It stated that peasants had rights and insisted on fair codes of behavior for all knights and soldiers in war and peace time. In addition, it guaranteed the safety of merchants and the sanctuary of churches.

**def•i•ni•tion**

**Excommunication** meant removal from full communion with the church. Since the sacraments were essential to the salvation of the soul, to be excommunicated was to be damned to Hell.

Later measures were taken during the eleventh century with the Truce of God. This new step was used to reduce bloodshed in Europe. It advocated armistices in blood feuds and prohibited fighting from Wednesday night until Monday morning. The truce was enforced by bands of militia and threats of church punishment including *excommunication*. First decreed at the Council of Elne in 1027, the Truce was amended in 1095 by the Council of Clermont. The council lengthened the prohibitions for fighting to include the Christmas season.

Both of these measures were ineffective in ending the bloodshed in Europe. But they did have an important role in convincing many knights under the threat of church punishment to atone for their sins by going on a crusade to the Holy Land. The Peace of God and the Truce of God also showed the cultural influence of the church in the daily life of Europeans.

# The Code of Chivalry

The code of chivalry can be described as a secular code of honor in a warrior aristocracy. Generally, this code followed by the knights of Europe flourished from the mid-eleventh century to the end of the Middle Ages. Several factors influenced its evolution into a complex set of rules and conventions that had a strong impact on medieval society.

But at first the influence of the church was great. The code itself can be traced to the softening of the epic virtues of the Germanic warriors found in tales like *Beowulf* to a gentler attitude which had some degree of respect for human life and dignity, even toward enemies. This was evidenced in the blessing of banners, the use of prayers before battle, clerical prayers for Christian knights fighting pagans, and a developing interest in warrior saints like Saint George and Saint Michael.

## Saint George and Saint Michael

Saint George was a famous saint and martyr of the church whose death was not really documented. Regardless, he became very popular and his legend underwent considerable transformation during the Middle Ages. Historians today generally accept him as a historical figure who was a Roman legion who may have been martyred in the fourth century near Lydda in Asia Minor.

The cult of Saint George first popped up in Europe during the sixth century. It had spread throughout England by the end of the eighth century. As time passed, George's story became very elaborate, with fantastic deeds including the slaying of dragons. One such example was written in the thirteenth-century tale *The Golden Legend*, which described Saint George's rescue of a maiden from a dragon. During the Crusades, he was idolized by the knights in the Holy Land, and tradition has it that he came to the aid of the knights during the siege and Battle of Antioch during the First Crusade. In general, Saint George was usually depicted in artwork with a sword or spear in his hand slaying a dragon. During the Late Middle Ages, George's cult still flourished and he was named the protector of the Order of the Garter in 1347 by King Edward III. Eventually he became known as the patron saint of England.

Saint Michael is one of only three angels that were mentioned in the Bible (the other two were Gabriel and Raphael). Traditionally, Michael was thought to have appeared during a plague in Rome, gathering the souls of those who had died. This was most probably the origin of the Christian spiritual hymn, "Michael Row the Boat Ashore." But during the Middle Ages, Michael became known as a warrior saint who protected knights and gave victory to the good over the forces of evil. Thus he was often prayed to by knights and kings alike as a sign of having God on their side. In art, like Saint George, he was usually shown with a sword, fighting or standing in victory over a dragon or snake.

The evolution of feudal society in the High Middle Ages brought even better conditions for the continuing growth of the code of chivalry. Developing its association with the nobles of feudal society, chivalry developed its institutions, rules, and conventions during the twelfth and thirteenth centuries with the help of poets as much as monarchs. Ceremonies of dubbing into knighthood at the age of 21, the giving of arms, and the adoption of a distinguishing emblem emphasized the secular attributes of the knight. It was only with the formation of military orders for the Crusades (which we'll discuss in a later chapter) that the code was brought back to a strong religious element.

## For the Love of a Woman

Another factor impacting the chivalric code was women. Women were present at the tournaments as spectators. Ideas of service to women and courtly love became entwined with the ideal of the knight. For example, a thirteenth-century poem laid out the duties for a knight:

- Eschew false judgment and treason
- Attend church every day
- Fast on Friday
- Always honor women

The ideas of chivalry even outlasted the loss of the Holy Land. In fact, they were augmented during the Late Middle Ages. The patronage of monarchs and dukes created chivalric orders like the Order of the Garter in England and the Order of the Golden Fleece in Burgundy. Young knights on a quest, both physical and spiritual, became part of the consciousness of the West to this day. Heraldry and genealogy, also a part of the chivalric code, ensured that traditions of descent and family remained a strong feature of Western civilization, especially with the ruling group.

In the end, chivalry slowly civilized the military aspect of feudal society and even Western society to some degree. Germanic warriors had been rude and violent, but by the end of the Middle Ages, knights were gentlemen. The behavior of knights usually fell short of the code of chivalry, but failure meant punishment, usually public disgrace. The knight could be stripped of his armor, have his weapons broken, and have a priest declare him "dead to honor." That sometimes worked. So it was definitely a start in creating a less violent world.

> **Notable Quote**
>
> "The good man took the sword, girded him with it and kissed him, telling him that with the sword he had given him the highest order that God had created and ordained, the order of knighthood, which ought to be blameless."
>
> —*The Legend of Perceval,*
> Chrétien de Troyes

# Minding Their Manors

The feudal system established a relationship between the lords and vassals, but the other 80 percent of the population was made up of peasants who worked the land and were essential to the economic system known as manorialism that developed during the Middle Ages.

Manorialism had its roots in Roman custom. Small peasant landowners turned over their holdings to nobles in exchange for protection and some of the crops. These estates, which became known as manors, were the center of the medieval community. As the Middle Ages progressed, the peasants, who were once free to come and go as they wished, became serfs, tied to the land for their living, as were their descendants. Eventually a majority of the peasants of Europe became serfs.

## To the Castle!

During the early Middle Ages, lords designed their houses for defense. The word castle comes from the Latin *castellum*, meaning "small military camp." In the beginning, these castles were made of thick wooden walls. Later, lords built their castles out of stone, on hilltops, and usually in a river bend or some other very defensible position. A castle often was surrounded by a moat or ditch filled with rainwater and other waste, including human waste. (The smell of a moat was horrible.) A bridge that could be raised and lowered gave the only access to the castle.

After some time, castles became quite large since they were designed to house the lord and his household. Space also needed to be available for the peasants who lived in the village near the castle walls to move inside in case of emergency. Just inside the walls was a central courtyard, where court was held when the weather was good. It also housed the workshops and kitchen necessary to supply the castle and its defenders. The castle had stables, storehouses for food and weapons, and jails for prisoners. Each castle kept enough food and water on hand for the inhabitants to survive a siege lasting several months.

The lord of the castle and his family lived in the inner defensible structure, in a stone tower called the keep. The most frequently used room of the castle keep was the great hall, a room large enough to house all of the knights who defended the castle. There the lord had great parties where people drank, sang, played games, or listened to stories by wandering minstrels.

The nobles ate fish, birds, wild game, and bread, usually washed down with wine or ale. Peasants, who had a much plainer menu, ate porridge, cabbage, turnips, and bread washed down with beer. Generally peasants did not eat meat because it was an expensive luxury, whereas nobles had access to a lot of meat through hunting on game preserves.

The great hall also had one or more fireplaces that had to be continually stoked to keep the hall even remotely warm. Most of the food served in the great hall was prepared in a separate kitchen and brought into the hall to be served. This was a practical arrangement, as kitchens tended to catch fire often—but food at the castle party was usually served cold.

## A Typical Manor

A manor was made up of a castle or manor house for the noble, the peasant village, a church, and the surrounding fields, pastures, and forests. Of course, the manor house was probably the largest building; these houses started out as two-story wooden houses but evolved into castles.

A small manor might have about 300 acres of land with 15 peasant families to work the land. A larger manor could have several thousand acres and over 50 peasant families. The peasant village was stocked with a variety of one-room homes built of dried mud and thatched roofs. Fires were centrally located in the homes with a hole in the roof for escaping smoke. The floors were made of earth, and usually there were no windows, only a door. The furniture was simple, with usually a plank table, a few stools, and one bed for everyone to sleep on.

The lands of the manor provided for the lord and his family as well as the peasants. A well, spring, or dammed stream provided water. The forests provided wild game for the lord and firewood for all. They used any open land to pasture the manor's domesticated animals.

The land used for crops was divided into two portions. The lord's portion was called the demesne. The peasants' portion of land was divided into small strips separated by footpaths. During the eighth century, peasants developed the "three-field system" as each peasant was responsible for three strips of land. In the fall, one strip of land was planted with wheat. In the spring, a second strip of land was planted with barley or oats. The third strip was left fallow or not planted for the year. This allowed the soil to replenish itself, improving production. Beyond their own lands, the serfs had to work the lord's demesne at least three days a week and more during harvest time.

At the end of the first millennium, the shortage of trade meant that most manors had to be self-sufficient and produce all the needed food and goods. Food was preserved by a variety of methods, including storage in root cellars, pickling, smoking, and salting. Wine and beer were made from fruits and grains. Bread for everyone was baked daily in the lord's kitchen.

## A Serf's Life

The serfs made all the clothing for the manor. They raised sheep for wool and planted flax to make linen. The women and children were kept busy spinning yarn and weaving cloth. They also used animal hides to make leather shoes and harnesses. Eventually this self-sufficiency created a specialization of labor on the manor. Some peasants became skilled workers, like carpenters, leather workers, blacksmiths, or bakers. Only later when towns were revived at the start of the second millennium did manors no longer need to be so independent.

To work the land, serfs had several different tools available, including hoes, plows, scythes, and sickles. Most of the tools were primitive and made by hand from pieces of wood and old iron. The serfs were not advanced enough to use fertilizer or oxen to help increase their yield from their fields. Since there was no surplus of food, the loss of a harvest to drought, famine, or an act of God meant starvation. Later in the Middle Ages, improvements in agriculture including the use of the heavy plow, the horse collar, horseshoes, and wind and watermills increased crop yields.

The constant struggle for survival took most of a serf's time. Still, everyone needs some enjoyment in life, and celebrations were held for many occasions, including weddings, births, saint days, holy feasts, and other holy days. On important religious days, the feasts were held at the lord's house. With food and drink, the serfs played games, danced, and talked. They gathered at the manor church for physical contests such as wrestling, jumping matches, shooting and throwing contests, and tugs of war. On some occasions, wandering poets came to the manor feast to sing and tell stories that entertained and informed the people of the news of Europe. During these times, the peasants of the manor got to see the jugglers and minstrels the lord had hired as entertainment.

The serf's life was hard. Peasants had to work the fields and serve their lord in war if need be. They faced harsh punishments for any offense toward the lord, his family, or lands. In addition, the lord was free to abuse the serfs at will because the lord was the justice of the manor. So the fear of death, war, disease, and starvation were a constant in a serf's short life.

## A Lord's Life

Lords, on the other hand, had it a bit better. The lord's word was the law; because he owned the manor, he could make the rules. He could also create taxes and levies whenever he needed to cover extra expenses, like a marriage or a new knight.

But with the power came responsibility. He had to dispense justice. Being fair always made one a favorite, and being a favorite meant the serfs felt a loyalty to their lord. If the loyalty factor was high, some lords would use stewards to supervise the manor, which was especially true with lords who owned large manors or had more than one.

## Recreation on the Manor

The people of the manor, like those before and since, looked for ways to entertain themselves. For the lords of the manor, the great entertainments were hunting and hawking. They would ride through the fields and forests of their manor chasing wild deer and boar. Hawking was another favorite but it did not originate in Europe. It developed in Asia and then spread to the Roman Empire through the interregional trade of the Silk Road. In Europe, hawks were trained to hunt and bring down rabbits, pigeons, and herons.

The lord of the manor also enjoyed the performing arts. Jugglers and jesters would perform for the lord of the manor. These performers were dressed in ridiculous costumes and gave wise-crack answers to questions. For their efforts, they would receive meals and a roof over their head. There were also minstrels who traveled to the manors telling stories for entertainment, to spread news and gossip, and to continue the legends of a region. In France, these minstrels were called jongleurs.

Popular and educational plays were also performed during the feast days. These plays were used by the church to teach the public, most of which could not read. They involved either stories about the Bible, saints, or virtues and vices. The stage for the play was often a box with the playing lasting only 10 to 20 minutes. The plays were supposed to be religious, but some got so obscene that the church would ban them from being performed in the churchyard.

Feudalism and manorialism gave Europe much-needed stability. For peasants and nobles, feudalism and manorialism brought better food, housing, clothing, protection, and security during a time of uncertainty. No, it was not all wine and roses for the people, especially the serfs, but these improvements did rest on the foundations of feudalism and manorialism until the Late Middle Ages.

From the Early Middle Ages to the High Middle Ages, Europe was more fertile than ever before. The three-field system when used cultivated the land more intensely and with better crop yields. From this agricultural production grew an economy that could support more population, trade, and towns. And until the thirteenth century, the people of medieval Europe enjoyed a greater degree of stability and security than that of the early Middle Ages and even Late Middle Ages.

## The Least You Need To Know

- ◆ Feudalism developed in response to the invasions of the late first millennium.

- ◆ Lords granted lands to vassals in return for military service; these knights became the main fighting force of the Middle Ages.

- ◆ Fortified houses or castles became the place of protection for the people.

- ◆ Manorialism developed between lords of the land and serfs. Serfs worked for the lord in exchange for protection and a share of the crops.

# Part 2

# The High Middle Ages (1000–1300)

With the new millennium, Europe saw some definite improvements over the previous 500 years. Politically, the kingdoms of Europe were becoming more effective in their rule. Part of this was because the threat of catastrophic invasions was waning. Additionally, the climate of Europe warmed up slightly, which, coupled with new agricultural innovations, allowed farmers to produce a surplus. With surplus food, the population and commercial activity of Europe increased twofold by 1300. With more people and commerce, new cities appeared and old cities grew larger. People were living, eating, and working better than ever before. With economic and social prosperity came intellectual and cultural developments. Universities educated a new professional intellectual class made of nobles and an emerging middle class. From these universities sprang ideas of self-awareness and rationalism fundamental to the modern Western mind.

# Chapter 8

# When the Big Three Were Little

## In The Chapter

- ◆ Ottonians, Franconians, and Hohenstaufens
- ◆ The lay investiture controversy
- ◆ William the Conqueror
- ◆ Anglo-Norman England
- ◆ The Capetians and France

After the invasions of the late millennium and the development of feudalism and manorialism, several kingdoms emerged that would later develop into the major nation-states of Europe. The centralization of the monarchies at the turn of the second millennium began this development.

## The Holy Roman Empire or the Holy Rollers

The Holy Roman Empire was able to centralize the power of the monarchy earlier than England and France, but less effectively. The empire created by the Treaty of Verdun developed from the eastern kingdom of

Charlemagne's grandson Louis. The people of the eastern kingdom were less influenced by Roman custom than the rest of Charlemagne's old empire. Of course, Louis was an ineffective ruler and so were his descendants.

By the time the last of Louis's descendants died in 911, the region was divided into five different duchies: Saxony, Franconia, Swabia, Bavaria, and Lorraine, each ruled by a duke. These dukes depended on bonds of loyalty and skill to rule their duchies. After the two centuries of invasions and the domination of feudalism, various nobles created many smaller estates out of these duchies. It took centuries of political work for the region to be centralized into the Holy Roman Empire—with only varying degrees of success.

## The Origins of the Ottonian Dynasty

When the last Carolingian, King Louis the Child, died in 911, the dukes of the duchies elected Conrad of Franconia to be their king, not because he was strong but because he was weak. Conrad held the title for close to eight years but did very little. He was a throwback to the do-nothing Merovingian kings. The Magyars were harassing the kingdom, and his nobles were out of control. However, as he lay dying, Conrad made one good executive decision when he recommended that his rival, Henry the Duke of Saxony, become his successor.

Henry of Saxony (876–936) became king of Germany in 919 and was the first king of the Ottonian dynasty. To protect the kingdom against the Magyar threat, he built a system of fortified defenses. Henry the Fowler, as he was called because he loved hunting wild fowl, then defeated the Magyars on the field of battle in 933 at the Battle of Riade. Although, like his predecessor, Henry was challenged by the nobility, he laid a strong political foundation for his son to succeed him.

## Otto the Great

After Henry, Otto I, or the Great (912–973) as he probably liked to be called, was crowned king of the Germans at Charlemagne's old palace at Aachen. As king, he carried out a military policy of expanding eastward from Saxony against the encroaching Magyars. Otto defeated the Magyars decisively at the Battle of Lechfeld in 955, putting an end to their aggressive tendencies.

Upon taking control of his eastern borders, Otto looked south toward Italy and invaded Lombard-controlled northern Italy to help free Queen Adelaide, the widow of a Lombard King, who was imprisoned by her enemies. (Very chivalrous!) After Otto defeated her enemies and rescued her, he married her and claimed the title of king of Italy. In 960, when the papal lands were under attack, the pope appealed to Otto, who was more than happy to march into Italy and sort out the mess, much as Charlemagne had done in the past. And just as with Charlemagne in 800, the grateful pope crowned Otto the Great as Holy Roman Emperor, which placed him in line of succession, in theory, with Roman emperors and Charlemagne. This beginning of a new Holy Roman Empire linked Germany and Italy for years to come.

At home, Otto strengthened his political position by allying himself with the church. He gave church bishops landholdings, and they gave him money and soldiers. This practice was feudal in principal and allowed the king to appoint bishops to the church. It also bound the bishops to their feudal lord, the king of Germany. So with church support, Otto was able to squeeze out the power of the nobles. He took the land of nobles who opposed his policies and usually gave it to the church. This feudal arrangement between church and state stifled the spiritual and cultural progress of the church in Germany.

## The Franconian Dynasty

However, Otto the Great's successors were not so great. They neglected their political position in Germany while attempting to control the Italian peninsula. The Slavs in the east and the Danes in the north took advantage of this time and raided German strongholds in both regions. When the last Saxon king died in 1024, the German dukes elected Conrad II (1024–1039) as king of the Germans and Holy Roman Emperor. And although the Franconian dynasty ruled for less than a century, they increased royal authority and centralized power.

The Franconian rulers reduced the political power of the nobles by replacing them with *minsterales*, a word coming from the Latin word for "servant." These officials' authority came from the king, and their offices were appointed, not hereditary, so their children could not claim the office. This prevented any one family from having too much power against the king. Conrad II and his successors also collected long-overdue taxes, giving the treasury a much-needed shot in the arm. This money was used to develop silver mines in the empire to mint more coins, again giving the empire financial strength.

**def•i•ni•tion**

Simony is the sale and purchase of church positions, a common practice during the Middle Ages.

The Franconian rulers also worked to reform the church in Germany by appointing capable people who were loyal to the empire in positions of leadership. Henry III (1039–1056) helped Pope Leo IX become pope. He did this in support of the pope's efforts to correct the abuses of *simony* and failure of priests to obey their vows of celibacy.

## The Lay Investiture Controversy

When the son of Henry III ascended the throne, he was six years old. With Henry IV, the empire was left in a weakened position as nobles seized royal property and took over many of the royal powers. As a result Henry IV constantly struggled to assert royal authority over his nobles. But this was not going to be his only struggle.

In 1073, a monk named Hildebrand who was part of the Cluniac reform movement was elected pope. Pope Gregory VII revitalized the office of the papacy in power and prestige. He wanted to end the abuses of the clergy and free the church from the control of kings. To do this he needed to put all members of the clergy under papal, not royal, control and end the practice of *lay investiture*. As a result, Gregory issued a decree in 1075 forbidding lay investiture with the threat of excommunication. Although this decree applied to all rulers of Europe, Henry IV was brought into direct conflict with the papacy over the issue.

**def•i•ni•tion**

Lay investiture was the practice of laypeople or secular rulers investing clergy with the symbols of ecclesiastical powers. This allowed secular powers to have control over the church.

With his errant nobility at home, Henry IV needed to appoint bishops and archbishops who were loyal to him. So in response, he accused Gregory of simony and other abuses and went so far as to call him a "false monk." Gregory shot back with papal envoys who warned Henry that he would not tolerate insolence like that. Henry responded by convening a synod of German bishops loyal to him to depose the pope. This was too much for Pope Gregory. He excommunicated Henry and released Henry's subjects from their oaths of allegiance.

The German nobles were overjoyed. They invited Pope Gregory to come to Augsburg to preside over the election of a new emperor. Knowing that he had lost the struggle, Henry sought forgiveness. In the winter of 1077, he crossed the Alps in the blinding snow to Canossa in northern Italy, where he sought to meet Pope Gregory before he reached Augsburg. After keeping Henry waiting in the snow for three days, Gregory lifted his excommunication, restoring Henry to the church.

But this did not end the struggle between the two men. In 1083, Henry captured Rome and made his own candidate pope. Gregory, who had fled, appealed to the nearby Normans in southern Italy. They did help capture Rome but pillaged the city. The people of Rome held Gregory responsible for the looting of the city, so he could not return to the papal throne. He died alone in exile in 1085. Henry also died alone after failing to regain the throne from his rebellious son.

> **Notable Quote**
>
> Laying aside all the trappings of royalty, he stood in wretchedness, barefooted and clad in wool, for three days before the gate of the castle, and implored with profuse weeping the aid and consolation of apostolic mercy.
>
> —Pope Gregory's account of Henry's penance at Canossa

## The End of the Franconians

The conflict between the popes and the Holy Roman Emperor did not end until 1122 at the Concordant of Worms. With the concordant, German nobles forced Henry V to compromise with the papacy to end the conflicts. In the terms of the treaty, the emperor gave up his claim to invest the bishops with the symbols of the office, which were the ring and staff, but he was allowed to invest them with a scepter that represented temporal power. In addition, the clergy had the right to elect their bishop but only in the presence of the emperor. On the other hand, the pope gave up control of religious estates in Germany and got full control over the appointment of bishops in Italy. The agreement did end the conflict, but it also weakened the Holy Roman Emperor considerably, especially his powers over the church.

After the last of the Franconians in 1125, civil war tore apart the empire as two noble families, the Welfs and Hohenstaufens, fought for the title of Holy Roman Emperor. In the end a Hohenstaufen prince, Conrad III (1138–1152), became the emperor, but not without a struggle. After gaining the throne, Conrad III went on the Second Crusade, which was not the best of moves. When he returned, he found the nobility fighting each other and him for political power.

# The Origins of the Hohenstaufen

Struggling to regain control of his empire after an unsuccessful crusade, Conrad died without an heir. To solve the problem of succession, the nobles chose Conrad's nephew, Frederick of Hohenstaufen, as emperor because his mother had been a Welf.

Frederick I, or Barbarossa (meaning "redhead"), took the throne determined to centralize royal authority. He forced nobles to reaffirm feudal oaths and tried to assert control over church office appointments. He shored up the borders defensively in the north and east and finally put down a rebellion led by his cousin.

Once Frederick had Germany under wraps, he turned his attention to Italy. He wanted control over the cities of Venice, Genoa, Pisa, and Milan because they were sources of trade revenue. These cities formed the Lombard League in anticipation of Frederick's desire for control. In addition, he wanted to control the papacy. So in 1168, Frederick and his army invaded Italy. He was able to defeat the pope and capture Rome, but he didn't get to enjoy his victory for long; he was forced to withdraw when an epidemic broke out.

The Italians had had enough. When Frederick and his armies came into Italy again in 1176, the combined forces of the pope and the Lombard League were able to defeat him. At the Battle of Legnano, Frederick was forced to flee for his life. In the next year, he signed the Peace of Constance with the Lombard League, granting the cities the right to self-government in exchange for feudal taxes to the Holy Roman Emperor. Additionally, Frederick and the pope agreed to terms, and he was reconciled with the church.

Through ambition and force, Frederick increased the power of the Holy Roman Empire. He worked hard to make strong feudal ties to himself, so that all feudal power came from the emperor. But he did not want to stop with Germany and Italy. When news reached Europe that Islamic forces led by Saladin had captured Jerusalem from the Christians, Frederick saw an opportunity; but unfortunately, he never reached the Holy Land because he fell off his horse and drowned in a small river in Asia Minor.

But for centuries after his death, people believed Frederick the Barbarossa did not die but had fallen asleep in a secret cave—which is suspiciously close to the fate of the mythological King Arthur.

Frederick's son, Henry VI, continued his father's work. He consolidated power over Sicily and planned even more conquests. But his plans never came to be; he died after a brief reign, leaving the throne to his very young son, Frederick II (r. 1220–1250). A civil war resulted as nobles tried to support other candidates to the imperial throne.

# Frederick II

Frederick II was only able to calm things down after gaining Pope Innocent III's support by giving up claim to Sicily. At that point, the pope proclaimed him the Holy Roman Emperor, and Frederick II immediately took control of his lands, defeating a powerful force of nobles in the political and military field. After he gained sure control of Germany, Frederick turned to Italy like those before him and tried to expand his power over the Kingdom of the Two Sicilies (Sicily and Naples). Since Frederick spent most of his life in Sicily, he was not too interested in his German lands. As a result, he gave control of many royal estates in Germany to local nobles and clergy, which created the environment later for Germany to become a region of small, independent states.

In Italy, Frederick regained the power over Sicily that he had lost to the papacy and took direct control over the government there. He reorganized the army and navy as paid forces rather than feudal obligations, making them easier to direct. He also set up an efficient treasury and established the University of Naples to train administrators in Roman law.

But it was not all roses for Frederick; like Henry IV, he also had trouble with the church. In 1227, Pope Gregory IX was elected to the papal throne. Alarmed at Frederick's growing power in the Italian peninsula, he ordered Frederick to fulfill a promise to lead a crusade to the Holy Land. Frederick, of course, knew the intent of the request and refused, so Gregory then excommunicated him.

To redeem himself with the pope, Frederick organized the Sixth Crusade in 1228. He was able to gain access for Christians to Jerusalem, Bethlehem, and Nazareth through the port at Sidon. Despite this success, his relations with the papacy only got worse. Returning from the crusade, he found his lands under attack by papal forces. From then until his death, Frederick was at war with the church. His conflict with the papacy and his neglect of German lands led to the disintegration of the Holy Roman Empire.

With the help of France, the pope succeeded in overthrowing the Hohenstaufen in Sicily. The last Hohenstaufen was captured and killed in 1268. In 1273, Rudolf of Hapsburg became the Holy Roman Emperor, establishing the Hapsburg dynasty that lasted until 1806. But the Holy Roman Empire was decentralized and weakened. Individual German princes took more political control of the empire, while the emperor only had nominal control by the end of the Middle Ages.

# Jolly Olde England

During the early Middle Ages, the Germanic tribes of Angles, Saxons, and Jutes settled on the island of Britain and came to dominate it culturally. These Anglo-Saxons formed several independent kingdoms across Britain, now called Angleland. The Anglo-Saxon kingdoms were not immune to Viking invasions of the late first millennium and lost power and lands to the Vikings.

King Alfred the Great of Wessex finally united the Anglo-Saxon kingdoms to drive out the Viking invaders, but the "united kingdom" of the Anglo-Saxons did not last for long. After the death of King Edward the Confessor, William the Conqueror, of Normandy in France, made a claim for the throne. In 1066, William and his Norman army defeated the other rival for the Anglo-Saxon throne, Harold Godwinson, at the Battle of Hastings. From then William the Conqueror and the Norman kings of England centralized the power of the monarchy.

## William the Conqueror

William the Conqueror was crowned king on Christmas Day, 1066. During his reign, he consolidated power over the Anglo-Saxons and the Normans who had invaded England with him. To protect his power, he gave the Norman knights small, scattered estates and demanded they recognize his supremacy. In addition, William limited the number and size of the castles that were built. William also used an oath of fealty called the Salisbury Oath to break feudal obligations. In this oath, vassals owed their primary allegiance to the king of England rather than the lord from whom they received their fief. This permitted William and his successors to start the process of nation building.

William combined the political and social institutions of Anglo-Saxon and Norman traditions in government and laid the foundation for a strong, centralized government. He created a Great Council that included all the great lords of England. He also established a council of royal advisors called the King's Council. Both of these institutions evolved into the English Parliament. William left the local Anglo-Saxon system of government in place, but had royal commissioners oversee the courts and sheriffs.

He also reformed the church in England by replacing Anglo-Saxon clergy with Normans. William allowed the church to create separate ecclesiastical courts to hear cases on religious matters. He enforced the rule of celibacy in the clergy and decreed that no papal letter could be read in England without prior consent of the king. In an effort to dissuade William from too much church reform, Pope Gregory VII asked him to swear an oath of allegiance and ordered all English bishops to report to Rome. William quickly rejected both demands. Gregory VII was too involved in his struggle with Henry IV to contest William's reaction and the matter was dropped.

---

### Illuminations

In 1086, William ordered a survey of the land ownership of England to be made. This survey was known as the *Domesday Book*. The word *dome* meant judgment; so the book was to be used in judging disputes in land ownership. More importantly, the book allowed William to inventory his economic resources because it included a record of all plows, forests, cows, pigs, and other properties in England.

---

## Anglo-Norman Culture

William's rule changed England culturally. Traditionally in the Anglo-Saxon past, Scandinavia and northern Germany had influenced the culture. Under William, that contact decreased and contact with France and western Europe increased. New Norman lords brought French artisans to England. Cathedrals were built in the Norman style. In addition, William introduced a more centralized and efficient form of feudalism to England.

All this change was most evident in the use of language. French became the language of the nobles and the king's court, although Latin was still used as the language of the church. And Anglo-Saxon or Old English was the language of the everyday folk of England. After several generations, the strong Anglo-Saxon and Norman cultures blended to create the Anglo-Norman culture of the Middle Ages.

William the Conqueror's successors continued the policies of centralizing royal power. They developed a corps of royal officials that administered the policies of the king. Better than feudal lords, these officials owed their positions to the king and could not give these positions to their offspring. Henry I increased the administration of royal justice when he sent judges out to hear law cases rather than have the courts of feudal lords and the church hear the cases. This took power from the lords and the church. He also was a vigorous tax collector and had royal officials collect taxes from across the realm keeping very accurate records.

### Illuminations

Royal officials who collected taxes tallied their records on a checkered table that looked like a chessboard. These officials eventually became known as the Exchequer, which later became the modern office of the treasury in England.

# Henry II

After Henry I died in 1135, a controversy arose over who was to succeed the throne. Henry's son had drowned in a shipwreck while his daughter, Mathilda, was married to the count of Anjou of France. The counts of Anjou did not get along with the Normans one bit. So in 1154, after a long civil war, King Henry II, son of Mathilda, came to the throne, establishing the Plantagenet dynasty in England.

As son of the Count of Anjou, Henry inherited many lands in France, including Normandy, Maine, Touraine, Brittany, and Anjou. In 1152 he married Eleanor of Aquitaine, the repudiated wife of Louis VII of France, bringing him greater estates in France. Henry's kingdom stretched from northern England down to the Pyrenees in France. These gains were enhanced with the homage of Malcolm III of Scotland and by Henry's recognition as the overlord of Ireland in 1171.

Henry's first task on becoming king was to end the chaos in the kingdom and dealt harshly with the lords who had built castles without the king's permission. He then opened up the scope of royal justice and jurisdiction in royal courts by having judges base their decisions on the common customs and traditions of the people, laying the foundations of common law. As time went by, common law came to refer to a body of legal principles based on the decisions of the royal courts. With this reliance on the royal courts, the need for courts of lords and the church diminished.

The earliest forms of a jury system also developed under Henry. One was created after a plaintiff purchased a royal writ or order for a hearing before a royal official. Twelve people under oath, called a jury, presented their case. The second jury was established by the Edict of Clarendon in 1166 and called for sheriffs to collect a group of 12 men to appear before royal justices to help present cases for judgment. This was the fore-runner of the grand jury we have today.

Henry's legal reforms put him into conflict with the church courts, which traditionally had jurisdiction over cases involving the clergy. Because Henry thought the church courts were too lenient on its own members, he issued the Constitution of Clarendon in 1164. This act included a provision that allowed members of the clergy to be indicted by the royal courts. In addition, a person could be tried by the church court, but punishment had to be issued from the royal courts. Finally, the act stopped the clergy from appealing sentences to the papal courts without the king's permission.

# Thomas Becket

Thomas Becket, Archbishop of Canterbury, once a friend and advisor to the king, opposed Henry's legal reforms in relation to the church. Becket thought no member of the clergy should be subject to the laws of England and vowed to oppose the Constitution of Clarendon as long as he lived. His stand became part of one of the classic confrontations between church and state in politics.

Oddly, Becket rose from very humble beginnings to end up challenging a king. He was born in London and studied at Paris under a noted teacher, Robert of Melun. He then entered the service of the English monarchy, working with the English sheriffs as a clerk. In 1141, he became a member of the household of Archbishop Theobald of Canterbury. Becket made a name for himself as a man with a considerable future. As a result, he was sent to study law at Bologna and Auxerre and in 1154 he was appointed archdeacon of Canterbury.

As a rising young star in English politics, Becket attracted the attention of King Henry II and they became fast friends. They had similar tastes and interests; both had a love of hunting, women, and luxury. Eventually, Henry gave Becket the position of chancellor of England. Becket wielded vast power in English government and, with his gift of administration, ruthlessly enforced Henry's political will.

As chancellor of England, Becket reduced the opposition of the English barons and centralized royal power, often to the detriment of the power of the church. Since the power of the church was always a problem for the king, it seemed logical for Henry to appoint his friend and confidante to the post of Archbishop of Canterbury with the death of Theobald in 1161. Becket was reluctant to take the office, but did after Henry's prompting in 1162.

After Becket was consecrated as archbishop, a change took place in him. He renounced his worldly ambitions and adopted an intensely religious life. Realizing that the interests of the church did not match those of the state, he resigned as chancellor of England.

Becket soon clashed with King Henry II on a number of issues. He excommunicated a baron, one of Henry's loyal vassals; opposed a tax proposal; and fought against the Constitutions of Clarendon. Becket also rebuffed Henry's claim that clerics who committed crimes should be tried in secular courts. Henry responded with some harsh measures of his own against his former friend. He had Becket condemned by a council of English bishops loyal to the king.

As a result of the condemnation, Becket fled the country and came under the protection of King Louis VII of France. He remained in exile from 1164 to 1170. During this period Becket appealed his case to Pope Alexander III, while Henry ran the Church of England through the bishop of York, who was loyal to the king.

In 1170, a reconciliation between Henry and Becket took place. Becket returned to England in November. The people of England, who saw Becket as a hero, lined the roads to greet him as he made his way to the cathedral in Canterbury.

But the reconciliation did not last. By December, the final break between Henry and Becket occurred. Becket refused to absolve any of the English bishops who supported Henry during his exile unless they took an oath of obedience to the pope. Henry, sore over the public displays of support for Thomas, greeted the news with rage and fury. In the end, Henry, angry and drunk, supposedly referring to Becket, asked some of his knights, "Is there no one to rid me of this troublesome priest?" Four of those knights took Henry's words as a command and murdered Becket as he prayed in the cathedral at Canterbury.

The death of Becket was universally condemned. Miracles were reported shortly after his death at Canterbury. Soon Pilgrims began appearing at Canterbury, making it into one of the most popular holy sites during the Middle Ages. Becket received sainthood quickly from Pope Alexander III in 1173. Henry was blamed for the popular Becket's murder and performed penance for his sin, which included being flogged naked by monks. The king also agreed to recognize papal authority in church law and to exempt clergy from punishment in the civil courts. But this did not end England's conflict between the church and state; later another chancellor of England, Thomas More, would suffer a similar fate.

## Richard the Lionhearted

Richard I, the Lionhearted (r. 1189–1199), was the third son of Henry II. He became the Duke of Aquitaine at the young age of 12. During his reign of England, Richard actually spent fewer than six months on the island. Shortly after his coronation, Richard, ever the warrior, set off on the Third Crusade. He did fairly well on the crusade but failed to recapture Jerusalem from the Muslim forces led by Saladin.

On his return, Richard was captured in disguise and held for ransom. The king's mother, Eleanor of Aquitaine, worked hard to convince the English people to pay the ransom through a tax. Finally, in 1194, Richard was freed. After only a few weeks in England, Richard went to war again to fight the king of France, who had seized some English castles in France. He died in France in 1199. Despite the fact that he bankrupted the treasury of England with his crusade, ransom, and war, he became a folk hero to the English people.

## King John and the Magna Carta

In 1199, Henry II's other wayward son ascended the throne. King John was a bad ruler and violated most of the principles of justice that Henry II had tried to create. He killed his nephew and stole his land; he took one of his nobles' twelve-year-old daughters for his wife despite public outcry; later he argued with the pope and got himself excommunicated. When the nobles protested his actions, he threatened harsh punishment. John even locked up women and children who protested his actions. His unpopularity was so widespread that the people of England began to look to the nobles for relief.

And the nobles were complaining just as loudly as the rest of the English people. Finally, Stephen Langton, the archbishop of Canterbury, who openly criticized the king, began gathering supporters. When John raised taxes to wage war in France, the nobles saw it as their time to do something.

By 1215, the war in France was going poorly, and John needed more money to continue it. He pleaded to the nobles of England for a tax increase, and on June 12, 1215, they responded by demanding a meeting with him. The nobles rode out to a meadow along the Thames River and met with the king. With them, they brought a document with a list of their demands on it in order for John to receive more tax revenue. After a week of debate, the king put his seal on the document which became known as the *Magna Carta* or Great Charter. The document spelled out the rights nobles were to have, including the right to justice, taxation only with consent, and a jury trial. Later the provisions in the Magna Carta extended to all citizens, not just nobles.

> **Illuminations**
>
> The Magna Carta, with its limits on the power of the monarchy, is one of the documents that influenced the drafters of the United States Constitution later in eighteenth-century America.

## Edward I and Model Parliament

At the time of King John's death, two components of the English government had been established. They were the use of common law and the concept that the king was subject to law. In 1300, the final lasting component was added: Parliament.

The controversy over taxation did not end with the Magna Carta. Later English kings tried to tax in order to finance wars in France. During the reign of Henry III (1216–1272), Simon de Montefort led the nobles who rebelled against the king's call for taxes. They succeeded in capturing the king and ruling in his name for over a year. In that time, Simon summoned an assembly of nobles, clergy, knights, and representatives from each chartered town. They called the assembly Parliament, and it represented one of the first forms of democratic government. And although Henry III was restored to the throne, kings of England continued to consult with Parliament whenever they needed more taxes.

Edward I (1272–1307) continued to centralize royal power with the help of Parliament. He annexed the kingdom of Wales in 1284, naming his son the Prince of Wales, but his efforts to acquire Scotland were not successful, and he died leading an invasion force into the region. During his rule, Edward saw that raising taxes and dealing with other problems through Parliament was much easier. In 1295, he called for the "Model Parliament," based on Simon de Montfort's model but with one difference.

Edward divided the nobles, knights, clergy, and burgesses into separate groups. By the fourteenth century, these groups developed into two houses: the House of Lords, which consisted of nobles and bishops, and the House of Commons, which consisted of knights and burgesses. Parliament became more powerful as it took on more responsibility for ruling England during the Middle Ages.

# The Capetian Dynasty and France

In France, the centralization of the power of the monarchy took much longer, probably due to the entrenchment of the feudal system there. In 987, the noble Hugh Capet seized the French throne from a weak Carolingian king. During the eleventh and twelfth centuries, the Capetian dynasty consolidated power and strengthened France and the monarchy. But the feudal system was deeply rooted in French soil; it took King Philip II, Louis IX, and Philip IV to overpower the system by weakening the power of the feudal lords and making the royal courts dominant over the feudal courts.

## Philip II

King Philip II of France (1165–1223) succeeded his father, Louis VII, in 1180, and began an aggressive policy of restoring and expanding the kingdom of France. To do so, he defeated the Count of Flanders and the Duke of Burgundy. In addition, he seized Artois and part of the valley of the Somme River.

At first, Philip was obliged to accept the homage of King John of England and give up control of the lands of Normandy, Aquitaine, and Anjou. But that arrangement did not last long, and Philip was able to recover Normandy, Anjou, Poitou, and the Auvergne for France. Later he defeated the combined armies of King John of England and the Holy Roman Emperor at the Battle of Bouvines in August 1214, establishing a stronger, unified France. In addition to these military successes, Philip devoted time and energy to reform the legal system of France and to revitalize and fortify Paris. By the end of his reign, royal power was well on the way to being firmly established.

## Saint Louis IX

Saint Louis IX (1214–1270) succeeded his father, Louis VIII, as king of France in 1226 and worked very effectively to consolidate and stabilize the country. Louis also had to deal with English territorial claims in France. He was very religious and built the Sainte-Chapelle in Paris to be the home of holy relics shipped in from Constantinople. Inspired by his miraculous recovery from a severe illness, he started the Seventh Crusade against Islamic forces in Egypt in 1248. Louis was initially successful on the crusade but was captured and held for ransom until 1250. But that did not dampen his crusading spirit; he later went on another crusade to Tunis, where he died of the plague.

Louis did much for the government and prestige of France. He expanded the administration of royal justice and established a supreme court of justice consisting of trained lawyers, nobles, and clergy. In addition, Louis was renowned for his fairness in mediating disputes between monarchs and common people. He was also generous in war and peace, demonstrated by the peace treaty that he signed with Henry III of England in 1259. All these attributes led Pope Boniface VIII to canonize him in 1297. His sanctity in the church gave a great deal of prestige to the Capetian dynasty and France.

## Philip the Fai

The last monarch to increase the power of the monarchy was King Philip IV, or the Fair (r. 1285–1314), who was the grandson of Saint Louis IX. He strengthened royal control over the nobles of France while improving law and justice in the realm. Philip was not called "the Fair" because he was just but because he was so handsome. In fact, he was a crafty and cruel monarch, ruthless in his pursuit of power.

Philip was constantly looking for ways to raise money for the royal treasury, including taxing the clergy in 1296. When Pope Boniface VIII resisted, a fight ensued. When Philip was excommunicated, he tried to have the pope arrested. The conflict did not end when Boniface died. The next pope, Clement V, a French cardinal, was under the king's control. As a result, the papal court was moved from Rome to Avignon in France, beginning 70 years of the "Babylonian Captivity." In addition, through Clement V, Philip suppressed the Knights Templar in France and seized their lands to pay off his debt. He also suppressed Jews and took their land.

Philip's focus on money during his reign actually brought about several key improvements in the powers of the French monarchy. He expanded the royal bureaucracy and set up a treasury to supervise the collection of taxes and keep accurate records of the royal income and expenditures. To raise taxes, Philip IV required the support of the nobility, so he created the Estates-General, an assembly of nobles, clergy, and merchants that also checked the power of the monarchy. As in England, the monarchy centralized power but also had to give some power away to keep the process of centralization going.

So with the three major kingdoms of Europe, monarchies worked to break feudal bonds and centralize power. The Holy Roman Empire was first out of the gate, but ended up falling short, while England and France were able to centralize the power of the monarchy and make nations out of kingdoms.

## The Least You Need to Know

- The Ottonian, Franconian, and Hohenstaufen dynasties all tried to increase royal power in the Holy Roman Empire.

- The politics of Germany and Italy became intertwined as the result of several of the emperors' interest in controlling the church and northern Italy.

- The Holy Roman Empire was unable to consolidate royal power over its nobles.

- William the Conqueror started a new era of Anglo-Norman rule in England.

- The English monarchy consolidated royal power through the use of the courts and Parliament.

- The Capetian dynasty of France consolidated royal power through financial and political means.

**9**

# The Struggles of the Other Kingdoms

## In This Chapter

- Spanish *Reconquista*
- An independent Portugal
- Portuguese expansion
- The Swiss
- Poland and Hungary

By the High Middle Ages, changes were taking place all over Europe. While the monarchs of England, France, and Germany tried to extend their power, other kingdoms on the fringes of Europe, including Spain, Portugal, the Swiss Confederation, Poland, Hungary, and Russia, struggled to do the same. Each kingdom's task in consolidating power was unique.

# Spain

In 589, when the Visigoth King Reccared accepted Catholic Christianity as his faith, Spain was on the way to developing a strong, consolidated kingdom. However, in 711, Tarik, an ambitious Muslim leader, crossed from North Africa to Spain with a large Muslim army and quickly and easily defeated the Visigoths; by 721, he had conquered the entire Iberian peninsula.

## Islamic Spain

For a generation, the Islamic rulers consolidated their power over the Iberian peninsula, but they were not to remain united for long. In 756, Abd-al-Rahman established a large independent state with its capital at Cordoba. This Cordoba caliphate, as it was called, survived until 1031. For Spain, it was a golden age. The government was administered well, and as a result, the economy boomed and culture flourished. In addition, the Islamic rulers were tolerant of Christians and Jews, making it one of the most prosperous and culturally creative periods in the Middle Ages.

> **Notable Quote**
>
> "Do not talk of the Court of Baghdad and its magnificence, do not praise Persia or China and their manifold advantages; for there is no spot on earth like Cordoba."
>
> —Arab historian on Cordoba

The city of Cordoba was extremely wealthy, with a population of over half a million people. Products from all over the Mediterranean came to the city, including delicacies like dates, olives, lemons, and peaches. At its peak, it was one of the richest and most beautiful cities of Europe. Islamic culture at this time was cosmopolitan, so Spain was linked to other centers of Islamic culture in North Africa and the Middle East.

The exchange of learning between Islamic, Jewish, and Christian scholars benefited Europe. Islamic scholars had preserved many Greek and Roman texts and translated them into Arabic. During the High Middle Ages, Christian scholars translated these texts into Latin, and as a result Europe recovered more of the learning from ancient antiquity.

## Reconquista

During the eighth century, Muslim rulers dominated all the Iberian peninsula except for a few small Christian kingdoms in the north. In these kingdoms, Christian efforts to retake Spain began. The first campaigns, if you remember, were made by Charlemagne in the early 800s. He conquered a small region in the north called the Spanish March, a buffer zone between the Muslims and the Franks. Unlike the rest of the Iberian peninsula, Christian and Frank culture mostly influenced the March.

When the Carolingian Empire broke up, the Spanish March was fragmented into the kingdoms of Catalonia, Galicia, the Asturias, Leon, and Navarre, which fought among themselves but also pushed south into Muslim territory. The push south, which lasted over 500 years, became known as the *Reconquista*. By the late tenth century, the kingdom of Castile emerged as the most powerful and vigorous kingdom in effecting the *Reconquista*.

## def•i•ni•tion

*Reconquista* is Spanish for reconquest and refers to a period in Spanish history during the Middle Ages when the Christian Spanish kingdoms took back territory from Muslim forces in Spain.

By 1031, the caliphate of Cordoba had fallen into disarray due to internal fighting. Islamic Spain was fragmented into 20 different kingdoms, which the Christian kingdoms of the north saw as an opportunity. Sancho the Great (1000–1035), the ruler of Castile, was the first to press the advantage. He united the local kingdoms and led an army against Islamic forces.

The *Reconquista* was seen as a Christian holy war. In 1063, the pope proclaimed a crusade for the reconquest of the Iberian peninsula. Knights from all over Europe flocked to Spain to answer the pope's call. Periods of fierce warfare were followed by relative peace. As Christian rulers retook the Iberian peninsula, they generally treated their non-Christian subjects with tolerance. As a result, Islamic culture still thrived in the Christian kingdoms as Islamic artisans and merchants continued to go about their business.

A rallying point for the crusades during this period of the *Reconquista* was the cathedral of Santiago de Compostela in northwestern Spain. Traditionally, it was thought that Saint James, one of the original 12 apostles, went to Spain to spread the gospel after the death of Jesus. King Herod of Agrippa later put James to the sword and martyred him in Jerusalem, but Spanish

### Illuminations

One of the most popular epics of the Middle Ages came from the *Reconquista* period. *The Song of Roland* detailed the heroic deeds of the Frankish knight Roland who stayed behind to fight the Muslims. The epic also fostered some of the general feelings of antagonism Europeans had toward Muslims.

Christians believed in a vision revealed to a shepherd boy during the early tenth century that his body had been transported to the cathedral at Santiago. As a result, thousands of Christians made pilgrimages to the cathedral. In addition, the slogan "Santiago!" became a rally cry for the crusaders in Spain.

### Middle Age Myths

It is highly questionable that Saint James ever came to Spain. No early Christian documents support either the claim that he preached the Gospel in Spain or that he was buried there. The fostering of the origin of the story of James coincides with the *Reconquista* period making it likely a public-relations creation of kings, bishops, and popes.

## The Cortés

As the Christian kingdoms of the north took Muslim lands in the south, the monarchs came across problems like those of the other monarchs of Europe. To help, the kingdoms created assemblies called Cortés, made up of representatives of the clergy, nobility, and towns. They had the power to vote on taxes and monitor spending. In addition, the Cortés could petition a monarch to make or reform laws. As a result, the kings of the Spanish Christian kingdoms were unable to establish strong, central governments.

Other reasons caused this lack of strength as well. First, the nobles took many political and military liberties during the fight with Muslim forces. Also, the independent organizations of knights made up to fight the Muslims seldom listened to the monarchs. Finally, the church had been given large landholdings and privileges for its help in the *Reconquista*, and as a result, it had a great deal of influence on the political landscape.

## The Three Kingdoms

By 1212, three Christian kingdoms, Castile, Aragon, and Navarre, had joined together to defeat Islamic forces at the Battle of Las Navas de Tolosa. Shortly thereafter, they captured Cordoba and Seville. This left only the Argave and the kingdom of Granada under Islamic control. The crusades had been a success and, during the next 200 years, the *Reconquista* slowed down. During that period, the Christian kings consolidated power in their kingdoms for one final push against Islam.

---

**Illuminations**

One of the more interesting and famous heroes of the period of the crusades in Spain was Rodrigo Diaz de Bivar. His adventures are detailed in the Spanish epic, *El Cid*. The poem showed Cid as a perfect Christian knight, but the reality was different. Diaz fought for money, which meant that he killed both Muslims and Christians. After he led a successful siege against the Muslim city of Valencia, Diaz became its ruler.

---

# Portugal

During the early Middle Ages, Portugal was not a separate kingdom and therefore shared the same political experience as the rest of the Iberian peninsula. Conquered by the Muslims, it was part of the Cordoba caliphate until its reconquest, at which point Portugal became part of the Christian kingdom of Castile and remained its province until 1095.

## Henry and Theresa

Alfonso VI, king of Castile, gave his daughter, Theresa, in marriage to Henry of Burgundy, who as a crusading knight had helped Alfonso fight the Muslims. For her dowry, Theresa (and Henry) received two counties located on the Atlantic coast called Portucali and Coimbra. These counties became the foundation of the kingdom of Portugal.

Henry and Theresa were united in their determination to convert their dowry into an independent kingdom. They fortified towns and led troops on campaigns to consolidate control over the kingdom. After their deaths, their son, Alfonso Henriques, continued the struggle, extracting a promise from the king of Castile that he could rule any territory he seized from the Muslims. Alfonso defeated the Muslims—but the king of Castile refused to honor the promise. Pope Innocent III mediated the dispute between the rulers but ruled in favor of the king of Castile. Recognizing the political needs of the papacy, Alfonso offered his kingdom as a fief to the new pope, Alexander III, if he would recognize him as king of Portugal. Alexander III agreed, and in 1143 Alfonso I (1158–1214) or the Noble took the rule of the kingdom of Portugal.

## Alfonso the Noble

Alfonso's rule started with internal strife and the frequent intervention of the neighboring kingdom of Navarre into the affairs of Portugal. This interference resulted in the joint attack by Navarre and Leon on the kingdom of Portugal, which Alfonso was able to divert. Alfonso's political relations with Aragon were always good, and as a result, the two kingdoms signed a pact in 1179 that settled the demarcation of the border between the two kingdoms once the Moors had been pushed out of Spain.

Because of Portugal's geography, the only way for the kingdom to expand was south against the Moors, and during the Second Crusade (1146–1149), some knights from northern Europe helped Alfonso do just that. They freed the cities of Lisbon and Santarem from Muslim forces, making the capital of the kingdom of Portugal Lisbon. Another war against the Moors absorbed Alfonso's energies from 1172 to 1212, and although he was humiliated by the Moors in 1195, he came back and won a great victory at the Battle of Las Navas de Tolosa in 1212 with the help of the king of Aragon. Thus, Alfonso did a great deal to destroy the power of the Moors in Spain. Sancho I (1185–1211), son of Alfonso I, also pursued a policy of expansion, which earned him the nickname "the Colonizer." He encouraged Christians to colonize the areas taken from the Muslims.

Alfonso married his daughter off to King Henry II of England, helping to establish an alliance between the two countries. Finally, Alfonso founded Spain's first university of higher education, providing the royal court with well-educated administrators.

Successors to Alfonso I and Sancho I worked to consolidate royal power and control the church and nobles. To that end, the kings of Portugal set up royal commissions to regain lands obtained illegally by the church. They also pursued a policy of expansion and captured the last Muslim fortresses in the Algarve region.

## Dinis the Farmer King

One of the most influential kings of medieval Portugal was King Dinis (1279–1325). He was known as the Farmer King because he encouraged his nobles to farm and distributed farmland to peasants. He also created a school of agriculture to help farmers develop better methods of growing crops, raising livestock, and stopping soil erosion. Partly due to his efforts, Portugal experienced a surplus in agricultural goods, which they could export abroad. To this end, Dinis created and organized an experienced and knowledgeable merchant marine.

Dinis also encouraged cultural and political stability. He had all official court documents written in Portuguese rather than Latin. In 1278, Dinis limited the power of the church by putting a cap on its holdings. He also supported the arts and humanities by founding the University of Lisbon.

During his rule, the kingdom of Portugal achieved territorial stability with its borders remaining the same to this day. The Cortés did exist in Portugal and tried to take a governing role, but it was less representative because only clergy and nobles were members. In addition, it met only when the king called it into session and did not have the right to make laws. As a result, the Cortés did not develop into a very powerful institution, and this allowed the king to consolidate royal authority very well during the High Middle Ages.

# The Swiss

While Spain and Portugal were creating strong unified kingdoms, other kingdoms were emerging in Europe. The disunity of the Holy Roman Empire enabled several small cantons to emerge to positions of power on the western frontier of the empire. These cantons in the region of present-day Switzerland formed the nucleus of the Swiss Confederation.

Late in the first millennium, the mountainous region of the Swiss came under the control of the Carolingian Empire. When feudalism took hold in most of Europe, its roots were not quite as deep in this region, so the peasants enjoyed more freedom and started to govern themselves through local assemblies. After some time, several towns located on the central European trade routes that carried goods from the Mediterranean to northern Europe developed into major cities, including Basel, Lucerne, and Zurich. In 1231, Frederick II granted the canton of Uri on Lake Lucerne a charter that gave the peasantry certain freedoms from local feudal lords in exchange for loyalty to the emperor. Afterward, the cantons of Schwyz and Unterwalden also received such a charter from the emperor.

In 1291, the recently chartered cantons drew up a treaty to end their feudal obligations to the Holy Roman Emperor. In addition, Uri, Schwyz, and Unterwalden agreed to defend each other if any one of them were attacked. This union became known as the League of Upper Germany and later became the Swiss Confederation and then Switzerland in the nineteenth century.

The struggle for independence for the Swiss was not easy. In 1315, Duke Leopold I of Austria invaded Schwyz through a narrow pass at Morgarten. Swiss peasants rolled boulders and logs down on the invaders from above the pass, then killed the pinned and trapped Austrians. Due to the League's success between 1332 and 1335, five more cantons joined, including Zurich and Lucerne. In 1386, Duke Leopold III attempted another invasion, but again the Swiss defeated the Hapsburg Duke of Austria and won recognition of their independence.

# Eastern Europe

During the Middle Ages several groups of migrating people settled in Eastern Europe, an area already populated by the Slavs and the Magyars. They included Germans, Prussians, Poles, and Lithuanians, which made the politics of the region a challenge for any king, to say the least.

## Poland

During the late tenth century, the West Slavs inhabited the plains of north central Europe. They lived between the Oder and Vistula rivers and were united under a powerful tribe known as the Polanians. Their chief, Miesko, signed a treaty with Otto I to prevent an invasion of the region by the emperor and his forces. Later in 965, Miesko married Dubravka, a Catholic princess from the kingdom of Bohemia. He, of course, converted to Catholic Christianity shortly after their marriage, as traditionally seemed to be the custom. As a result, the Catholic Church became an important cultural force in the future kingdom of Poland.

In 1000, Boleslav I or the Great (992–1025), the son of Miesko, became the first Polish ruler to have the title of king, but the monarchy of Poland, at that point, was not very strong. In 996, Boleslav conquered the region of Pomerania and then occupied the Czech city of Cracow. He further built his influence by harboring the religious fugitive Adalbert of Prague, and by his coronation in the year 1000 by the Holy Roman Emperor Otto III. After the emperor's death, Boleslav tried to expand the kingdom of Poland. As a result, he took lands up to the Elbe River and occupied a majority of Bohemia. Later, right before his death, Boleslav took on the grand duke of Kiev, whom he defeated on the banks of the River Bug. The river then formed the boundary between Russia and Poland.

During the High Middle Ages, dynastic struggles left the kingdom of Poland weak and divided. Additionally, invasions by the Prussians from the north and Mongols from the east created more problems. In 1241, the Mongols swept through Russia into Poland, leaving little behind as they burned down towns and churches and killed the population. To make matters worse, Teutonic knights from Germany invaded the kingdom and expanded their power in the region.

During the fourteenth century Poland had several rulers who strengthened royal power. Wladislav I (r. 1320–1333) arranged an alliance to ensure peace for the kingdom. His son, Casimir III, tried to establish a strong central government by reorganizing the administration of the courts and creating a comprehensive and uniform code of laws.

At the time of Casimir I or the Great's ascension to the throne in 1333, the kingdom of Poland was having difficulties. Even though Wladislav I united the kingdom, there were still many regional differences that were a source of conflict. In addition, Poland faced war on two different fronts: Bohemia and the German Teutonic knights in the region of Pomerania. But by 1350, Casimir was able to make peace with both groups. He also enlarged the kingdom by adding Red Russia and Masovia. Casimir then fortified his borders through marriage by marrying his daughters to the kingdom's powerful neighbors.

Within Poland itself, Casimir pursued a program of draining marshes and clearing forests to create new farmland. He stimulated trade by building new roads and bridges. In addition, he increased the economic potential of the kingdom by creating several royal towns with wide trading privileges. Culturally, he helped Poland by supporting the development of the University of Cracow, which secured for Poland a place in the intellectual world of Europe. Casimir also started the work of uniting the provinces under a central administration. As part of that initiative, the written law of Poland was codified and a special court established in Cracow. Thus, until the end of this reign in 1370, Casimir strengthened the monarchy in Poland.

# Hungary

Another state that developed in Eastern Europe during the Middle Ages was the kingdom of Hungary. The Magyars had settled in this region after their defeat by Otto the Great in the Battle of Lechfeld. Later the Magyars converted to Christianity, and tradition holds that on Christmas Day of the year 1000, Pope Sylvester II crowned Stephen the first king of Hungary.

The first king of Hungary was the son of a Magyar chieftain named Geza. Stephen succeeded his father to the throne in 997. Because he had been raised Christian and married a Christian, the daughter of Duke Henry II of Bavaria, Stephen promoted Christianity vigorously. He conquered the pagans in the region, the Black Hungarians, when they rebelled against Christian missionaries. He later forcibly converted them to Christianity. Thus, during Stephen's reign, the church became a powerful force in Hungary both socially and politically.

Of course, as discussed earlier, Stephen was anointed king of Hungary by Pope Sylvester II, who gave him the symbolic cross and crown that became famous symbols of the Hungarian state. Stephen advanced education and learning in his kingdom. He built churches and supported Christian missionary activity in the East. Finally, Stephen established a standing army to defend the kingdom.

Although Stephen laid the foundation for strong royal power, his successors were less effective. Dynastic struggles for succession were the rule, weakening royal power. Without a strong king, nobles fought for control and lesser nobles suffered as a result under the tyranny of the high nobles. As a result, a group of nobles forced King Andrew II (r. 1205–1235) to grant the *Golden Bull*. This gave remedies for many of the abuses of the nobles by prohibiting them from holding more than one position in the government. It also guaranteed nobles a right to a trial before the king. If the king ignored any of the provisions of the Golden Bull, nobles had the right to resist him.

With the decentralization of power in Hungary during the thirteenth century, the country also fell victim to the Mongol invasions. In 1241, Mongols pillaged the Hungarian countryside and killed half the population. Bela IV, the king of Hungary, took charge after the Mongols withdrew. He reorganized the army and built a chain of fortresses along the borders of the kingdom. But despite his successful efforts at defending Hungary from the Mongols, Bela and his successors were unable to break the power of the nobles.

By the fourteenth century, Hungary reached its largest size. A new ruling house established by Charles Robert of Anjou (r. 1342–1382) brought Hungary into a better place. Although Charles couldn't break the nobles, he did manage to impose regulations on them. He also established a new capital at Buda on the Danube River and even expanded Hungarian power into the Balkans. When his son became king in 1370, Louis the Great also became king of Poland. Louis strengthened royal power until his death by bringing the Hungarian nobles under royal control. But after his death, royal power and prestige again suffered in Hungary.

# Kievan Russia

The territory of Kiev, settled by a combination of Vikings and Slavs, developed into an organized collection of city-states or principalities. Each city-state had its own self-government as long as it paid taxes and respect to the Grand Prince of Kiev. Democratic forms of government were also adopted in the city-states. Some city-states had councils of nobles called boyars who assisted the prince of the principality. Others had assemblies that represented all free adult male citizens.

The growth of the principality of Kiev and its governmental structures attracted the attention of the Byzantine Empire, which considered organized Slavs a bit more troublesome than unorganized Slavs. In response, the Byzantine Empire sent missionaries to convert the Slavs to Orthodox Christianity, which was inseparable in some respects from the empire itself.

Olga, a princess of Kiev, was one of the first nobles to convert to the new religion. Later in 989 when Prince Vladimir wanted to marry the Byzantine emperor's sister for political purposes, he had to accept Eastern Orthodox Christianity for himself and his people. So Eastern Orthodox Christianity became the religion of the principality of Kiev. With this acceptance, Kiev, in a sense, became a satellite of the Byzantine Empire, depending on the empire to varying degrees culturally and politically.

With the development of a strong governmental system and the addition of the cohesive force of the Christian religion, the principality of Kiev, like most civilizations, enjoyed a Golden Age during the tenth and eleventh centuries. Two rulers were also in part responsible for this peak in the Kievan Rus. Vladimir the Great, who ruled Kiev from 980 to 1015, was responsible for converting the principality to Eastern Orthodox Christianity by proclamation. He also expanded the western borders of the principality.

The other contributor to the Golden Age of Kiev was Yaroslav the Wise, who ruled from 1035 to 1054. Yaroslav had a long struggle to become ruler of Kiev with his brother Svyatopolk, and not until 1035 and the childless death of another brother, Mstislav, did he gain total control over the principality of Kiev.

When Yaroslav ascended the throne, it started a boom period for Kievan Russia. Despite a short war with the Byzantine Empire called the Russo-Byzantine war (1043–1046), Kiev developed strong ties with the Eastern Empire. Christianity also took a strong hold in Kiev. But the church's position was regulated by the principality. As a result, building activity increased for the church, including the cathedral of St. Sophia in 1037.

Other improvements were made at the legal, political, and cultural levels. The laws of Kiev were codified and clarified for the people. Yaroslav organized the Kievan legal system under the title *Pravda Russkia*, meaning Russian Justice. This earned him the nickname, "The Wise," a biblical reference to the wisdom and justice of King Solomon. The legal progress in Kiev was matched by progress abroad. The Russian borders were extended and consolidated while political ties with the West were maintained through different royal marriages. Sadly, after Yaroslav's death, the authority of the principality was fragmented among the family and Kiev's fortunes began to decline.

Kiev's dependence on the Byzantine Empire, culturally, commercially, and, to some degree, politically, led to its decline. When the Byzantine Empire experienced economic, military, and political instability, it had a ripple effect on Kiev, which also

**Notable Quote**

They [the Mongols] attacked Russia, where they made great havoc, destroying cities and fortresses and killing men; and they laid siege to Kiev, the capital of Russia; after they had besieged the city for a long time, they took it and put the inhabitants to death.

—*History of the Mongols*, John of Plano

suffered, at least economically. So as the Byzantine Empire and trade declined, Kiev declined until in 1240 Mongol invaders from the plains of central Asia conquered the weakened principality.

Spain, Portugal, the Swiss Confederation, Poland, Hungary, and Russia struggled to consolidate power. This included royal power with the exception of the Swiss Confederation. And just like Germany, France, and England, they faced very unusual situations in accomplishing the task of acquiring power. Some were able; others were not. This period helped to decide the winners and losers of the nations of the Middle Ages.

## The Least You Need to Know

♦ The Spanish Christian kingdoms started out small but, during a period of 500 years, retook territory from Muslim rulers.

♦ The kingdom of Portugal established independence and expanded territorially during the *Reconquista*.

♦ The Swiss Confederation established a unique democratic form of independence for itself from the Holy Roman Empire in central Europe.

♦ The kingdom of Poland became independent but didn't have a strong monarchy.

♦ The kingdom of Hungary also established independence but could not create a strong monarchy.

♦ The city-state of Kiev rose to power during the tenth century to dominate the region of Russia for over 200 years.

# The Church During the High Middle Ages

## In This Chapter

◆ The sacraments

◆ Canon law

◆ Monastic reforms

◆ The Lateran Councils

◆ Reforming popes

◆ Popular Christianity

The Middle Ages have been known as the Age of Faith because Christianity did much to shape the hearts and minds of the people. In addition, the church as an institution dominated life in medieval times. At the top of its game under Pope Innocent III, the church claimed its supremacy as *the* power on earth.

The church used several methods to hold this power. First, through its sacraments, it held the key to the people's spiritual salvation. Second, through its courts, it acted as a judicial power. It also gained spiritual and political power through the reform movements that swept across Europe. And finally, the church maintained political power with the people, as was evidenced in the launching of the Crusades.

# The Civil Role of the Church

When the Roman Empire collapsed at the end of the sixth century, the people of Europe had to look for new leaders to fill the void. Beyond the Germanic warlords and kings, the people looked to the church to take this role. The Germanic tribes had never been good at administration, so the church, because of its bureaucratic nature, took the job. As a result, it operated a majority of the schools, hospitals, and orphanages of Europe. Churches and monasteries also offered sanctuary to all people of Europe in need.

> **Notable Quote**
>
> No king can reign rightly unless he devoutly serves Christ's vicar. The priesthood is the sun, and monarchy the moon. Kings rule over their respective kingdoms but the Lord … over the whole world.
>
> —Innocent III

By the High Middle Ages, the church also became the largest landowner in Europe, at least in Western Europe, as secular lords gave it tracts of land as acts of charity or penance for misdeeds. The lands helped the church fulfill both its spiritual and earthly missions by creating a permanent asset, which made the institution very rich and powerful because power in the Middle Ages was mostly measured by land ownership. At times, bishops and abbots were more powerful than secular lords and rulers, which invariably put the church into conflict with secular powers. Thus the church, ostensibly a spiritual institution, became a very powerful political institution as well.

## The Sacraments

Most people accepted the church's central role in their spiritual lives. It stood as the mediator between the people and God, in the form of prayer, attendance at mass, and participation in the sacraments or sacred rituals of the church. Only the priests could perform and sanctify the seven sacraments: baptism, confirmation, marriage, penance, last rites, Holy Orders, and the Holy Eucharist, also known as communion, a commemoration of the last supper that Jesus had with his 12 apostles.

Only through the sacraments were people able to obtain salvation in the next life. Generally, people could be denied the sacraments for doing evil acts or disobeying the church, and those denied the sacraments were shunned in this life by the people and in the next by God. The church used the threat of excommunication or being outside of the sacramental life to maintain social order and public morality. It also became a powerful weapon in the hands of church leadership in political struggles. Many powerful lords and kings were forced to yield to the church politically when threatened with the penalty of excommunication or, even worse, interdict, in which no one living in their territory could participate in the sacraments of the church.

To administer the sacraments, the church developed a hierarchical structure that reached all levels of medieval society. At the lowest level were the local parishes. The people depended on the parish priests for the daily officiated sacraments necessary for salvation. At the higher offices were bishops, archbishops, and cardinals, but the ordinary folk of medieval Europe knew little or nothing of these men.

## Canon Law

To add to the power of the administration of the sacraments, the church also performed many functions of the secular state. After the fall of Rome, when the kingdoms of Europe were disorganized, most of Roman law was forgotten or replaced with Germanic law. As a result, canon law and the church courts administered most of the justice. Later as Germanic law developed in the emerging European kingdoms, civil law, and courts developed and grew in power. Church courts tried both criminal and civil cases involving the clergy and even the people. Decisions were based on canon law, a combination of Roman law and church regulations that had been handed down over the years. The church courts made decisions about marriage, divorce, and wills. On these issues, church decisions were accepted as law by Christian lords and monarchs and thus enforced by public officials.

But tension grew between secular rulers and the church in jurisdiction. One of the most disputed issues was whether secular or church court would try members of the clergy charged with criminal offenses. As in the case of Henry II and Thomas Becket, this issue created bitter struggles between church and state that still resonate into the twenty-first century.

# Monastic Reforms

By the High Middle Ages, monasteries had developed into powerful and wealthy institutions, and with power usually comes corruption. Some monasteries ignored the disciplined religious rules set down by their founders. Abbots used their positions to obtain and retain wealth and power. Many monks and nuns broke their monastic vows, and the practice of *simony* spread throughout the church. In addition, priests were often poor and uneducated and, as a result, paid little attention to their duties and ignored their priestly vows. The effect of all these abuses was a religious revival during the High Middle Ages led by monastic and church leaders who worked for reform, helping to reestablish the church's spiritual power over the people.

## def•i•ni•tion

Simony is the sale and purchase of church offices.

### Age-Makers

David Knowles was born Michael Clive Knowles, David being his religious name, in England in 1896. Educated at Cambridge, he was ordained a Benedictine monk at the Downside Abbey, where he pursued his interest in the history of medieval monasteries, particularly those of England. Eventually, his research on the subject became authoritative. This led to his appointment to a position at Cambridge. Oddly, Knowles was at first unable to take the position; his abbot insisted he stay at the Downside Abbey, that vows of obedience included even authoritative medieval scholars. Eventually, Knowles appealed to the pope, who let him take the position at Cambridge, which he held until his death in 1974.

## The Cluniacs

A good deal of the reform movement that started in the High Middle Ages received its impetus from the order of Cluny in France. In the early 900s, the monastery of Cluny was created as a disciplined spiritual center separated from the secular world. By becoming direct subjects of the pope, the monastery avoided feudal entanglements and so was free of any secular influence. In addition, they reinstated the high moral standards of Saint Benedict's monastic rule, but with less emphasis on physical labor and more on time devoted to spiritual and intellectual pursuits. Finally, they took their vows seriously, with no exception.

The monastery at Cluny became a model for other abbots and church leaders who also saw the need for reform. At its height, the Cluniac order had established over 2,000 monasteries in France. In addition, over 100,000 Cluniac monks were scattered throughout Europe in Cluniac houses in the urban centers. Beyond the strict rule of their monasteries, these monks worked to reform the church by stopping abuses of power and the practice of simony.

## The Cistercians

Beyond the Cluniacs, another reform movement, led by the Cistercians, tried to regain the monastic discipline of the early Benedictine monks. The Cistercians order was founded in 1090 at Cîteaux in France, and the most famous of the reforming Cistercians was Bernard of Clairvaux (1090–1153).

## Bernard of Clairvaux (1090-1153)

Bernard of Clairvaux, born to a noble family of France, was one of many children and the one chosen by his mother to be in the service of the church. Later her death influenced him so deeply that at the age of 17, he left the cathedral school he was attending and entered a monastery at Cîteaux, France.

There, Bernard met several others who were as eager as he to experience the monastic life and who would later help him with all that he was to accomplish. Bernard threw himself into the religious life of the community, declaring that "God was conscious of the need of my weak nature for strong medicine." He was an extreme ascetic, denying himself food and sleep for many days. His devotion to this type of mortification caused him severe health problems, which plagued him the rest of his life.

At the monastery, Bernard was instructed by the noted abbot Stephen Harding, who chose him in 1115 to select a new site for a brother monastery. Bernard chose a site in Clairvaux, France, which became the center for the Cistercian order. Soon, Bernard gained fame for being a brilliant abbot and respected mystic at Clairvaux and, as a result, was sought out by many in the church and government for advice.

Bernard's influence only grew over the years. In 1128, he was secretary to the *Synod* of Troyes; in 1130, he helped Pope Innocent II with his problems with the antipope; he preached against heresy and for the Second Crusade. In defending the church, Bernard spoke out against the famous scholar Peter Abelard, who was condemned with Bernard's urging at the Council of Sens in 1140.

Bernard was also very interested in the spiritual well-being of the church. He wanted all of Christendom to devote their lives to the contemplation of God and God's guidance. Additionally, he thought God's love was so great that even the worst sinners could gain salvation by having faith in God and his goodness.

**def•i•ni•tion**

A **synod** is a meeting of church officers from one region or realm.

Bernard insisted that monasteries be built in rural locations so monks could lead simple lives and not be tempted by the sin of the towns and cities. He also stripped Cistercian monks of all worldly possessions and only permitted them to own a small amount of clothing.

Sadly, the last years of his life were marked with disappointment, especially over the failure of the Second Crusade. Bernard ended the days of his life in 1153 at Clairvaux, where he had sought to accomplish so much.

Despite his disappointment, by the end of this life Bernard had become one of the most influential and powerful church leaders of the Middle Ages. His authority came from his office and his personal will, even though to some he was considered a hard and uncompromising man. Bernard did not flinch in taking positions that others thought unpopular or unrelated to daily life—for example, Bernard's call for prayer and the condemnation of the persecution of Jews in Europe. In 1174, he was canonized for sainthood and given the title *Doctor Mellifluus* or the Honeysweet Doctor.

## The Cistercian Way

In part because of Bernard's efforts, by the time of his death there were over 300 Cistercian monasteries. The General Chapter, a governing body made up of all the abbots of the monasteries, linked these together. The General Chapter moved forward with Bernard's work, and by 1300 had established an additional 400 monasteries and several convents for nuns who wanted to follow the Cistercian order.

Every monastery and convent included a library where one could pursue intellectual and spiritual quests. They also continued to have scriptoriums where monks copied and illuminated manuscripts. The monks who copied the manuscripts vowed to fight the devil with pen and ink, hoping that with every letter and line a sin was forgiven.

The Cistercian monks drained swamps and turned them into productive farms. They also raised livestock, becoming very efficient at it. In England, the Cistercians were so efficient that they controlled a large portion of the wool trade.

# Mendicant Friars

During the thirteenth century, Pope Innocent III (1198–1216) established two new orders, the Dominicans and the Franciscans, who continued the spirit of reform created by the Cluniacs and Cistercians. The members of these orders were called *friars*, from the Latin for "brother." The friars saw the need to do the work of God in the world, not behind monastery walls, and dedicated their lives to working with the needy, mostly in the urban centers of Europe.

To finance that work, the friars begged for alms or money/food which eventually led people to call them mendicants or beggars. In addition to caring for the needy, the Dominican and Franciscan friars preached and defended the teachings of the church and combated heresy wherever they encountered it. The excitement of doing God's work in the everyday world attracted many talented thinkers and writers. For example, the Dominican theologian Thomas Aquinas (1225–1374) detailed some of the most precise arguments for the existence of God yet and is still widely studied to this day.

## The Dominicans

The Dominican order was established in 1216 by none other than Saint Dominic (1170–1221). Born in Spain, Dominic, like most leaders of the church, was the son of a noble family. He entered the church in 1196 and became a prior of a monastery near his home by 1201. At his position, Dominic soon grew to be highly respected by the local bishops. As a result, in 1203, he was appointed to head a papal delegation to preach to the *Albigenisans* in southern France.

There Dominic won over many converts through his sincerity and goodness. However, not satisfied by the success of Dominic and others with the Albigenisans, Pope Innocent II launched the so-called Albigensian Crusade, which was marked by barbarism and cruelty and lasted from 1209 to 1229. Throughout this time, Dominic tried to convert the Albigenisans through peaceful methods but with little success—and at a threat to his life.

### def•i•ni•tion

The **Albigenisans**, sometimes called Cathars, adhered to the belief in a dualism between good and evil much like the Manicheans. They taught that Jesus was an angel and the events of the New Testament were only allegorical, not actual.

Although discouraged by the crusade, Dominic was encouraged when he was joined by a number of like-minded individuals in his travels in southern France. He was also encouraged when in 1214 Simon de Montfort, the military leader of the crusade, gave him use of a castle near Toulouse as a headquarters. Dominic hoped that a religious order devoted to the peaceful conversion of Albigenisans could be established, with the castle at Toulouse as a base of operations. After gaining local approval for his order, Dominic gained final approval from Pope Honorius III for the establishment of the new mendicant order.

Dominic spent the rest of his life traveling, preaching, and promoting the Dominican Order. Dominican friars were sent to France, Italy, and Spain and also had houses attached to universities across Europe. This would be a key to the Dominican influence on the intellectual and spiritual movements of Europe and the church. In 1221, Dominic set out to preach to the people of Hungary, but on the way, he fell sick and returned to the city of Bologna where he later died. Dominic died as a great figure in the history of the Middle Ages. Although he has always been overshadowed by his friend Saint Francis, he made a lasting impact on the revitalization of the church during the Middle Ages through his vision and innovation.

After Dominic's death, the order continued to gain many followers. By the end of the thirteenth century, there were close to 400 houses throughout Europe and the Holy Land. As time progressed, the Dominicans stopped their wandering preaching altogether and focused their energies on establishing schools and universities across Europe and later around the world. They also established convents for Dominican nuns. Known for their dedication to stamping out heresy, the Dominicans were often picked to help with church courts. To this day, the Dominicans remain one of the largest and most influential orders in the Catholic Church.

## The Franciscans

The second order established by Pope Innocent III, the Franciscans, was founded by Saint Francis (1182–1126). Francis was born in Assisi, Italy, and unlike many other church leaders, he was the son of a cloth merchant, not a noble family. Francis worked for his father until the age of 20, taking frequent business trips to France. He was a very popular hometown boy because of his carefree and fun-loving attitude.

## The Life of Saint Francis

Francis's life changed dramatically in 1202 when he joined a campaign against a rival Italian city-state. The campaign did not go well, and he was captured in battle and spent time in prison. After being released from prison, Francis saw life as empty and unappealing. This feeling increased after a lengthy illness. Later, he called this time his conversion period.

Francis began to pray and work among the poor. But the watershed moment for him came when he came across a leper; being repulsed by the man's ugly appearance, Francis turned away from him. He then stopped himself, gave the man some money, and then kissed him on the cheek as a sign of love and compassion. Afterward, Francis went on a pilgrimage to Rome. On the way, he gave his clothes away to beggars and spent his day in Rome begging for alms in front of St. Peter's Basilica.

Francis returned home to Assisi and made it his routine to pray at the Church of San Damiano. There he heard the command from God telling him, "Repair my house." Of course, Francis wanted to obey this voice. To pay for the repair of the church, he, without prior permission, sold bales of his father's cloth. Infuriated by Francis's actions, his father locked him in his room, but Francis was released by his sympathetic mother. At that point, the break between father and son became really bad. Francis's father went to the local bishop and demanded his money for the cloth back. As a result, Francis stripped off his clothes and said they, too, belonged to his father. From then on, Francis dressed in a rough wool cloak tied at the waist to remember the cloak given to him that day by the bishop.

After the break with his father, Francis spent his time rebuilding the Church of San Damiano with his own hands. In 1208, inspired to travel and preach throughout Italy, he soon got considerable attention and was called "The Little Poor Man." Other like-minded individuals joined him as disciples. Francis then composed a simple rule of life for himself and his disciples to follow. Later in 1210, he took his rule to Rome, where he won approval from Pope Innocent III to form a mendicant order. The pope's initial reluctance was dispelled supposedly by a dream of Francis. Thus, Pope Innocent III sanctioned the establishment of the Order of Friars Minor or the Franciscans, who practiced rigorous asceticism and poverty and relied upon alms of the people as they wandered across Italy and eventually Europe preaching.

After organizing the Franciscans in Italy, Francis decided to travel to the lands of the Middle East, including the Holy Land. On the way to Palestine in 1214, he was shipwrecked and then fell sick. Finally in 1219, Francis reached Egypt. There, he witnessed the siege of Damietta by the crusaders of the Fifth Crusade. Desperate to see the Holy Land, Francis went to the camp of the Sultan of Egypt and asked for special access to the Holy Land despite the ongoing war. The Sultan was so impressed by Francis that he gave him permission almost immediately.

Francis returned to Europe to find his newly founded order in deep trouble. The rapid growth of the order across Europe caused irregularities and conflicts. As a result, Francis revised his rule of the order, which was approved by the pope in 1223. Afterward, Francis withdrew from society and left the affairs of the Franciscans to others. He died in 1226, and two years later Pope Gregory IX made him a saint.

After Francis's death, the Franciscan order became even more popular and influential in the reform movement of Europe. One reason was Francis himself, who was a genuine example of kindness and piety. The other reason was the order's simplicity, which reminded many of the early work of the apostles. So by the end of the thirteenth century, there were over 1,500 Franciscan houses across Europe.

Francis also helped to inspire the creation of a new order of nuns known as the Poor Clares. Clare, a noblewoman impressed by Francis and his teachings, renounced her inheritance and, with Francis's help, founded the new order of nuns. Like the Franciscans, the Poor Clares lived in poverty, cared for the poor, and provided shelter for travelers. And also like the Franciscans, the Poor Clares spread their influence across Europe.

# Other Reform Movements and Reformers

Not only was there a monastic reform movement sweeping across Europe to help create a more spiritually and politically powerful church, but there was also a movement within the church itself with the Lateran Councils and three especially reform-minded popes.

## The Lateran Councils

Five church councils were held to address problems within the church at the Lateran Palace in Rome between the twelfth and sixteenth centuries. At the First Lateran Council in 1123, the ninth ecumenical council, summoned by Pope Callistus II, confirmed the Concordant of Worms, ending the Investiture Controversy. In addition, the group created 22 new disciplinary canons to help reform some of the abuses in the church.

Sixteen years later, in 1139, the tenth ecumenical council met as the Second Lateran Council. This council was convened by Pope Innocent II to condemn the *antipope* Anacletus II and followers of Arnold of Brescia after the schism resulting from Innocent's election.

## def•i•ni•tion

An **antipope** is a pope whose election is disputed by the church.

In 1179, the eleventh ecumenical council met as the Third Lateran Council at the request of Pope Alexander III. The job of this council was to erase all traces of the schism involving the antipope Callistus III. But more importantly, the council made a decree for papal elections. In this decree, a College of Cardinals was created that would elect popes by a two-thirds majority vote. Finally, the council ratified a treaty with Frederick I (Barbarossa) and charged that each bishop conduct schools for clerics under their charge.

The Fourth Lateran Council convened in 1215 at the summons of Pope Innocent III. This council was one of the most important councils of the Middle Ages. It made several declarations, including one for an annual confession of the laity, a definition of the doctrine of the nature of Communion, Communion during the Easter season, a condemnation of the heresies of the Cathars and Waldenses, and the requirement of special attire for Muslims and Jews, which was enforced by the kings of Europe.

Of course there have been other church councils since the Middle Ages, but these councils and their reforms helped to cement the church's spiritual and political position in Europe. Other factors also aided this process, including three very notable medieval popes.

## The Three Popes

Pope Gregory VII (1073–1085), Pope Urban II (1088–1099), and Pope Innocent III (1198–1216) all worked for reform in different ways, with varying degrees of success, but all made a distinctive mark on medieval Europe.

## Gregory VII

Gregory was born to a poor family of Tuscany, Italy. When he was young, the family moved to Rome, where he acquired an education at the palace of the pope. As a result, Gregory became a priest and was appointed chaplain to Pope Gregory VI (1045–1046), and accompanied him into exile at Cologne in 1046. After the pope's death, Gregory entered the monastery. But his abilities would not allow him to be away from Rome long. Two years later, Pope Leo IX (1049–1054) called him to Rome to become an administrator of the Patrimonium of Peter. This prestigious position signaled the beginning of his rise as a powerful member of the church.

Gregory had enormous influence over the popes, including Victor II (1055–1057), Nicholas II (1058–1061), and Alexander II (1061–1073), as he represented the papacy as a papal legate to France and Germany. Also under Alexander II, he was chancellor of the Holy See. Finally all of his administrative duties and abilities paid off, and he was elected to succeed Alexander in mid-1073.

Gregory was committed to church reform. He made his central policy the moral renewal of the church, which had been part of the work of his immediate predecessors in which he had played a part. The reform movement that started during this time took its name from him, the Gregorian Reform. Gregory attacked the practice of simony and other abuses of the church by appointments of loyal papal legates and the Lenten Synods. He also asked for help from the secular rulers of Europe while his papal legates pushed reluctant or recalcitrant bishops.

Gregory's program of reform caused considerable controversy and opposition, especially from bishops in Germany and France. But the bigger issue was the political fallout caused by Gregory's work at the Synod of Rome in 1075 when he condemned lay investiture. Gregory became locked in a political battle with Henry IV over lay investiture that dominated his papacy. The final result of the lay investiture controversy was that Gregory fled Rome to Salerno, Italy, where he died in 1085. His dying words were: "I have loved justice and therefore die in exile."

Gregory was an able and stern reformer who was guided by a sincere and pious commitment to revitalizing the church. When he died, his reforms were far from complete, but other succeeding popes continued where he left off, in particular Urban II (1088-1099). But his successes and even failures set Gregory apart as one of the greatest popes of the Middle Ages.

## Urban II

The man who would become Pope Urban II was born in France, the son of a noble family. He studied to become a member of the clergy at Reims, and around 1068 entered the famous reform monastery at Cluny. By 1078, Urban's reputation for hard work and reform paid off, and Pope Gregory VII appointed him as cardinal. He also served as one of Gregory's papal legates to France and Germany. Thus, Urban was loyal to the message of Gregory's reforms.

Urban was elected successor to Pope Victor III after considerable delay in 1088. Once pope, he announced his intentions to continue the Gregorian reforms. So at the Council of Melfi in 1089, Urban issued 16 canons or church laws against simony and lay investiture. But trouble was on the horizon for Urban.

Before he was pope, Urban had successfully expelled the antipope Clement III at the Synod in Saxony in 1085. But Clement III gained the support of some powerful allies, including the Countess Matilda of Tuscany. As a result, Urban was forced to flee Rome in 1090 and was not able to return until 1093. During this time, Urban cultivated a relationship with the Normans of Italy and Sicily, which proved to be very valuable in his conflict with the Holy Roman Emperor Henry IV when they gave him a safe haven.

By 1095, Urban's troubles were over, and he was in a much stronger political position in Europe. Accordingly, he was able to convene two important church councils at Piacenza and Clermont. At the Council of Piacenza, Urban continued the Gregorian reforms and condemned heresy. At the Council of Clermont in November 1095, he proclaimed the Truce of God, which forbade warfare and fighting from Wednesday night to Monday morning with the threat of church punishment. This was supposed to help put an end to violence in Europe. But more important, answering the plea for help from the Byzantine Emperor Alexius I, Urban declared the First Crusade to liberate the Holy Land from Islamic hands and free the Holy City, Jerusalem (see Chapter 11).

Beyond these measures, Urban also reorganized the finances in the papacy, and with a decree in 1089, he created departments that assisted with the business of the papacy. This reform of the papal government centralized the church's administrative ability, which added to the power and prestige of the church and made him one of the most important popes of the Middle Ages.

## Innocent III

Innocent was born in northern Italy of a noble family. A cardinal when he was elected to the papacy in 1198, his goal was to restore papal supremacy and to bring reform to the church. At the start of his reign, he assumed an exalted position for the papacy, using the title Vicar of Christ to justify his claims of being "set midway between God and man, below God but above man." Despite his title, Innocent III stressed the spiritual authority of the papacy and was rather reluctant to dabble in worldly matters save where moral issues needed to be resolved.

However, political entanglements were a part of Pope Innocent III's reign. He reduced the power of the Italian aristocracy and regained control over the Papal States. He forced King Philip II of France to reconcile with his wife and queen. Also, he made King John of England accept Stephen Langton as Archbishop of Canterbury. In addition, Innocent III supported the Fourth Crusade, which turned against his wishes when the crusaders sacked Constantinople. Later, in 1204, he accepted the overthrow of the Byzantine Empire by the crusaders in hopes of a reunification of the Eastern and Western churches (see Chapter 11).

In the ecumenical realm, Innocent III was a reformer. He introduced changes to the church by encouraging reforming councils and insisting on the proper behavior of the clergy. In addition, he issued over 6,000 letters and decrees, and summoned the Fourth Lateran Council, discussed earlier. He also supported the Franciscans and Dominicans, making them a recognizable source of reform in the church. Finally, he combated heresy in the church, including directing a crusade against the Albigenisans in 1208. By the end of his reign and life, Pope Innocent III had become one of the foremost pontiffs of the Middle Ages.

# The Problem with Reform

Despite all the reform of the High Middle Ages, the beliefs of many European Christians remained very simple and primitive, often more superstitious than faithful in nature. This was especially the case in rural areas, where Christianity was a combination of legends and paganism that did not quite mirror the official doctrine of the church. Some people believed in demons, devils, ghosts, witches, and any other Halloween monsters that haunted the world of the living.

## The Bones of the Saints

An emotional form of Christianity based on blind belief and xenophobia saw biblical signs and miracles in everyday life. Throughout Europe, legends circulated of nuns and monks who cured diseases, of crying and bleeding statues, and other miraculous demonstrations of the divine, such as holy relics.

To medieval Europeans, a relic was an object that connected one to the divine because of its association with a holy saint. When a saint died, he or she left behind a physical body as well as a few material possessions. Such objects, including the body, were considered sacred and believed to hold great power to heal and bless the people who came into contact with them.

By the High Middle Ages, this cult of relics had developed a huge following, with literally thousands of relics floating around Europe—some of questionable authenticity, including the Crown of Thorns worn by Jesus, splinters of the Cross, hay from the manger in Bethlehem, hair from Noah's beard, and various bones and teeth of the apostles. Churches and cathedrals competed for relics because a powerful relic attracted pilgrims bringing substantial economic rewards to a city or town.

Of course, many of the circulating relics were fakes. The bones of some farm animal could easily be passed off as those of a saint. In addition, several churches or cathedrals might claim to have the same relic, such as the head of John the Baptist. This caused even more confusion and questioning of the cult of relics, prompting some of the more reform-minded popes to question the use and authenticity of relics.

## The Mary Cult

Another cult developed during the High Middle Ages, known as the Mary Cult. Mary, the mother of Jesus, had become very popular with the common people of Europe by the twelfth century. As a result, they began to pray to Mary to intercede for them with Jesus. In their mind, if one found it hard to go to the king, it might be easier to speak with the king's mother, who had influence over the king.

The Mary Cult produced many interesting new stories about Mary, nearly all of which were false. On the positive, the cult began to change the status of all women in Western society that early Christianity had started. Women, according to the Mary Cult, were to be seen as daughters of Mary and treated with respect. Of course this was only a small step in the road toward the equality of women, but at least it was a start.

## The Least You Need to Know

- ◆ The use of the sacraments and canon law aided the civil role of the church.

- ◆ The monastic reforms of the Cluniacs and Cistercians created a revival in the spirituality and political power of the church.

- ◆ The mendicant friars known as the Dominicans and Franciscans also helped to revive the spirituality and political power of the church.

- ◆ Several Lateran Councils and popes also aided in the process of reforming and strengthening the church.

- ◆ Despite the reforms, many Europeans continued to practice certain forms of Christianity that were outside the norm throughout the Middle Ages.

# Chapter 11

# Let's Go Crusading

## In This Chapter

- The origins of the crusades
- Motives for crusading
- The First Crusade
- Saladin and Richard the Lionhearted
- The rest of the crusades and the final effects
- Other crusades and inquisitions

The reasons for and the results of the crusades of the Middle Ages have triggered many debates. In general, the centralization of the monarchy and the power of the church combined to produce a mass migration of people to Palestine. When these people finally left the Middle East, they connected isolated Europe with the global civilization of Islam, which had a major impact on the history of the world.

## Origins of the Crusades

The major reason for the European crusades involved the city of Jerusalem, a holy city not only for Christianity but also Judaism and Islam. In the

600s, Jerusalem and the region of Palestine left Christian hands and fell to Arab invaders. These Arabs tolerated Jews and Christians in the city, so there was little problem with this new development; but later in the early eleventh century, Seljuk Turks who were also Islamic took control of the city and region. In an overzealous act, they closed the city to the religious traditions of Christianity and Judaism. Once news of the closing of Jerusalem reached Christian Europe, the crusades were underway.

## The Call

In 1095, the Byzantine emperor wrote Pope Urban II, asking for a few armored knights to help open the Holy Land and defend against the Seljuk Turks who had taken the Levant, or Palestine, from Byzantium. So Pope Urban II made his official, impassioned plea to a large crowd at Clermount, France, calling for a crusade or holy war against the Islamic forces in the Holy Land and promising penance for the crusaders.

> **Notable Quote**
>
> There was a great stirring of heart throughout all the Frankish lands, so that if any man ... could make no delay in taking the road to the Holy Sepulchre as quickly as possible.
>
> — *The Feats of the Franks*

As a result, armies of crusading knights and peasants started the trek to the Holy Land. The crusader symbol became a (usually) red cross on their tunics. Many historians estimate that at least 10,000 knights, 50,000 foot soldiers, and an equal number of civilians participated in the First Crusade. In fact, the response was so overwhelming that the pope forbade women to go with their husbands. He even had to stop the elderly and children from taking up the cross.

## Motives for the Crusades

Now there were many motives for going on crusade. Some did look on the crusades as a Christian obligation. The word crusade comes from the Latin word *crux*, meaning "cross." Many Christians even today feel they should "take up the cross" for God. Others hoped to gain wealth and/or land, especially knights who did not inherit an estate from their family. Some went for adventure or the chance to escape the life of a peasant. But still many devout Christians saw it as a penitential act for their sins in the hopes of gaining salvation.

The papacy had its own motives for the crusades. The pope hoped to extend control over the Eastern Orthodox Church, which had split from the Catholic Church in 1054. An added bonus was that quarrelsome nobles were sent to a distant land, removing a serious problem from Europe. To this end, the pope promised that the church would protect all crusaders' property while they were away. The papacy also excused crusaders of taxes and forgave many of their debts as an incentive.

# The First Crusade (1096–1099)

The message of the First Crusade spread quickly in part because of a hermit named Peter. Peter the Hermit was a preacher who rode around the French countryside on his donkey. His homilies or sermons convinced many to leave their work and follow him and his banner to the Holy Land with the intention of freeing it from the Muslims or *infidels*. By April 1096, five different divisions of common people had formed and started east to the Holy Land.

Two of the groups, led by Walter the Penniless (not someone I would be inclined to follow!), arrived in Constantinople on the edge of Eastern Europe in July. The others arrived a couple of weeks later, by which time all were weak, tired, and hungry. But the emperor of Byzantium was in no mood to entertain such a rabble of people within the walls of Constantinople—even if he had called for help. He quickly had them ferried over the Bosporus to Asia Minor (modern-day Turkey), where the Seljuk Turks quickly wiped them out and placed their bodies in a pile to bleach in the sun.

## def•i•ni•tion

**Infidel** literally means person without faith. During the Middle Ages, Christians applied this label to both Muslims and Jews.

## The Real First Crusade

Peter the Hermit's rabble of common folk were not the only ones to respond to Pope Urban's call for a crusade. Nobles Godfrey, Bohemund, and Robert led Norman, French, and German knights who had gathered separately. They traveled to the Holy Land by land and sea in a much more orderly fashion than Peter the Hermit's sun-bleached crowd, and their motives were less religious and more ambitious. As a result, the leaders of the First Crusade were divided, jealous, and often worked against each other. Lucky for them, the Muslim forces of Palestine were just as bad off.

## Miracle at Antioch

By 1099, after a long siege, the crusaders captured the city of Antioch. Not the best at strategy, they entered the city and were quickly surrounded by another Muslim army.

When the situation could get no worse (under siege, no food, no water), a miracle occurred—although it might have been man-made. A knight found what was said to be the lance that pierced Jesus' side on the cross, which they viewed as a sign that God was truly with them, so the crusaders rallied and broke the siege.

**Notable Quote**

"After taking Antioch the Franks camped there for twelve days without food. The wealthy ate their horses and the poor ate carrion and leaves from the trees. Their leaders, faced with this situation, wrote to Kerburqa to ask for safe conduct through his territory, but he refused, saying: 'You will have to fight your way out.'"

—Ibn al-Athir (1160–1233)

## The Capture of Jerusalem

After Antioch, they marched to Jerusalem, easily overcoming the defenders of the city's walls. Once in the city, the crusaders killed almost everyone they could: Christian, Muslim, and Jew alike. When the smoke had finally cleared, Godfrey was offered the title of king of Jerusalem but took the more modest title of Defender of the Holy Sepulcher.

After the capture of Jerusalem, the crusaders established three kingdoms at Antioch, Tripoli, and Edessa and tried to implement the feudal system in Palestine. These states were not very economically or politically strong and depended on a variety of outside sources for help.

# Military Orders

To help move Christian pilgrims to and from the Holy Land and to keep knights there, the crusaders established three religious-military orders that became very influential in the Holy Land and Europe.

In 1118, a group of knights in Jerusalem organized the Knights of the Temple, named after their headquarters site, the ancient Temple of Solomon. These knights took a vow of poverty, chastity, and obedience. They also promised to help Christian pilgrims in their journeys. After time, the Templars, as they were called, became wealthy in land and money, leading to their entrance into the field of banking by the thirteenth century.

A second order called the Knights of Saint John or Hospitalers was established in 1083 in the Benedictine abbey at Amalfi in Italy. The mission of this group was to provide shelter and food for Christian pilgrims, but later they expanded their operations to include fighting the Muslims in the Holy Land. There, besides fighting, they built places to house the wounded and dying called hospitals. After the crusaders were expelled from Palestine, the Hospitalers moved to Cyprus to build a base of operations. They, too, became wealthy and entered into several different power struggles with the monarchs of Europe.

The last order, called the Order of Saint Mary of the Teutons or the Teutonic Knights, was created in 1127 in Jerusalem by knights from Germany. Founded as a charitable order, it later became involved in military and political exploits. By the thirteenth century, the Teutonic Knights were crusading against the pagan Slavs in Eastern Europe. They conquered lands along the eastern Baltic coast as far north as to present-day Finland, establishing a German presence in the region.

# The Second Crusade (1147–1149)

The crusader states were constantly fighting and disunited, never much more than a few shattered outposts in Palestine surrounded by Muslim forces. As a result, the crusaders built huge, costly fortified castles to protect their territories. At first these castles, manned by a few crusaders, seemed to do the trick. Eventually, though, Muslim forces became determined to drive the Christians from Palestine.

The Muslim forces gained their first victory with the recapture of Edessa in 1144. This scared Europe into action. The pope ordered Bernard of Clairvaux to call for a Second Crusade against the Muslims to recapture Edessa. King Louis VII of France and the Holy Roman Emperor, Conrad III, responded, raising armies and marching to the Holy Land. Once there, they besieged Damascus, but the siege failed and both monarchs returned to Europe without ever seeing Jerusalem. Edessa remained in Muslim hands.

# The Great Saladin

In the next decades, the Muslims of the region found a brave, gifted leader who united them and expelled the crusaders. Saladin conquered Syria, Iraq, and Egypt, surrounding the crusader states on three sides. In 1185, he declared a holy war against the Christians in Palestine, then took advantage of quarreling crusaders to invade the kingdom of Jerusalem.

The disorganized crusaders met Saladin on the field of battle, where he defeated them easily and captured the king of Jerusalem, Guy of Lusignan. After that, the crusader strongholds fell quickly to Saladin, sometimes without even a fight. Finally, he captured Jerusalem, leaving only a small port city to the crusaders.

# The Third Crusade

The fall of Jerusalem shocked the people of Europe, and several monarchs saw it as their obligation to save the Holy Land. Philip II of France, Frederick Barbarossa of Germany, and Richard the Lionhearted of England responded to the perceived need for a Third Crusade. With the encouragement of Pope Innocent III, the kings created new taxes, known as the *Saladin tithe*, on their subjects to help with the financial burden of the crusade.

Frederick Barbarossa was the first to make his way to the Holy Land. He and his army marched overland through Hungary and the Byzantine Empire, but he never reached the Holy Land. Frederick fell off his horse into a river and drowned under the weight of his armor. With Frederick dead, most of his German army returned home.

Richard and Philip joined forces in Sicily. While on the way to the Holy Land, Richard conquered the island kingdom of Cyprus. The wealth of his conquest helped him finance the rest of his crusade to the Holy Land. Richard then joined Philip and French forces in the siege of Acre in June 1191. During the siege, the crusaders constantly bickered among themselves, nearly having their armies fight a pitched battle. Finally, they reached common ground together and in July Acre fell. By that time, Philip had had enough of crusading and returned to France. Richard knew he had to be quick, or Philip might try to seize English lands while he was away on crusade.

Richard stayed in the Holy Land partially because he enjoyed the life of warfare but also because he saw in Saladin a new, challenging enemy to fight. Saladin and his forces stopped Richard's army from taking Jerusalem in 1191. From there, Richard was forced to retreat to Ascalon. Using the city as his base of operations, he tried to recapture Jerusalem three more times but failed each time.

Finally, running out of time and realizing that if he did capture Jerusalem, he would have to spend his life defending it, Richard agreed to a treaty with Saladin that guaranteed Christian pilgrims access to the city. Richard never saw Jerusalem himself, vowing he would only see it when it was truly in Christian hands again.

**Middle Age Myths**

Robin Hood robbed from the rich and gave to the poor because the sheriff of Nottingham was ruling unjustly during King Richard's absence. Evidence does show that there were two Robin Hoods: one an outlaw and the other a king's servant during the time. Neither can be tied to the legend of Robin Hood, which has grown since the Middle Ages. Tales of Robin Hood and his merry men are probably just good stories.

# Later Crusades

The enthusiasm for the crusades went up and down like a business cycle. The later crusades had even less to do with religion and more to do with politics.

## The Fourth Crusade

The Fourth Crusade (1202–1204) was called for by Innocent III, who got promises from several prominent nobles, including Baldwin of Flanders, Boniface of Montferrat, and Geoffrey of Villehardouin, that they would support the cause of Christ. The plan of the crusade was to sail to Egypt and then push to Jerusalem. Transportation would be provided by the Venetians under their doge, Enrico Dandolo.

The crusade appeared to be doomed from the start. The anticipated numbers of knights failed to come to Venice, and those who did could not pay for the transportation to Egypt. At that point, the Doge Dandolo craftily suggested that they might earn money doing another job first. The job was to seize the Hungarian kingdom of Zara, a Christian kingdom that Venice wanted to add to its territory.

The crusaders thought it over and agreed to the venture despite the protests of Pope Innocent III. So 12,000 crusaders were transported to the Balkans to attack Zara, and Innocent excommunicated them because the city was Catholic. Once the crusaders took over Zara, they were offered money to topple the imperial Byzantine government at Constantinople on behalf of the son of the deposed Byzantine emperor. So in June 1203, the crusaders arrived at the walls of Constantinople and besieged it. In July they were able to remove Emperor Alexios III in favor of the young Alexios and his father. By April 1204, when the young emperor could not pay the crusaders for their services, they took over the city and sent its riches back to Venice as payment.

After Constantinople was sacked, the crusaders set up the Latin Empire of Constantinople, which lasted from 1204 to 1261. The pope was appalled by the results of the Fourth Crusade and disavowed it, but later tried to use it to reunite the Roman Catholic and Eastern Orthodox churches. This action failed and only deepened the rift between the people and churches of the East and West. Meanwhile, the Doge of Venice cleaned up. He gained the riches of Constantinople for Venice and secured Venetian trading interests in the Mediterranean.

---

### Illuminations

The Children's Crusade of 1212 also ended in disaster. In France and Germany, kids got caught up in the spirit of the crusades. Led by a peasant boy named Nicholas, they believed their innocence and love would allow them to gain Jerusalem without a fight. Many of the children died crossing the Alps on the way to the port cities of Italy. There unscrupulous merchants promised the children that they would transport them to the Holy Land. Instead the merchants put them on ships to North Africa to be sold into slavery.

---

## The Fifth Crusade

In 1215, Pope Innocent IV called call for the Fifth Crusade (1217–1221), but did not live to see it happen. His successor, Pope Honorius III, picked up where Innocent IV left off. The target of this crusade was Egypt and then the march to take Jerusalem. The Holy Roman Emperor Frederick II promised to send troops on the crusade to aid the King of Jerusalem and his forces and the Teutonic Knights under Hermann von Salza. But the emperor would never come through with his troops for the venture.

When the crusaders landed in Egypt, they immediately besieged the Egyptian city of Damietta and finally captured it in November 1219. When the Holy Roman Emperor's still-anticipated troops did not show, the crusaders decided to march on Cairo. As they advanced, the crusaders dealt with the flooding Nile River, the heat, and heavy Muslim resistance. As their numbers diminished, they decided to negotiate with the Muslim forces. In the end, the crusaders accepted an eight-year truce and a few holy relics to withdraw their forces.

## The Sixth Crusade

There were no battles in the Sixth Crusade (1228–1229) because the Holy Roman Emperor Frederick II was able to gain Jerusalem through political means. Having incurred enormous backlash from his lack of support for the Fifth Crusade, Emperor

Frederick decided it was high time that he fulfill his pledge and take the Holy Land. He and his army started the journey by ship in 1227. But fever broke out on the ships and he returned to Sicily.

When Pope Gregory IX heard about Frederick's delay, he excommunicated the emperor. The undaunted Frederick ignored the pope and set sail for the Holy Land again in 1228. The pope, taking the failure of Frederick to respond to his excommunication as a snub, put out the word that no Christian should help with the Fifth Crusade. So when Frederick reached the Holy Land, none of the crusader kingdoms were willing to help him retake Jerusalem.

Despite his lack of support, Frederick pressed on. He opened negotiations with the Muslims in Palestine and secured the rights for Christians to control Jerusalem, Bethlehem, and Nazareth. When the pope received the news, he refused to accept the treaty. In the end, Emperor Frederick crowned himself king of Jerusalem in 1229 with only his loyal men and the Teutonic Knights in attendance. Things fell apart quickly after he left Jerusalem to return to the Holy Roman Empire. Political factions fought each other for control, leaving Jerusalem poorly defended and weak. The city fell to Muslims in 1244 and would never again be held by a Christian ruler.

## The Crusades of Saint Louis IX

The Seventh Crusade (1248–1254) was led by Saint Louis IX of France. Inspired by the pleas of Pope Innocent IV, who was disheartened by the fall of Jerusalem in 1244 to the Ottoman Turks, Louis decided to follow the plan of the Fifth Crusade and concentrate his invasion on Egypt. King Louis and his French troops landed in Egypt and quickly captured Damietta by June 1249.

With his initial success, Louis and his forces advanced on Cairo. On the way, Louis fought against the Muslim forces at the Battle of Mansura in February 1250. At first in full control of the battle, the king was forced to retreat. Louis was unable to avoid capture in the hostile environment of Egypt, and, in April 1250, his forces were beaten and he was taken captive. For his freedom, Louis was forced to pay a large ransom. Bruised and beaten, the king and his army sailed back to France, leaving Louis to be haunted by his defeat in the Seventh Crusade.

While King Louis agonized over his loss, events were changing the political situation in the Middle East. In 1260, the Mongols, who conquered much of the region from Muslim forces, were defeated at the Battle of Ain-Jalnut by the Mamelukes, a group of former Egyptian slave soldiers led by the sultan Baybars. With the Mongols out of the way, Baybars embarked on a systemic campaign to end the remnants of the crusader kingdoms, starting with Antioch in 1268. When King Louis got word of the fall of Antioch, the Eighth Crusade was on.

In 1270, King Louis chose Tunis as the landing site for his invading army, because the local ruler expressed a desire to become Christian if he could get support. These expressions were quickly proven to be false, so Louis and his son Charles of Anjou laid siege to Tunis. The siege did not go well. Plague hit his camp and King Louis died. His son took command of the French army and sailed back to France. This proved to be the last of the efforts to save the Holy Land for Christians. Baybars and the Mamelukes were free to dismantle the last of the crusader kingdoms, which they did from 1271 to 1291. The city of Acre was the last Christian crusader stronghold.

# The Results of the Crusades

By the fall of Acre in 1291, the crusades had precipitated the decline of the Byzantine Empire, which had reason to regret their original request for help back in 1095. The idea that religious wars were pleasing to God had caused a great deal of bloodshed and persecution among minority groups in Europe.

Politically, the crusades actually helped to strengthened Islamic power in the Levant, since they reorganized and worked together to defeat the crusader advances. The crusades also did little to expand the kingdoms of Europe, although for a brief time they did enhance the power of the papacy, which had united the crusaders for the efforts in the Holy Land.

The most beneficial aspects of the crusades by far were economic and cultural. The merchants of Europe benefited because the crusaders extended the European maritime domination into the eastern Mediterranean and the Black Sea. The crusades established European commercial endeavors in these areas, especially in association with the Italian city-states. The crusades also brought Europeans into closer contact with the Eastern world. It was no accident that Arabic was studied in Europe during the twelfth century or that the universities of Europe began to acquire texts that had long been lost to the West. They had been taken from Muslim and Byzantine libraries and translated in Latin.

Finally, the crusades helped advance technology, including more accurate maps, magnetic compasses, crossbows, and improvements in military techniques.

# Crusades and Inquisitions

While the crusades were fostering the growth of militant Christianity abroad, it also was rising in Europe. Europeans viewed as heretics faced new threats, as did Jews and even other militant Christians. In the thirteenth century, popes called for crusades against the forces of Islam but also against fellow Europeans, including one Holy Roman Emperor.

The Albigensian Crusade, fought against the Cathar heresy in the early thirteenth century, was the ugliest of these local holy wars. If you remember, the Cathars or the Albigenisans adhered to the belief in a dualism between good and evil much like the Manicheans. Their beliefs came from the teachings of a third-century religious teacher in Mesopotamia named Mani. He tried to reconcile Christianity with Persian theology by interpreting the world as a battleground between the powers of good and evil or the spirit of life and the spirit of flesh. The result was a theology that rejected basic Christian theology including the role of God in the creation, the humanity of Christ, and the resurrection of the body. Because of the Cathars' mistrust of material things that were thought to be of the devil, they renounced most non-procreative sexual activity, practiced vegetarianism, and refused to submit to secular authorities, especially when it came to oaths.

Cathars first came to Western Europe from Bulgaria during the early eleventh century. By the thirteenth century, their population in southern France was substantial, centered at Albi in Languedoc. Within the religious population, they had their own church with priests and bishops. Pope Innocent III saw the Cathars as a threat to the unity of the Catholic Church and tried to end the heresy with all of his available powers. Innocent removed bad members of the clergy in France, urged the nobility to help suppress the Cathars, and tried to revitalize the spirituality of the church with men like Saint Dominic.

When none of these actions succeeded, Innocent called for a crusade against the Cathars—a crusade against Europeans! The Albigensian Crusade lasted from 1209 to 1229. It was a savage crusade that ended Albigensian heresy only after decades of fighting and bloodshed. In the end, the French monarchs intervened to help bring the crusade to an end, which helped to establish royal authority in southern France.

The region of southern France recovered quickly, but a north-south divide in France remained long afterwards. Later the search for heretics in southern France gave rise to the inquisition during the High and Late Middle Ages.

## Inquisitors and Inquisitions

Although heresy was not a new phenomenon during the Middle Ages, not until the time of the Cathars did the papacy believe it necessary to establish better methods to combat it. It had been generally seen as the bishops' job to inquire into heresy in their own diocese, but during the 1230s Pope Gregory IX began to add to church inquiries by appointing men called *inquisitors*.

Most of these men were Dominican or Franciscan friars, very educated and deeply devoted to Christianity. The inquisitors were also, more importantly, responsible to the pope alone—not local bishops. Thus they were given sweeping authority. As they traveled southern Europe looking for heresy and heretics, they employed torture, secret testimonies, denial of legal counsel to the accused, and many other actions that tested the limits of church and secular law. To them, these types of practices were necessary; it was a war on heresy.

**def•i•ni•tion**

An **inquisitor** was a church official that was given special powers by the pope to find and punish heretics.

Many inquisitors were opposed by regional bishops and lords on humanitarian grounds, but inquisitors also simply overrode their powers. Some inquisitors did try to act justly, but many were eventually imprisoned and punished for their actions. Fewer still were condemned to death by the church and handed over to secular authorities for punishment. Oddly, the Dominicans, which were founded to preach to and convert heretics, became the leading inquisitors.

The actions of the inquisitors can never be justified, but for historians they can be explained. For Christians in Europe, heresy was the ultimate crime. It was a betrayal of Christ and the church. It resulted in damnation of the soul to hell and could spread like a plague to other souls. Many inquisitors thought that they were fighting for the souls of the people. To them, heresy was a clear and present danger. Sadly, they were not the only ones in history unable to respond with peace and love to beliefs that were different from their own.

## The Templars

During the early fourteenth century, charges of a different kind were leveled against another group: the Knights Templar. The Templars were born out of the crusades but were destroyed by one of its effects: the development of militant Christianity.

King Philip IV of France accused the Templars of blasphemous and homosexual acts. He then tortured them to secure confessions and forced the pope to agree to the suppression of the order. Finally, in 1314, he burned all of their leaders at the stake. Philip's goal was to gain their landholdings in France, and he did, for the most part. Other lands of the Templars were transferred to the Hospitalers, who are still around today as a charitable organization called the Knights of Malta.

## Minorities in Europe

While most Europeans were white and Catholic, there were small groups that were not, and tolerance was not a virtue in the medieval world. People who were different were seen as a problem and were treated badly by the majority white Catholics. One of the minority groups that received most of the discrimination were the Jewish people.

Most Jews lived in the Middle East, but there were exceptions and some did migrate to Europe. A few were farmers, but most were artisans and tradesmen. The church did not allow Christians to lend money if they charged interest, so the Jews filled the void and became bankers. Jewish bankers made loans at high interest rates—not because they were greedy, but to defend against defaults. But this practice definitely did not make them a favorite of the community!

After the First Crusade, anti-Jewish feelings swelled in Europe, and Jews became the victims of mob violence. Some Jews turned to secular rulers for help and got it. But those rulers usually charged higher taxes in return for their protection. In 1215, as previously mentioned, the Fourth Lateran Council required that Jews live in designated areas and wear a yellow label. In addition, giving in to anti-Jewish feelings, England and France expelled all Jews from their borders in the 1290s. Many of those Jews migrated to Germany.

The transplanted Jews learned the German language and combined it with Hebrew words. This new language conglomeration was written in Hebrew and became the modern Jewish language Yiddish. But life in Germany was not always safe for the Jews, and some kept moving east to Poland and Russia, where conditions were often no better. Some Jews converted to Christianity, while others followed the teachings of Judah Halevi, who talked about the day when Jews could return to Jerusalem. Jews continued to face hardships in Europe well into the twentieth century.

The Europe of 1300 was very different from the Europe of the millennium. The frontiers of swamps and forests had been cleared, and European influence had pushed to the east and south. Europe dominated in different ways such cities as Toledo, Antioch, Cordoba, and Constantinople. After the crusades, Europe was connected like never before to the culture and commerce of Islam and Byzantium.

Europe was opening up to a wider world. This led to many other developments, including Marco Polo's trip to China in 1271, Portuguese exploration of the West Africa coast during the fifteenth century, and Christopher Columbus's voyage to America.

But sadly, although European culture seemed to be opening up to new influence, it was also shutting down. Europeans looked for a uniform culture that was hard to obtain and dangerous to enforce. Intolerance for diversity was growing within Europe. This seed of intolerance would later prove to be Europe's downfall.

## The Least You Need to Know

- The Christian crusades originated with Pope Urban II's call for a crusade in 1095 to recapture Jerusalem and the Holy Land.

- The First Crusade was successful; it did recapture the Holy Land.

- Crusader kingdoms were carved out of the territory of the Holy Land after the First Crusade.

- King Richard the Lionhearted led the Third Crusade in response to the recapture of Jerusalem by Saladin and his Islamic forces.

- The crusades after the Third Crusade were not very successful and only served to deplete Europe of monarchs, men, and money.

- The crusades did open up Europe to the interregional trade routes, stirring a renewed interest in trade.

- Other crusades were internal, including the Albigensian Crusade in southern France during the thirteenth century.

- Minority groups, especially the Jewish people, were persecuted for their different beliefs and culture.

# Chapter 12

# The Church Goes to School

## In This Chapter

- ◆ Education in the Middle Ages
- ◆ Medieval universities
- ◆ The scholastic movement
- ◆ Medieval science
- ◆ Medicine of the Middle Ages

During the early Middle Ages, education and learning fell to an all-time low except for brief episodes with people such as Bede or Alcuin. But with Charlemagne's stable reign and promotion of education, seeds which were planted slowly took root. By the High Middle Ages, several factors helped to foster a renaissance of learning in Europe. Commerce and trade in urban centers started to flourish. The bonds of feudalism had been weakened. The church reform movements of the High Middle Ages helped to separate the church from the secular state, which allowed some members of the church to explore more intellectual and spiritual pursuits.

A central issue in this renaissance was the debate over faith and reason. Thomas Aquinas thought there was no conflict between the two. Others disagreed, and the debate signaled a revitalized medieval Europe.

# Going to School in the Middle Ages

Unlike today, when education is associated with the state, during the Middle Ages education was generally associated with the church. Monastic schools educated young noble boys to serve as monks in the monasteries of Europe. Cathedral schools prepared young noble boys to become priests. Not every boy who attended these schools became a monk or a priest, but for noble boys, the monasteries or the cathedrals were the choices for an education. Noble girls had a different choice. Orders of nuns provided education for them to be ladies of the manor. The instruction included reading, writing, account keeping, needlework, surgery, and first aid. But these choices were for noble boys and girls. Most other children remained uneducated and illiterate.

## Other Ways to Get an Education

Some other forms of education were not associated with the church. Sons of nobles were trained as pages and squires in preparation for knighthood, but the reading requirements for wielding a sword and swinging it were, as you can guess, minimum. Many other boys in towns became apprenticed to artisans and tradesmen. Peasants taught their children how to farm and perform work on the manor. But very few children learned to read and write outside of the church. This began to change, however, during the High Middle Ages when literacy became more common among the nobility and wealthy merchants of the urban centers.

## The Course Requirements

The curriculum of most cathedral and monastery schools consisted of the study of the Bible, the church fathers, and the decrees of various church councils. During the High Middle Ages, influenced by the curriculum of Cassiodorus, schools began to broaden their curriculum to include the liberal arts, divided into *trivium* and *quadrivium*. The *trivium* was made up of Latin grammar, rhetoric, and logic, and arithmetic, geometry, astronomy, and music composed the *quadrivium*. Just as Latin was the language of the church, it was also the language of education and scholarship, a tradition that remained until modern times.

## Old and New Textbooks

During the early Middle Ages, books were rare and terribly expensive because they were reproduced by hand on vellum or parchment. And of course, some of the original works were written in poor Latin and copied incorrectly. One of the most copied books of the Middle Ages was a textbook on Latin grammar titled *Ars Minor* written by Donatus, a fourth-century Roman. It was *the* Latin textbook for over a thousand years. Other texts used for instruction included *A Handbook of Sacred and Secular Learning* by Cassiodorus, the Latin Vulgate Bible, *The Consolation of Philosophy* by Boethius, and *Etymologies* by Isidore of Seville.

Later, during the High Middle Ages, as the religious schools started to expand, more noble sons applied for admission to the schools, not to join the clergy but to learn to read and write and apply knowledge to other pursuits. And on occasion an intelligent son of a peasant might be admitted to school. One such example was Gerbert.

## Gerbert

With the help of a monastery school, Gerbert became an excellent scholar and teacher, although he originally intended to become a monk. Because Gerbert did so well academically, his abbot sent him to Spain, where he studied under Islamic and Jewish scholars whose knowledge was much deeper than those of medieval Europe.

After returning from Spain and completing his education, Gerbert became the master of a cathedral school at Aurillac in southern France. As a result of his advanced knowledge of science, math, and philosophy, some people regarded him as a magician. In his new position, he opened the curriculum of the school by declaring that the church fathers were not the only source of knowledge. He required students to read pagan classical authors and also to use an abacus (definitely a pagan invention!) to solve math problems. Later in 999, Gerbert was elected pope and took the name Sylvester II in honor of Pope Sylvester (314–335), who had had an excellent relationship with the Roman emperor Constantine the Great.

As pope, Sylvester proved to be very capable of defending the rights of the church while maintaining good relations with the Holy Roman Emperor Otto I. He worked to reform simony and marriages of the clergy and helped establish the church in Hungary and Poland. Tradition has it that Sylvester sent the famous Crown of Saint Stephen to the Hungarian king in 1000. But most importantly in relation to schools, he promoted education because of his notoriety and a superior knowledge of astronomy, math, science, and Latin. Thus Sylvester, a man of humble origins, ruled the church very aptly until his death in 1003.

# The Growth of Universities

During the twelfth century, the cathedral schools of France and Italy developed into universities, due in part to increased political and subsequent economic stability. People needed to be trained in law, medicine, and other subjects not related to religion. Since few people knew how to teach such subjects, students had to move to where the teachers lived. As a result, students from a variety of backgrounds congregated around teachers and one another to exchange ideas, which encouraged intellectual growth and a further demand for learning and education. Eventually, students and scholars who came together formed schools that were separate from the cathedral and monastery schools.

Sadly, some scholars were not so well educated, and sometimes the students who converged on a town were not such a welcome sight. So to counter these problems, students in Bologna, Italy, created an association to protect their interests, which they called a *universitas*. The *universitas* at Bologna managed the living arrangements of its members, established a curriculum, made scholars follow standards of teaching, and soon became a model for universities in southern Europe.

## The University of Paris

In France, the University of Paris became the model for universities in northern Europe. Little is known about its origins other than it developed during the twelfth century, probably evolving from the Notre Dame cathedral school, which had a reputation throughout Europe for its teaching of Latin, logic, and theology. Evidently when enrollment exceeded the capacity of the Notre Dame cathedral school, the bishop of Paris granted teachers permission to have classes at other locations in the city. Even with this new independence, the bishop retained some power by hiring teachers and supervising examinations.

Eventually the University of Paris became so popular and large that it was impossible to control. In 1200, the king of France, Philip Augustus, made the university into a separate institution, independent of the bishop of Paris and Notre Dame cathedral school. Later the University of Paris moved to the south bank of the Seine River; to this day, the neighborhood is known as the Latin Quarter because Latin was the language of scholarship.

## Other Universities

As universities developed during the High Middle Ages, some became known for certain subjects. Bologna was a center for the study of law, while the University of Paris was known for the study of theology. During the twelfth and thirteenth centuries, other universities were established at Oxford, Montpellier, and Naples. Soon more were established as learning and education became a sought-after commodity. Other universities were established because of student discontent. Oxford University was established by discontented students of the University of Paris. When Oxford closed in 1209 because of student riots, many students moved to Cambridge to form Cambridge University.

# University Life

To townspeople, the university was seen as a dangerous and chaotic place. During the day, young men met with scholars and discussed worldly subjects. At night, the young students sometimes became unruly by drinking and gaming to excess. (Not very different from today's university scene!) Generally women were not allowed to attend universities, although some privately studied with scholars.

## Town and Gown

Towns often resented the universities because they operated as a separate and independent organization within the community. This separation was demonstrated in the use of academic robes or gowns that university students and scholars wore. The traditional robes were worn partly for warmth but also to disguise the differences in wealth and class among the students and scholars. Thus the tension between the townspeople and the university was sometimes referred to as "town and gown." Tensions arose in the towns when students spent more time drinking and gaming than studying. As a result, town authorities had to be vigilant of student excesses, which caused even more tension. Eventually many universities incorporated their classrooms and housing behind enclosed walls for protection from the townspeople.

However, it was not all fun and games at the university. Students did have a standard course of study. And because textbooks were costly, students were expected to attend lectures of the scholars and memorize their words. Lectures would last six or seven hours, during which the scholar would read the textbook and expand on its contents to the students. Afterward, students would rush back to their housing to commit what they learned to parchment while the light lasted.

## Getting a Degree

To be granted a degree from a university, a student had to jump through several hoops. First, he had to complete from three to five years of study. At that point, he was eligible to take a comprehensive examination. If he successfully completed this exam, he was granted the designation *baccalaureatus* or bachelor, which indicated that he had done enough to have the first degree. But a bachelor's degree had little status, so it was generally best to continue. If the student continued study for several more years, he was eligible to submit a "masterpiece" to complete his studies. If the student successfully defended this work in an oral examination, he obtained the title "master" and could become a teacher at a university himself. The university system we have today is still loosely based on this system. For example, instead of a masterpiece, students today submit a Master's thesis.

# Scholasticism

The growth of learning and education during the High Middle Ages helped to generate an interest in applying reason or logic to faith. During the early Middle Ages, the church fathers provided all the official answers in the dogma of the church. But the new scholars or scholastics of the High Middle Ages questioned the accepted *dogma*. They wanted to prove that Christian principles could be known by logic and reason as well as divine revelation.

The scholastics developed this approach through access to Latin translations of pagan Greek philosophers (Aristotle being the most prominent) whose texts had come to Europe through Islamic Spain. Aristotle and the Greek philosophers taught that theory must be based on facts, and, to know a thing, one had to know its causes. In addition, the scholastics took on the teaching methods of Socrates known as the Socratic Method. Instead of making statements, teachers posed a series of questions to resolve contradictory beliefs, and this method became central to scholasticism. Five scholars in particular helped to give momentum to the scholastic movement. They were Anselm (1034–1109), Peter Abelard (1079–1142), Peter Lombard (1100–1160), Albert the Great (1200–1280), and Thomas Aquinas (1222–1274).

**def•i•ni•tion**

**Dogma** is a collective group of accepted doctrine, beliefs, or tenets usually religious in nature.

# Anselm (1034–1109)

Anselm of Canterbury was one of the first and leading members of the scholastic movement. Anselm was the son of a Lombard family, but he entered the famed monastery of Bec in Normandy in 1059. Under the tutelage and influence of Lanfranc of Pavia, he took his monastic vows in 1060 and later succeeded Lanfranc as prior of Bec. Later in 1078, he became abbot of the monastery.

Anselm gained great respect for his spirituality, writings, and teaching ability. As a result, he was the top choice to become Archbishop of Canterbury in 1089. But because of several disputes with King William II of England, his consecration was delayed until 1093. As archbishop, Anselm was in constant conflict with William and Henry I over the rights of the church in England and more particularly the issue of investiture. Twice, in 1097 and 1103, he was exiled from England. Finally, in 1107 at the Synod of Westminster, Anselm and Henry I were able to come to a compromise that allowed him time to focus on other theological issues.

As a theologian, Anselm was a very capable leader of the scholastic movement. He created an *ontological argument* for the existence of God by using the simple idea that the existence of the idea of a Creator proves his being. Thus Anselm created the phrase, "I believe in order to understand," which anticipated the theological and philosophical arguments of Thomas Aquinas and even Descartes of Enlightenment Europe. Anselm was a prolific writer whose most notable contributions include *Monologue, Why Did God Become Man?*, and *Addition*. But most importantly, Anselm made the first tentative steps in the use of faith and reason during the scholastic movement.

## def•i•ni•tion

An **ontological argument** asserts that the conception of a perfect being implies its existence outside of the human mind.

# Peter Abelard (1079–1142)

Peter Abelard was one of the most controversial philosophers and theologians of the scholastic movement. Born in Brittany, he studied at Tours and Paris under Anselm and other scholastic leaders. Although he was a brilliant student, Abelard butted heads with many of his teachers and their views. For example, he was able to refute his formidable teacher William of Champeaux's ideas on philosophical realism.

After his studies, Abelard gained fame as a teacher of philosophy and theology at the University of Paris, where he really got into trouble. Being a very popular teacher,

Abelard was asked to tutor Heloise, the niece of Canon Fulbert of the Notre Dame cathedral. Heloise had a brilliant mind and was very astute and quick to raise questions. She was also very attractive, maybe the most attractive woman in Paris. Abelard and Heloise, tutor and tutee, fell in love. Soon they entered into a forbidden affair that resulted in a secret marriage and the birth of a son named Astrolabe. Uncle Fulbert was so outraged that he hired thugs to castrate Abelard while he slept, and Heloise was forced into a convent as a nun. Abelard left Paris in shame but continued to teach after he entered the monastery. Tragically, the two, although physically separated, continued to love and care for each other until their passing as evidenced by their letters.

Despite Abelard's personal calamities, he produced some outstanding philosophical and theological works. His first work, the *Theologia*, examined the nature of the Trinity, although his views within the book were considered so unorthodox that he was condemned at the Council of Soissons in 1121. In his second work, *Sic et Non (Yes and No)*, Abelard further stressed church officials by collecting the various contradictions of church teachings. Again his work was condemned. Abelard then added to his body of writings with another *Theologia, Know Thyself* or *Ethica*, and *Dialogue between a Philosopher, a Jew, and a Christian*. Again, his writings, while being genius, were criticized by theologians and philosophers alike. Finally, the Council of Sens in 1140 condemned several of his propositions with the help of Bernard of Clairvaux. As a result, Abelard went to the monastery of Cluny for shelter and to be reconciled with the church.

There he completed his autobiography, titled *History of My Calamities*. At peace with his various personal mistakes, Abelard died at Cluny but was later buried at Père-Lachaise cemetery next to Heloise.

> ### Notable Quote
>
> In my case the pleasures of lovers which we shared have been too sweet—they can never displease me, and can scarcely be banished from my thoughts even during Mass …. I should be groaning over the sins I have committed, but I can only sigh for what I have lost.
>
> —Heloise in a letter to Abelard

# Peter Lombard (1100–1160)

Peter Lombard was born in Italy, got his education at several locations: Bologna, Reims, and Paris, and subsequently taught at the cathedral school of Notre Dame. Described by his contemporaries as a master scholar, Peter's abilities enabled him to take part in the Council of Reims in 1148 and allowed him to eventually be named bishop of Paris in 1159. Around this time he wrote the *Book of Sentences*, or simply

*Sentences.* Holding the office of bishop only briefly, Peter taught and wrote the rest of his life at the cathedral schools of Paris. Some of his other writings included commentaries on the Psalms and the epistles of Paul as well as sermons and letters.

But *Sentences* was what earned Peter fame and respect in the scholastic movement. A collection of the church fathers' writings, opinions of respected theologians, and important scriptural traditions, *Sentences* became the standard text for theological study during the High Middle Ages. Peter divided the text into four books: God and the Trinity; creation and sin, angels, demons, and the fall of man; the Incarnation; and the sacraments; and the Four Last Things, which were death, judgment, heaven, and hell.

Many scholars, blown away by the depth of Peter's scholarship, wrote commentaries to Peter's *Sentences*, including Thomas Aquinas. It remained an essential textbook in the new universities until it was replaced by Aquinas's *Summa Theologica*.

## Albertus Magnus or Albert the Great (1200–1280)

Albert was born in southern Germany in a town on the Danube River. As the son of a noble family, he was able to attend the University of Padua, where Albert was drawn to the Dominican order. After joining the Dominicans in 1223, Albert continued his studies in Padua and later in Germany before obtaining a teaching position in the city of Cologne. In 1245, he attended the University of Paris and earned a doctorate. During his time at Paris, he came across the writings of Aristotle, which were trickling up from Spain and the Byzantine Empire, and met his future student and friend Thomas Aquinas.

After getting his doctorate, Albert returned to Germany and, in 1248, established a house of studies at Cologne, serving as its headmaster until 1254 when he was elected the chief of the Dominicans for Germany. While in Cologne, Albert was helped by his brilliant student Thomas Aquinas as they worked with others to defend the place of the mendicant orders in the church and the universities and advance the Scholastic movement.

Albert's vigorous defense of the mendicant orders earned him the attention of the pope. As a result, Pope Alexander IV appointed him bishop of Regensburg. Later, Pope Urban IV asked him to help preach for the Eighth Crusade in Germany. After this fruitless task, Albert, tired of church politics, was allowed to retire to Cologne and teach part-time. In his last years, he seldom left his beloved city and died there in 1280.

During his life, Albert was called the "Great" for several reasons. He wrote a large collection of volumes on theology, logic, philosophy, ethics, and metaphysics. Albert also wrote commentaries on Aristotle, the Bible, and *Sentences*. Although he was not as intelligent and orderly as his friend Aquinas, many considered him easier to understand. As an important leader of the Scholastic movement, he tried to unite faith and reason. This unity developed further in the Scholastic movement and found its fullest expression in Albert's student Saint Thomas Aquinas.

## Saint Thomas Aquinas (1225–1274)

Thomas Aquinas was one of the most important of the scholastics. The son of Count Landuff of Aquino, Thomas was born in northern Italy in 1225. He began his studies at the age of five at the famous Benedictine monastery of Monte Cassino on a fast track to becoming a Benedictine monk as his parents planned. But after studying for a year at the University of Naples, Thomas decided to become a Dominican friar. Of course, this did not go over well with his parents, and they held him prisoner in hopes that he would change his mind. Legend has it that they even hired a prostitute to seduce him in his home prison but to no avail. So his parents gave way, and in 1245 Thomas began his studies in Rome and in Paris as a member of the Dominican order.

> **Notable Quote**
>
> You call him a "dumb ox" but one day you will hear Thomas Aquinas bellow across Europe.
>
> —Albert the Great on Thomas Aquinas's nickname

At Paris his classmates called him the "Dumb Ox" (he was a large man who was slow to speak), but his teacher, Albert the Great, recognized his intelligence and took him to Cologne, where he was ordained in 1248.

After he was ordained, Thomas returned to Paris to lecture on scripture and theology and was also forced to defend the new mendicant orders from the attacks of critics. After Thomas received his doctorate in theology in 1257, he began writing the *Summa Contra Gentiles* for Dominican missionaries, but in 1265 while in Rome he began his greatest contribution to theology and philosophy, the *Summa Theologiae*. In this work, Thomas combined the logic and reason of Aristotelian philosophy with the Christian faith in an effort to uncover the Christian faith. Another important period of scholarship for Thomas was in Paris between 1268 and 1272, when he defended the proper use of Aristotelian philosophy, which defined the tone of scholasticism from that point forward.

In 1272, Thomas returned to Italy, where he established a program of studies in Naples and continued work on his *Summa Theologiae*. In late 1273, Thomas had a mystical experience that led him to say, "Everything I have written seems like straw compared to what I have seen and what has been revealed to me." After that experience, Thomas put down his pen and never wrote or taught again. He died traveling to the Second Council of Lyons in 1274.

It is impossible to overstate Thomas's contribution to theology and philosophy during the Middle Ages and to this day. Although his ideas of systematically combining faith and reason were new and quite controversial during his time, he was later declared a Doctor of the Church, a high honor only held by a few. In addition, his philosophical style called "Thomism" became a major branch of the Scholastic movement.

# Bonaventure (1221–1274)

Bonaventure was another leader of the Scholastic movement and a contemporary of Thomas Aquinas. Born Giovanni di Fidanza in Italy, he changed his name to Bonaventure once he joined the Franciscan order. After joining the order, Bonaventure studied at the University of Paris. By 1248, he was teaching at Paris and continuing his studies there. During that time he became a well-known preacher and theologian. In fact, he was as famous and popular as Thomas Aquinas, who was one of his closest friends. Bonaventure was delayed in obtaining his doctorate of theology from the University of Paris over a disagreement between the professors and the mendicants of the university. Finally, in October 1257, he was given his doctorate on the same day Thomas Aquinas received his. During that same year, he was appointed to minister-general of the Franciscan order.

Bonaventure was an excellent leader for the Franciscans. He worked unceasingly to restore the order into a united group and ended the controversy over the standards of poverty set by Saint Francis. His work on that issue, codified in 1260, made many consider him the second founder of the order. Later in 1263, Bonaventure wrote a new biography of the life of Saint Francis, which became the approved and official biography of the first founder of the order.

Bonaventure became a highly respected leader and church official with his work with the Franciscan order. He was offered the position of Archbishop of York but declined. Later, he helped secure the election of Pope Gregory X, ending a period of time in which there was no elected pope. As a result, Gregory made him a cardinal in 1273. Traditionally, with the office of cardinal comes a symbol of great honor, a red hat. The story goes that when several papal legates came to Bonaventure at his residence to present him the red hat, they found him washing dishes. Bonaventure, ever the good servant, asked the legates to hang the hat on a nearby tree and finished washing dishes. Later the cardinal's hat became his symbol. Just before his death, Bonaventure was asked to aid in the negotiations with the Eastern Church at the Council of Lyons in 1274. He died during the council proceedings.

Bonaventure was a gifted theologian and philosopher who wrote several works, including *Journey of the Mind to God, On the Reduction of the Arts to Theology,* and *A Short Treatise.* In addition, he authored several other religious works and a commentary on Peter Lombard's *Sentences.* As a philosopher, he rejected many of the elements of Aristotle's philosophy that were such an important part of his friend Aquinas's philosophy. Bonaventure thought philosophy was not able to discover the divine on its own. Philosophy needed the supernatural, or more specifically church theology. As a result, he believed that the Greek pagan philosophers were not reliable sources on issues of philosophy or theology. On the other hand, he was willing to accept many of Plato's ideas if they came to him through the pen of Saint Augustine. Because of these beliefs, Bonaventure often came into conflict with Thomas Aquinas. Despite those differences, both men remained close friends.

### Middle Age Myths

You've always heard that the people of the Middle Ages thought the world was flat, and when Columbus sailed in 1492, many thought he would fall off the face of the Earth. In reality, most people of Europe knew the Earth was round. Bede described the Earth as a globe. Roger Bacon and Thomas Aquinas, leading thinkers of the Middle Ages, thought the same. Medieval monarchs held orbs with crosses upon them to demonstrate their authority over the Christian world. The flat-earth theory was popularized during the nineteenth century, but it was not based on fact.

# Medieval Science

During the High Middle Ages, not only were advances made in philosophy, theology, and law, but there were also significant advances in the field of science. During the early Middle Ages, science was based on a few surviving works of classical antiquity, which often contained many inaccuracies that mixed superstition with fact.

With the rise of the universities in the twelfth century, scholars became familiar with the scientific works of Islamic thinkers who had borrowed much from the ancient Greeks. These works came to Europe in the form of Latin translations via Spain and

Sicily. The Islamic learning about the natural world was much more advanced than anything in Christian Europe, especially in the areas of optics, math, and medicine. Due to the scholastic movement's affinity with Aristotle and the Greek philosophers, the "new" scientific learning seldom clashed with Christian principles. As a result, European scholars were able to use it as a start for their own scientific inquiries. Two medieval scientists, Robert Grosseteste and Roger Bacon, took the lead with this new learning.

## Robert Grosseteste (1168–1253)

Robert Grosseteste served as bishop of Lincoln and also chancellor of Oxford University. But he is most remembered as the "founder of modern science." Grosseteste advocated for the objective study of the natural world and emphasized the importance of math in scientific inquiry. Influenced by his readings of Aristotle, he developed a passion for observation and experimentation to verify scientific findings.

But like most of his medieval contemporaries, Grosseteste tried to reconcile his science with Christian theology. In his most important work, *Concerning Light*, he argued that, since God is the source of all light, knowledge of the properties of light helped a person know God.

## Roger Bacon (1214–1292)

Roger Bacon was the most influential scientist of the Middle Ages. Born in Somerset, England, he studied at Oxford University under Robert Grosseteste before going to the University of Paris, where he lectured on Aristotle for a number of years. Tired of the daily grind of teaching, Bacon resigned his position at the University of Paris in 1247 to devote himself to scientific experimentation. He returned to Oxford in 1250, and in 1251 joined the Franciscan order.

Even as a Franciscan, Bacon continued to conduct scientific experiments and study astronomy, alchemy, optics, languages, and math. His experimental ideas aroused many suspicions with the Franciscans. As a result, he had to petition Pope Clement IV for aid when questioned about his orthodoxy. To help his petition, Bacon sent the pope his volume titled *Great Work* and several other writings, hoping to gain approval from the pontiff to continue his work. Sadly Clement IV died, and Bacon was condemned and imprisoned in 1277. He subsequently wrote about his troubles in the *Third Work*.

Bacon was definitely ahead of his time in the field of science, possibly inventing an early telescope, a flying machine, gunpowder, and glasses. In addition, he wrote many works on math, philosophy, theology, and Greek and Hebrew grammar. In his scientific philosophy, Bacon thought all aspects of knowledge were interlinked. According to him, the study of the natural sciences was as important as the study of religion and philosophy. And like his former teacher Grosseteste, Bacon believed that the person who understands the principles of light and optics would understand the divine plan of the universe.

# Medieval Medicine

The field of medicine also expanded during the High Middle Ages. Like philosophy and science, it was greatly affected by the influx of "new" learning from Islamic and Greek texts. Medicine during the Middle Ages was not considered a science but a branch of philosophy. Medieval doctors did not perform experiments or surgical operations; surgery was the field of barbers, who were organized into guilds of barber-surgeons. The medieval physician's role was to prescribe for patients the cure for their disease based on a knowledge of medical texts from antiquity. So medicine of the Middle Ages was based on the medical writings of the ancient Greeks, the most important of which was Galen (130–200 C.E.).

The Latin translation of Galen's medical encyclopedia made its way to Europe during the early twelfth century, and he became the authority for the field of medicine during the Middle Ages. One of his most influential theories was that health depended on a balance among four bodily fluids called humors: blood, mucus, black bile, and yellow bile. Disease and illness were the result of a person's having too much or too little of one of these fluids. So the practice of medicine lay in diagnosing which fluid was out of proportion and correcting it. To correct the proportions, a variety of methods could be used, including drugs, diet, rest, and bleeding the patient. Many medieval physicians believed that reducing one's blood supply could bring the humors back into balance.

Despite the inaccuracies of the field of medicine, some progress was made in the late Middle Ages. The University of Salerno and the University of Montpellier taught the field as a science, and students learned to dissect animals and human cadavers. These university studies led to better skill in surgery.

When the epidemics of the High Middle Ages swept through Europe, taking huge death tolls, people realized that diseases needed to be controlled. Some towns appointed physicians to oversee the health of the town. To combat raging epidemics, other towns set up quarantines for visitors and newcomers. At the quarantines, a physician examined the people and required the sick to remain in quarantine for a set amount of time to prevent any disease from spreading. Some cities had hospitals set up near the monasteries outside the walls of the city.

In rural Europe, most people never saw a physician. Generally they relied on folk medicine, which combined magic and witchcraft to prevent illness with traditional home remedies such as roots and herbs. In addition, because illness and disease were often connected to the devil and evil spirits in the Bible, people used Christian prayers, penances, and pilgrimages to seek relief.

## The Least You Need to Know

♦ Cathedrals and monasteries, in an effort to train priests and monks, directed most of the education and learning in the Middle Ages.

♦ During the High Middle Ages, universities developed as a need for learning grew with economic expansion and political stability.

♦ The scholastic movement that came out of the universities tried to reconcile Greek philosophy with the Christian faith.

♦ The field of science benefited from the growth of universities as new approaches of scientific inquiry developed that formed the basis of modern science.

♦ Medieval medicine made some advances during the late Middle Ages despite its dependency on the inaccurate theories of the Greek physician Galen.

# Chapter 3

# Books and Blocks

## In This Chapter

- ◆ Literature of the Middle Ages
- ◆ Romanesque churches
- ◆ Gothic churches
- ◆ Medieval artists
- ◆ Gregorian chants

The flowering of culture in medieval Europe not only affected the church, education, and learning but also had a substantial impact on the literature, architecture, art, and music of the Middle Ages. Again this was due in part to the relative political and economic stability Europe experienced during the High Middle Ages.

## Medieval Literature and Romances

When the Romans moved into Europe and conquered the Germanic tribes, they brought the Latin language with them. With time, Latin became associated with the educated and kept that exalted position even after the Roman Empire passed away. The church used Latin as the language of

# def•i•ni•tion

> **Liturgy** is simply the ritualistic order of a church service. **Vernacular** is the language of everyday speech in a certain region, considered a common language.

the *liturgy* and for church business. Eventually, areas of Western Europe, influenced by the use of Latin, developed their own languages combining Latin with the local language. Those languages became known as the *vernacular*.

We can divide the literature of the early Middle Ages into two types. The first includes written works in Latin, such as poetry and theological works. The other consists of many traditional legends and myths that were passed down orally from generation to generation. Later these oral traditions were written down in Latin or, by the High Middle Ages, in the vernacular.

Before these early vernacular stories were written down, wandering minstrels carried them from town to town, castle to castle, and monastery to monastery. The minstrels told or sang the stories to provide entertainment, spread news and gossip, and continue the legends of a particular region. In France, these minstrels were called *jongleurs*. Their songs or *chansons* developed into long narrative poems about the deeds of heroes and warriors. Many stories focused on the rule of Charlemagne, which many in France considered a golden age. While nominally based on historic events, the minstrels frequently embellished their accounts to be more entertaining.

## The Song of Roland

The oldest and most popular of the *jongleurs'* tales was *The Song of Roland*. In the tale, Roland, the nephew of Charlemagne, was an officer in Charlemagne's army, which was trying to drive out Islamic forces in Spain. The army did not succeed and, while withdrawing to France, was attacked by the dangerous Basque tribes of the Pyrenees Mountains. Roland, in command of the rear guard forces, led a delaying action to allow the rest of Charlemagne's forces a chance to withdraw. Roland and his rear guard were killed to the last man, but the rest of the army withdrew to fight another day, which they did. Charlemagne, so inspired by Roland's bravery, marched an army right back into Spain, captured the city of Saragossa from Islamic forces, and created the Spanish March as a buffer zone between the Carolingian kingdom and the Muslims.

*The Song of Roland* was probably told quite frequently at the monasteries along the pilgrim route to the shrine of Saint James at Compostela in northwestern Spain, because the event might have taken place close by. The epic became very popular with the knights and monarchs of Europe because it glorified the role of Christian knights in fighting the infidel Muslims and also symbolized the classic victory of good over evil.

Notable Quote

"Now that Roland felt death approaching, he confessed his sins, and began praying to God for salvation and to the archangels Michael and Gabriel to guide him. Seeing that all attempt to destroy his sword was to no avail, he decided to hide it under his body, as he sat against the pine tree, facing the direction of his enemies in Spain. And then, he died."

— *The Song of Roland*

## Other Epics

The Spanish had an immensely popular epic titled the *Poem of Cid*. Written down during the High Middle Ages, it detailed the adventures of the *Cid* or the lord Rodrigo Díaz de Bivar, who led crusades against Islamic forces in Spain.

The Germans also had their own epic: *The Song of the Nibelungs*. Told in a sophisticated thirteenth-century High German, it combined the popular legends of the migration age that were common to much of the Germanic world and in Scandinavia in Viking poetry. The epic tells the tale of the hero, Siegfried; his killer, Hagen; Siegfried's wife, Kriemhild; Queen Brunhilda; and the treasure of the Nibelungs. It borrows heavily from the traditions collected from the early history of the Burgundians and their defeat by Attila and the Huns in the fifth century. Immensely popular, *The Song of the Nibelungs* had a strong influence on German cultural life, including poetry, prose, and eventually music.

> **Illuminations**
>
> During the nineteenth century, the German composer Richard Wagner used *The Song of the Nibelungs* as a basis for his epic opera *The Ring of the Nibelungs*.

Sadly, the English were not able to produce the epics that the Germans, Spanish, and French were able to. The early Anglo-Saxon epic dated from the eighth century, *Beowulf*, which recounts the deeds of the warrior Beowulf, was quickly culturally overshadowed by the Norman conquest in 1066. The Normans spoke French, and therefore did not perpetuate the Anglo-Saxon epic into the High Middle Ages. During the twentieth century, J.R.R. Tolkien lamented this fact and tried to produce an epic for England, which resulted in *The Lord of the Rings*.

## Love Stories

In addition to epics, love songs and romantic poems and stories became popular during the High Middle Ages. Most of these songs originated from France where troubadours sang them for eager audiences. Later, William of Aquitaine and his daughter Eleanor introduced the tradition of troubadours to the royal courts, and their popularity spread across Europe. Eventually, the love songs of the troubadours became associated with the code of chivalry held by the knights of the era. Two of the most popular romantic stories/poems of the High Middle Ages were *Tristan and Isolde* and the *Romance of the Rose*.

## Tristan and Isolde

*Tristan and Isolde* was rooted in the traditions from the period of Viking rule in Ireland around the tenth century but was given artistic form in Anglo-Norman England in the twelfth century. Written originally in French, the story was later translated into German by the poet Gottfried von Strassburg and also English and Old Norse.

The lengthy romantic prose incorporates much of the cultural background of Arthurian legend as it compares the skill and reputation of Tristan to Lancelot as knights and lovers. The region of Cornwall in southern England provides the central background for the romance, which was the same area in which the Arthurian legend was set. The story also moves around the Celtic world from Cumbria to Ireland and to Brittany, acquiring that Celtic flavor of Arthurian stories.

The chief characters are Tristan, the warrior and nephew; King Mark of Cornwall, Tristan's uncle; Isolde of Ireland; and Isolde of Brittany. The parts of the story, mixed in different versions, make up the essence of a true medieval romance and involve a lost nephew, a trusting king and husband whose trust is broken, love potions, poisoned cups and weapons, magical remedies, tragedy, dragons, and death. The final element that still brings tears to people's eyes today is the survival of love even after death.

## The Romance of the Rose

During the early thirteenth century, a French poet named Guillaume de Lorris wrote a poem of 4,000 lines called *The Romance of the Rose*. The poem was written in the form of a dream vision, a popular form of presentation during the Middle Ages. Personifications of human traits fill the poem, and characters have names such as Sir Mirth, the lord of the garden, his lady Dame Gladness, and a helpful person named Fair-Welcome.

In the poem, the poet/dreamer comes to a garden enclosed by a high wall. In the garden there is a fountain. In the fountain are two crystal stones. The crystals in reflection reveal a rose garden. In the center of this garden is one perfect rosebud. Seeing it from afar, the dreamer falls in love with it. The bud is, for the poet, a symbol of a woman he loves, Rose. But his efforts at trying to reach the bud are blocked by the personified vices of jealousy and shame. This allegorical garden is, for the poet, an analysis of the psychological state of true love.

*The Romance of the Rose* was so enormously popular during the thirteenth century that, like today's demand for movie sequels, by the end of the century another 18,000 lines were added to the story by the French poet Jean de Meun. The styles of the two poets were very different. Guillaume was an idealist, and his characters were light and graceful. To him, the theme of proper love was tied to proper social order. Jean de Meun drew on other thirteenth-century thought and scholastic philosophy for his writing. His addition used the methods and interests of the academic and legal culture. As a result, his personifications gave long and contradictory speeches and argued scholastic philosophy. At the end of the poem, the dreamer wins the woman Rose after a military siege of Rose's castle. And although the poem is written with allegorical and literary conventions, the conclusion is clearly sexual.

The poem, like *Tristan and Isolde*, is a good example of thirteenth-century romance literature. Its knightly characters, caught between God and the world, developed philosophies to satisfy both. In addition, the poem was written to satisfy themes such as the power of love, personal loyalty, and devotion to God.

## Fabliaux and Fables

All these epics and romances were generally told among the nobility. No peasant literature survives from the High Middle Ages. But the stories and oral traditions of the peasants might be embedded in ballads, proverbs, and songs that were written down centuries later, for example, those in Grimm's Fairy Tales, whose origins are difficult to trace.

Some urban literature was produced in the towns and cities of the High Middle Ages. As trade grew and towns expanded, merchants, artisans, and tradesmen created a vernacular literature of their own design. One result was the *fabliaux*, which were short satirical poems filled with vulgar humor that ridiculed conventional morals. In these poems, priests and monks were presented as sexually perverse; merchants' wives were portrayed as promiscuous; merchants were seen as greedy; and young men were depicted as handsome and clever upstarts. The heroes of the poems were the young men who made fools out of the others.

Medieval towns also created fables, allegories in the style of the ancient Greek tradition of Aesop's Fables. In these fables, various characters of medieval society (priests, nuns, monks, lords, ladies, merchants, and serfs) were thinly disguised as animals. The most popular of these fables involved Renard the Fox and were collectively known as the Romance of Renard. The tales parodied the chivalric ideas of the nobles, with Renard continually outwitting King Lion and his loyal (and stupid) vassals. It was much like a medieval version of Bugs Bunny versus Elmer Fudd. These forms of urban literature became very popular and eventually spread into the countryside through trade.

# The Three Greats

As literature of the High Middle Ages evolved, there was a move away from traditional vernacular epics to new forms. Three noted authors of the High Middle Ages: Chrétien de Troyes (1135–1183), Dante Alighieri (1265–1321), and Geoffrey Chaucer (1340–1400) became leaders of this movement.

## Chrétien de Troyes (1135–1183)

Chrétien de Troyes wrote for the cultivated audiences of the aristocratic courts of France from 1165 to 1180. In this task, he stood out as one of the most influential and innovative writers of vernacular in the High Middle Ages. Chrétien was the founding father of the romance story and, as such, his stories were translated and imitated by many. He drew much of his inspiration from Arthurian legend and from contemporary court society.

Chrétien's most well-known work is *Perceval*, which was unfinished at his death. In the story, he details the quest of Perceval, a knight of King Arthur's Round Table, for the Holy Grail, which was the miraculous cup of Jesus Christ. Of course, the love for a maiden is also in the story. Both the maiden and the search for the Grail have an ennobling effect on the knight. Although the story was unfinished, Chrétien's gift for psychological observation, analysis (mostly of love), humor, and irony gave the story a sense of elegance and complexity and made it one of the most popular tales of the Middle Ages.

## Dante Alighieri (1265–1321)

Dante Alighieri was one of the great poets of the Middle Ages and arguably all of Western civilization. He spent his early years writing and transplanting old romances into the vernacular for the rising middle-class audience of Florence. Dante pared down most of the elements of the romances to stress the bare essence of love. This work complemented his own love for Beatrice, a kindly woman whom Dante had only seen a handful of times (both were married), yet who inspired his writing. The death of Beatrice in 1290 was a great emotional blow to Dante, and as a result he wrote *La Vita Nuova* or *A New Life*, a work of adoration for a woman he never could know or have as his wife.

Later Dante was introduced to the writing of Boethius and the philosophy of Aristotle and became very involved in the politics of Florence. Dante was a member of the Guelphs, the political and family party that was divided into bitter factions. In this political role, he was elected to the *priori*, one of the highest offices. As *priori*, he visited the papal court of Boniface VIII, but while he was at court a coup d'état erupted in Florence, putting the Guelphs out of power. As a result, Dante was banished from the city he loved with the threat of death.

As he wandered the Italian peninsula looking for answers to his grief, he continued to work with the philosophy of Aristotle, producing the *Convivio*, based on Aristotle's *Ethics*. The work was aimed at laymen who wanted a glimpse of the works of ancient and new philosophies. About 1309, Dante started to write the *Monarchia*, a statement of his political views, especially those concerning a world monarchy. In this work, he used Aristotelian and Platonic ideas of perfection to create an elaborate defense of the Holy Roman Empire. His work, like others of the High Middle Ages, sought to remove the temporal power of the church.

During Dante's 15 years of wandering, the *Divine Comedy*, a masterpiece of Western literature, took shape. Consisting of three sections, *Inferno*, *Purgatorio*, and *Paradiso*, it is the story of Dante's journey through hell, purgatory, and heaven, the three levels to which souls can be assigned by God after dying. He is first guided through these levels by Virgil, the Roman poet, and finally by the kindly woman Beatrice, the love of his live. It is in and through Beatrice that Dante sees a reflection of the love of God. Throughout the poem Dante intricately puts together the elements of allegory and realism with the historical figures and characters of Florence now forgotten. In the end, Dante produced a haunting poem about the faults of human beings and the power of love.

> **Notable Quote**
>
> "In the middle of the journey of my life I came to myself within a dark wood where the straight way was lost."
>
> —Dante from *The Divine Comedy*

# Geoffrey Chaucer (1340–1400)

Geoffrey Chaucer, along with being one of the great English poets, was a man of business who traveled across Europe, including Italy, and an active participant in the courts of London, principally under the patronage of John of Gaunt, the duke of Lancaster. Chaucer's business controlled several important aspects of the customs services in London, making him a wealthy man. He was also, for a time, a clerk of works at the palace of Westminster, at the tower of London, and at St. George's Chapel in Windsor. So Chaucer was definitely a man who knew how the "real world" worked.

Chaucer developed his chief work, *The Canterbury Tales,* from 1385 until his death in 1400. The tales, which probably came from many of his own life experiences, were of 29 pilgrims traveling from London to Canterbury to pray at the tomb of Saint Thomas Becket. To pass the time, each pilgrim told two tales on the way to Canterbury and two tales on the return to London. Of the 120 projected stories, Chaucer only completed 24 before he died. The stories he did set down present a vivid picture of medieval England that blend realism, imagination, and comedy.

### Age-Makers

William of Malmesbury (1090–1143) was an English Benedictine monk and historian who devoted his life to historical writing. He wrote several works, including the *Historia Novella* or *Modern History,* which details the first Anglo-Norman kings of England. William dedicated himself to trying to reveal historical truth with an eye for a good story and is one of today's chief sources of the early history of the English.

# Religious Drama

During the Middle Ages, drama developed out of the plays performed in the churches of Europe. During the late first millennium, the church dramatized the stories of the Bible to teach people who could not read. In the beginning, the clergy acted out the stories only on holy days with the play in Latin and in the church. As the popularity of plays grew, the performances were moved to marketplaces to accommodate a larger audience.

Eventually, the casts of the plays included laypeople and used the vernacular language of the region so more people would understand the story being acted out. These performances came to be called mystery plays because they detailed the mysteries of the

Bible and life of Jesus. Later, the lives of some of the saints were also acted out. These plays were called miracle plays, as they detailed the miracles associated with each saint. Finally, the plays were expanded even further to include morality plays, whose plots surrounded particular moral instructions the audience needed to be taught.

# Medieval Architecture

During the early Middle Ages, very little building was done outside of the fortified manors and castles for defense, and religious buildings such as monasteries and churches. But the political and economic stability of the High Middle Ages brought a surge of construction. In addition, returning Crusaders, who had seen the beautiful structures of Byzantine and Islamic civilization, wanted to transform their own dark and dingy manors and castles into palaces or a close facsimile thereof. Also, the church had accumulated vast wealth and assets that it used to build new cathedrals, churches, chapels, and monasteries. With this outpouring of money, new styles of architecture developed and spread across the landscape of medieval Europe.

## The Romanesque Style

During the early Middle Ages, churches were built in the style of the old Roman basilicas, which were, in fact, courts of law. Later, this style became known as Romanesque. In general, the basic building plan of a Romanesque church was a large rectangle surrounded by thick walls of brick or stone with very small windows. Usually a light wooden roof was supported by the outside walls with two rows of columns that ran the length of the building. In between the rows was a wide central space called a nave. In addition, an aisle lay between each column and the outside walls. The columns were always taller than the walls and, as a result, the central part of the roof was supported by the columns and was higher than the sides of the building. This allowed the small windows to be placed on the two levels of the roof to help with lighting the interior of the building.

Building impressive Romanesque churches became a competitive issue for bishops and abbots, so eventually, driven by the competitive spirit, they made modifications in the basic plan. They rearranged the columns so that the floor formed the shape of a cross. A new aisle or transept perpendicular to the nave and longer than the width of the church was added to each side to help complete the cross. As a result of this development, churches became so wide that wooden beams could no longer support the roofs, so they used barrel vaulting. In addition, the central part of the church was made

## def•i•ni•tion

A **buttress** or **flying buttress** stands apart from the roof that it supports and is usually connected to the supporting walls by arches.

taller. This forced builders to use *buttresses* and later *flying buttresses* outside of the walls to carry the weight of the roof and support the walls.

Bishops and abbots also tried to have the most beautiful and elaborate ornamentation and art designed for their churches, so they decorated their churches inside and out, with many different mosaics, sculptures, and paintings that showed scenes from the Bible or detailed the lives of the saints. In general, a stylized standard form was adopted for each holy person of the Bible. This helped worshippers, as they entered any church, to easily and immediately recognize the event or person that the art was detailing.

## The Gothic Style

With the rise of cities and towns during the High Middle Ages, churches changed in style and size. With more prosperity, cathedrals, large, monumental structures that required much more skill, labor, and sacrifice than before, were built in the new Gothic style of architecture. This style emphasized openness by using many large windows to let huge amounts of light into the building. In addition, the builders used tall, slender arches and very narrow columns to make the cathedral dominate the skyline of the city. Dozens of large stained-glass windows used light as a means of worshipping the divine as most of the windows depicted some scene from the Bible or tale of a saint like in the art of Romanesque churches.

One of the first Gothic-style buildings was the abbey church of St. Denis, near Paris. Directed by the famous abbot Suger, St. Denis was built in 10 years from 1140 to 1150. By the mid-thirteenth century, St. Denis's style was copied and spread across Europe. The French produced most of the Gothic-style churches, with the Notre Dame in Paris and the cathedrals of Reims, Amiens, and Chartres. All of these dwarfed the landscapes and townscapes around them. For example, from the floor to the top of the cathedral's central nave, Notre Dame was 107 feet; Chartres rose to 118 feet, and Amiens stood at 144 feet.

The rivalry between bishops, abbots, towns, and cities to build the largest and tallest cathedrals accounted for the great heights of the cathedrals. In addition, the church wanted the cathedral to be the central focus of the city with no other building in the town standing higher. God, represented by the cathedral, was the most important thing to the town. Of course, this mentality could backfire; in 1284, the choir walls of the cathedral at Beauvais, France, built to a record height of 157 feet, collapsed, killing several church members.

## Pillars of the Earth

To build a cathedral was a long and arduous task, often taking decades to complete. Unskilled labor dug the foundations and moved massive stone blocks into place. Later more skilled workers and tradesmen carved the stone and artwork that went into the cathedral. All told, this process took a lot of money and effort. For many bishops, abbots, and tradesmen this was also a lifetime of concern and work. During the High Middle Ages, hundreds of Gothic cathedrals were built. In France, over 100 cathedrals were built in 100 years from 1170 to 1270, while across Europe, over 500 cathedrals were built in a 400-year period of European history.

For all the troubles of building a cathedral, they were worth the time and effort. Cathedrals provided a place of worship for the Christians of Europe, where often over 5,000 met for special masses. In addition, the cathedrals were a source of pride for their respective towns and the sites of many pilgrimages. Usually each contained a holy relic, which helped draw pilgrims. And they gave the towns some economic vitality as pilgrims spent at the markets near the cathedrals.

# Medieval Art

Beyond the artistic crafts associated with the churches, cathedrals, and monasteries, there were very few opportunities for artists to make a name for themselves. But during the High Middle Ages, there developed some exceptions to this rule.

## Cimabue (1240–1302)

One exception was a painter named Cimabue. He was the son of a rich noble but, unlike many nobles, he wanted to do something worthwhile and artistic with his life. As a result, he become a painter. His paintings grew in popularity, especially his paintings of Mary, which demonstrated a new dignity and realism. One was so popular that the king of France traveled to Florence expressly to see Cimabue's work.

Even more important than his paintings was his ability to recruit new talented painters. One legend has it that Cimabue was walking down a road when he noticed a boy drawing pictures on a rock. Cimabue was so struck by the boy's talent that he made him his assistant on the spot. The assistant's name was Giotto.

## Giotto di Bondone (1277–1337)

Born in Tuscany, Giotto was trained in Florence by Cimabue to be a painter and architect. His contemporaries, including Dante, Petrarch, and Boccaccio, recognized him as the best artist of his time. Giotto combined Byzantine painting and Gothic sculpture, and his work was noted for its simple solution to the problem of representing the human figure within space. Giotto was also considered a master of the dramatic narrative in art.

Only three signed pieces of work can be definitely attributed to Giotto. These altarpieces, which are paintings that sit on the church altar and inspire worship, are *Stigmatization of St. Francis*, *Madonna and Saints*, and *Life of St. Francis*. In these works, Giotto represents the end of a long development of Italian Gothic painting but also points to the possibility of the new trends of art in the early Renaissance.

## Fra Angelico (1400–1455)

Another famous painter of the High Middle Ages was Fra Angelico. This painter and Dominican monk bridged the stylistic gap between the medieval and Renaissance styles. Angelico worked with many types of art including miniature drawings and large paintings. One his most important contributions to Western art was the addition of *perspective*, a technique of making some objects or figures look closer or more distant than others.

# Medieval Music ... or Basically Just Gregorian Chants

Most of the important music of the Middle Ages involved the church, although there was folk music, which varied from region to region. The people of Europe wanted their church music to please the ears and also the soul. As a result, the Gregorian chant became popular.

The Gregorian chant was traditionally thought to be organized and arranged by Pope Gregory I (590–604), from whom the name of the chant is derived, although most historians question Gregory's actual involvement in its development. In general, it is accepted that the chant comes from Jewish sources and developed as the music of the mass under the members of a school of singers founded by Pope Gregory.

The Gregorian chant was (and still is) a vocal form of music that used a conventional scale of eight notes. Often the Latin text that was to be sung determined the tone of the chant. The chant grew in popularity from the time of Gregory and was adapted to different regions. By the time of the High Middle Ages, it had become increasingly ornate and complex with the addition of musical instruments to accompany the vocals. Eventually its complexity meant that only very well-trained choirs could master its style. This led to the chant's demise as fewer churches used it as an expression of worship.

## The Least You Need to Know

- With the political and economic stability of the High Middle Ages, literature, architecture, art, and music flourished.

- Epic poems in the vernacular, such as the *Song of Roland*, were popular forms of literature of the Middle Ages.

- Church architecture expanded during the High Middle Ages from the Romanesque to the Gothic style.

- Much of the art of the Middle Ages was associated with nameless artisans, but artists like Cimabue and Fra Angelico made names for themselves.

- The music of the liturgy, which came in the form of the Gregorian chant, dominated the music of the Middle Ages.

Chapter **14**

# Cities and Commerce of the Middle Ages

## In This Chapter

- The growth of towns
- The rights of women
- Agricultural revolution
- Technological innovations
- The growth of guilds and trade
- Money and banking

During the early Middle Ages, towns and cities of the Roman Empire diminished in size. Only in the Byzantine Empire and in Islamic civilization did cities continue to grow and flourish. But after the invasions of the ninth and tenth centuries subsided, the towns and cities of Europe experienced a revival. By the High Middle Ages, the conditions of Europe had changed quite dramatically. Feudal warfare had declined and trade had increased. The Crusades brought interest in new goods from the East.

In northern Italy, city-states such as Venice, Genoa, and Pisa took the lead in bringing goods from the East to Europe. Other European cities such as London, Antwerp, Milan, and Florence prospered from the developing wool trade. With a revival in trade and travel, much-needed improvements were made in transportation. Old Roman roads and bridges were added to or repaired, which allowed merchants to move their goods cheaper and easier. Trade centers developed along the rivers of central Europe, such as Mainz and Strasbourg along the Rhine River. Other cities grew into major ports, including Hamburg, Calais, and London.

# The Rise of the Burgs

By the eleventh century, villages, towns, and cities began to form around fortified castles or burgs, whose name comes from the Latin word *burgus* meaning "fortified castle or place." Eventually, the people who lived in these burgs became known as burgers in Germany, the bourgeoisie in France, and burgesses in England. In the burgs were many opportunities, so serfs escaped their lords and came to the towns in search of jobs and freedom for, according to custom, any serf who lived in a town for a year was considered free. Other people of the towns were former serfs who had bought their freedom, merchants, tradesmen, and artisans.

## The City Plan

Most villages that had grown up around the castles of Europe were only a hodgepodge of cottages. As these villages evolved into towns, homes were often crowded into small areas, usually because the lord limited the amount of land for housing. As a result, newer houses were built two or three stories high. In addition, the walls of the castles were extended to include the new developing towns. This again limited the size of the town and also increased crowding. Eventually, the small and narrow paths between the houses developed into the streets of the town. Also to have more space in the houses, builders projected the second and third stories outward over the developing paths and streets. This happened to such a degree that in some towns, people living on different sides of the street could reach out their windows and touch. The end result was that the streets of the town were narrow, dark, and evidenced little planning.

As we've learned, the tallest building in any town of Europe was the church or cathedral. And the largest open space in most towns was the marketplace, usually located next to the church. Tradesmen, artisans, and merchants put their shops close to the marketplace, and most of the town's water supply came from several wells also in or near the marketplace. Thus, during the daylight hours, merchants, tradesmen, artisans, and pilgrims gathered there to exchange goods and gossip.

Of course, the largest and fastest-growing towns were those located next to important rivers, roads, or ports. Other factors in the growth of a town included the importance of the cathedral or church and if there was a university. Due to problems with over-crowding, many new townspeople had to settle outside the town walls. Eventually these people would demand protection, and the town walls would have to again be extended to enclose a new section. Sometimes the old town walls were torn down to make new space for housing or to create wide boulevards to help alleviate traffic prob-lems in the town.

### Middle Age Myths

In 1284, the town of Hamlen, Germany, had a rat problem, and the mayor offered a rich reward to anyone who could stop the problem. A piper played such a lovely tune that the rats followed him to the river and drowned. When the mayor refused to pay up, the piper played a new tune which led the children out of the town to their deaths. Fact or fiction? Either way, it had a good moral: pay the piper or suffer the consequences.

## Big City Life

In the towns, the living space for most families was relatively small. In comparison, the houses were not much larger than the cottage of a peasant. Due to overcrowding and poor planning, sanitation was poor and people threw their waste into the muddy streets. Because of these conditions, disease and fire could spread rapidly through a town.

Despite these conditions, more and more people wanted to settle in the towns of Europe. The protection of the town was worth the problems of the town to most. Some peasants worked in the fields outside of the town during the day but lived within the protective walls at night.

## Going to the Market

Despite the height of the church or cathedral, the life of the town centered on the marketplace. There farmers exchanged their surplus produce, and merchants set up booths to sell local and not-so-local goods. People worked from sun-up to sundown.

Most went to bed when it got dark; only the wealthy could afford candles to light their homes. The day of rest, of course, was Sunday and sometimes holy days, when townspeople attended mass and enjoyed their friends and families.

## Keeping It Straight

Because few people in town could read, symbols and sound had a great deal of importance. The monks and priests kept track of time using marked candles, water clocks, and sundials and kept the people up-to-date by tolling the church bell every hour. But the bell was important for more than telling time, as it was used to sound an alarm for danger, mark the death of a person, and announce important occasions.

Merchants, tradesmen, and artisans had another way of making announcements. They used hanging signs with the symbol of their goods over their shops. For example, a boot was for the shoemaker; a twisted pretzel for the baker; and an anvil for the blacksmith. As street names developed, they acquired the name of the activities on the street. For example, the Spicery was the place where spices were traded, while Goldsmiths Lane was where the goldsmith and jewelers were located.

> **Notable Quote**
>
> "Let it be known to all of you that I have given and conceded, and by this my present charter confirmed to all my citizens of Chester, their guild merchant, will all liberties and free customs."
>
> —Charter for the city of Chester by the Earl of Chester, thirteenth century

As towns grew in size and importance, town leaders became more important as they negotiated with feudal lords who actually owned most of the towns. As the expense of warfare rose during the High Middle Ages, the lords levied higher taxes on the towns that they controlled. Town leaders responded by demanding contracts and charters that guaranteed certain rights and privileges. This was the beginning of a new independence for the towns and also aided the breakdown of the feudal system.

## Speaking About Rights ...

One group of people did not enjoy the rights and privileges that towns started to offer: the women. Women during the Middle Ages were very limited as to how they could live their lives. From the day a woman was born, she had a man tell her what she could or could not do. Marriages were usually only for convenience and arranged in order to gain land or property. At times, women were arranged to marry as young as four or five years old. This practice of arranging marriages was so widespread that the church created a canon to prevent it, which stated that children in the cradle could not be married. If a woman did not acquire an arranged husband during childhood, her adult choices were either to get married or to go to a convent and become a nun.

In marriage, the man ruled the family. On certain days, the wife was required to bow at the feet of her husband and beg his forgiveness for anything she had done to him or failed to do for him. Wife abuse was also a common occurrence. Of course, the rules for wife abuse stated that the beating should be reasonable. But despite all of this, women were important to family life, and in Italy, especially, they were a powerful member of the family circle.

Women did much of the labor of the Middle Ages. They tended the fields alongside men. Women, including noble women, spun cloth and made the clothing for the family. Women in towns and cities had a wide variety of jobs in commerce and industry. Sometimes when their husbands died, they were able to continue to operate the family businesses.

Most of the women were illiterate like their male counterparts, but some education was available for women. Remember, Heloise was being tutored by Peter Abelard, a renowned theologian and philosopher, when she fell in love with him. Of course, this romance cost him his job and a few other things and her education was halted. But Heloise's opportunity to be tutored was an exception, not the rule. In general, women were barred from attending most of the universities of Europe that emerged during the High Middle Ages, and many cited the romance of Abelard and Heloise as justification for this educational discrimination.

An exception with women and education was in Italy, where women were allowed to attend universities if they had the proper financial backing. In fact, Maria di Novella became a professor of math at the University of Bologna at the age of 25. Her professorship at such a young age would have been an incredible feat for a man, but for a woman during the Middle Ages it was nothing short of miraculous.

# A Revival

The growth of towns significantly changed the landscape of medieval Europe. People were no longer isolated in self-sufficient communities and manors but, instead, became connected to the outside world. This expanded their opportunities, and as a result, the culture and commerce of Europe grew by leaps and bounds. During the High Middle Ages, Europe experienced massive economic progress. Many historians think it was one of the most impressive achievements in European history.

During the early Middle Ages, if you remember, Europe did not have it so good. Invaders raped and pillaged. Most of the people lived and died on the manors or land on which they were born. Life was a daily struggle. Food was scarce; trade was almost nonexistent; coinage had disappeared as a medium of exchange; and the towns shrank in size and population. But by the end of the High Middle Ages, this bad picture had changed dramatically. More and better food was available; trade was booming; coinage was again used as a medium of exchange; and towns were growing and new ones were springing up. This huge change in Europe happened for several reasons.

## A Revolution

One major reason for the economic progress of the High Middle Ages was the agricultural revolution of the eleventh century, which changed the way Europeans grew their food. Peasants grew and ate more food, which brought about a population explosion. By 1300, Europe had three times as many people as it did at the end of the first millennium. This revolution, of course, encouraged the growth of trade and cities, since people didn't have to spend as much time in the fields of the manor.

Several factors created this agricultural revolution, and the first was the political stability that developed after the ninth- and tenth-century invasions. With the decline in feudal warfare and the emergence of strong monarchies came political security that helped encourage people to clear more land for farming. Another factor related to the climate, which had become warmer and drier from the tenth to the thirteenth centuries. This new climate favored farming, and peasants cultivated more land in northern Europe.

## New Inventions

Also due to the political stability, Europeans took advantage of some important new inventions. With the heavy plow, peasants could more efficiently till the heavier soils, and with the harness and tandem harness, they could yoke oxen and horses together to pull heavier loads and plow more fields. Finally, horseshoes allowed horses to have an easier time and better footing on rough terrain.

## The Three-Field System

Another factor in the agricultural revolution was the use of the three-field system. Before modern fertilizers, part of a farmer's land had to lie fallow each year, so as not to exhaust the soil. During the early Middle Ages, European peasants copied the

Roman model of leaving half of their arable land uncultivated every year. But by the eleventh century, peasants divided the arable land into three parts. Every year, one third of the land would lie fallow, one third would be sown with grain in the fall, and one third would be sown in the spring. As a result, medieval peasants had two harvests a year, increasing their food production. In addition, the spring crop was usually beans or oats, which made for a much healthier diet. When combined with bread, a staple of the peasant's diet, beans made a good source of protein.

With the increased grain production, peasants also increased the number and variety of livestock they kept. More livestock, like pigs, cattle, sheep, and goats, meant more meat, milk, cheese, butter, and eggs. This also made for a much healthier diet and provided extra income if needed.

## A Technological Revolution

Beyond the agricultural revolution, many technological advances helped spur the economic advancement of Europe. A variety of mechanical devices were invented to convert flowing water into power. Using gears, cams, and pulleys, Europeans were able to convert the circular action of a water wheel into an up-and-down action or into the faster motion of a small wheel. With this new knowledge, water-powered mills sprang up alongside rivers and streams. The mills allowed Europeans to do a variety of tasks more efficiently: grind grain, tan leather, and forge iron. Later, windmills were invented for regions that did not have ready access to rivers but still wanted the power for their tasks.

Two important technological advances occurred during the thirteenth century. The spinning wheel revolutionized the making of cloth, and commercial coal mining began. Coal was mined in Belgium to be burned as a source of energy. The people of Europe could no longer rely on forests for fuel, since more and more land was cleared to feed the growing population.

By the late fifteenth century, new mining techniques allowed for the extraction of minerals and ores more effectively than ever before. Timbers supported horizontal and vertical shafts in the earth, while water-power or horse-power was used to pump water from the mines. Water-powered bellows were created to increase the temperature of the fires used to smelt the ores. This produced cast iron, used to make strong tools for farmers and tradesmen.

Other technological advances of the High Middle Ages made sea travel safer and more efficient. In the thirteenth century, the compass and the astrolabe had finally reached Europe from China. Sailors also charted the shores and harbors of Europe. With the compass, astrolabe, and better charts, sailing became much safer. Also during the thirteenth century, shipbuilders created the caravel, a three-masted ship with a rounded bottom that could be operated in shallow water and steered into a crosswind. Eventually larger ships called galleons were developed for even heavier cargoes, all of which facilitated more trade between the ports of Europe, Africa, and Asia.

# An Explosion of Trade and Commerce

With the foundation of the agricultural revolution and technological innovation, trade and commerce expanded. Because manors produced more food than they needed, the lords could trade that surplus for luxury goods a manor was unable to produce. The silks and spices that came into Europe as the result of the Crusades in the East increased the desire for luxury goods. As the High Middle Ages progressed, trade spread throughout Europe.

With the Crusades, merchants from Venice, Genoa, and Pisa created profitable trading companies, which bought luxury goods from the Middle East to the ports of Italy and southern France. Many of these goods had their origins in India, China, Persia, and Africa as well as the Islamic lands of the Middle East. The main port in Southern France was Marseilles. From there, merchants transported the goods into the interior of France using a combination of roads and rivers. The same happened with the cities of central Germany as merchants bought goods from Venice or Genoa and transported them across the Alps. Goods that reached northern Europe were then shipped from northern ports to England and the Scandinavian kingdoms. The merchants in southern Europe traded their luxury goods for products of the north, including grain, leather, and wool.

## Flemish Wool and the Flanders Fleet

With the expansion of trade and commerce, the Lowlands region of the North Sea became a commercial powerhouse. In the western Lowlands called Flanders, the Flemish raised sheep, which thrived on the plentiful marsh grasses of the area. The Flemish had always been known for their cloth as early as Charlemagne's day. Now the cloth became a medium of exchange. To improve their position, the Flemish merchants imported wool from the English. Eventually the Flemish and English wool trade became interlinked and interdependent.

By the fourteenth century, the merchants of Venice created the Flanders Fleet, which traveled the coastlines of Europe from Venice to Flanders, a way that was less expensive than the traditional overland route. As a result, Venice became an even stronger commercial city with control of trade to the Middle East and to northern Europe. It became a thriving market with goods from most of the known world. Venice was then the most cosmopolitan city of Europe. If you could not get it in Venice, you couldn't get it anywhere.

## Let's Go to the Fair

Also as the trade of the High Middle Ages expanded, towns along the European sea and land trade routes set up trade fairs. At the fairs, merchants from many different regions met to settle accounts and make deals for future trades. Eventually, a few fairs stood above the rest, and these were the annual fairs held at Champagne, Ghent, Leipzig, and Winchester. The nobles who owned the lands on which the fairs were located also participated, but in a unique way. They provided services, such as special courts to settle disputes, guards for merchants and their goods, clerks for the paperwork, and buildings where people met.

The fairs were as important for the diffusion of ideas as for the exchange of goods. Trade fairs were international events, and ideas from around the world got tossed around in many conversations. With time, these fairs helped to end the isolation of the peasants and lords of Europe.

## The Growth of Guilds

As the towns and trades grew, merchants, artisans, and tradesmen started to unite in associations known as *guilds*. Over time, these associations acquired a lot of power in the towns. They controlled the quantity and quality of the goods produced, set the price for those goods, and protected the interest of the guild members. During the High Middle Ages, two types of guilds developed: the merchant and craft guilds.

The first guilds on the scene were the merchant guilds, whose main goal was to control trade in a particular region or town. Thus all the merchants in a town would join together to supervise trade, make sure foreign merchants paid taxes, and regulate the weights and measures of the town. If a

**def•i•ni•tion**

**Guilds** were organizations through which town trades and crafts were supervised in training, quality, and sales.

dispute arose, the guild courts settled it. Guilds also helped to protect merchants on their travels. In addition, they negotiated with other guilds in other towns on issues of trade and debt. The guild also served several religious, social, and charitable roles as they usually held special festivals in honor of the patron saint of the guild. At guild meetings, members had some of the best food and entertainment available. And finally, the guild helped with funeral and burial expenses of members who passed away or even helped families of members who had been incapacitated.

The second type of guild was the craft guild, which by the end of the Middle Ages had superseded the merchant guilds. Tradesmen and artisans in trades such as weaving, leatherworking, metalwork, and baking organized themselves into guilds and then only allowed people practicing their trade to join the group. Like the merchant guilds, the craft guilds supervised the production of goods and created a monopoly. If a guild member made or sold poor-quality goods, he would be fined or expelled from the guild. This quality control protected consumers, which in turn guaranteed their patronage and loyalty.

Each craft guild also limited its membership to control the trade. To become a member, a person had to pass through three stages of membership. Apprentices were boys who had been accepted for training and received no pay but only food and shelter. As a young apprentice, a boy watched and learned the skills needed to perform the craft. If the boy passed his examination, he was then admitted to the guild as a journeyman and could be paid for his work. When a journeyman reached the age of 23, he was eligible to submit his masterpiece to prove his skill in his craft. If the masterpiece was acceptable, the journeyman became a master craftsman and was officially admitted to the guild. From there, the master could open his own shop and take on his own apprentices and journeymen.

As guilds grew in power, they took on leading roles in the governing of towns by hiring guards to patrol the streets of the towns, donating large sums of money to the churches to fund new building, and setting up schools and hospitals for the townspeople. But with these benefits in the growth of guild power came some negatives. The guild system was very rigid and restrictive. Membership to them was sometimes limited only to the sons of members. Many young men had to remain journeymen or laborers for their entire lives. As a result, the trust between journeymen and masters suffered and was replaced with bitterness, which even led to riots during times of economic hardship.

## The Hanseatic League or HL

During the early fourteenth century, the merchants of the coastal towns of the Baltic and North seas formed a super guild to secure trading privileges for its members in foreign ports. This guild became known as the Hanseatic League and eventually attracted members from over 200 cities. It monopolized the trade and commerce of northern Europe for close to 300 years as it acquired control of a variety of businesses from England to Russia and even created its own naval force to protect its ships, ports, and interests. Finally, the league made its own system of weights and measures to standardize business transactions among its members. The league was ruled by merchant representatives from each of the member cities although they seldom met. Regardless, the league had a great deal of political influence because of its wealth.

## Money! Money! Money!

Money transactions slowly replaced the barter system as trade revived. And for the first time since the fall of the Roman Empire, coins were used as a medium of exchange and not for religious rituals.

By the thirteenth century, the use of coins as a medium of exchange was widespread. Medieval kings and the city-states of Italy all issued their own coinage to establish a monetary system. With the demand for coinage on the rise, lords sold some of their lands for coin. Townspeople also used money, as did the developing trade fairs.

Some coins were much more widely accepted than others. Most merchants accepted the ducats of Venice and the florins of France. To prevent counterfeiting, rulers ordered the gold or silver coins be stamped or minted with their seal, which represented a standard in size and weight, to ensure the value of the coin. Because many merchants (and some rulers, too!) were very adept at shaving gold off coins and substituting the weight lost with tin or copper, some Italian merchants made their livelihood evaluating coins. They would weigh and analyze the coins on *bancs* or benches, and later their businesses became known as banks.

> **Notable Quote**
>
> "I will not have you be money lenders, and for this reason, that God would not have you so. If you have lent your money ... advanced a loan to someone from whom you expect to receive interest ... as I said you expect to receive back more than you gave, you are a usurer, and in this respect you deserve blame and not praise."
>
> —Saint Augustine on usury

## Banks and Loans

With the revival of trade and coinage, some Europeans developed a surplus of cash, while others wanted to borrow. Kings needed money to wage more and more expensive wars. Merchants needed to finance more and more complex trade networks. And nobles wanted to buy more and more luxury goods. The problem was that the church considered the practice of *usury* a sin. Not everyone was completely deterred, however. Some Christians lent their money through Jewish middlemen who were not restricted by the same set of rules. As such, money lending was one of the few occupations Jews were allowed to have in medieval Europe. Most Jews could not own land, practice a trade, or join a guild.

**def•i•ni•tion**

**Usury** is the practice of loaning money to other people in return for interest.

But by the late Middle Ages, the Jews were not the only people lending money in Europe. The Italian merchant-bankers had gotten into the act. As trade and production increased, merchants found it necessary to borrow, standardize, secure, store, and transport money. The Italian bankers became specialists in just such services. With the importance of this work recognized by everyone, the church lifted some of its moral restrictions on loaning money as long as these merchants maintained reasonable interest rates.

Other ideas about wealth were also affected by the economic boom of the High Middle Ages. When guilds first assembled, they established a just price for a product. Following church teachings, the just price included the cost to make the good plus a small profit. After this price was set, the guild did not change it. But as the economy expanded, the attitudes of merchants and guilds changed considerably. It became possible to charge higher prices; in fact, profiting from whatever customers were willing to pay was no longer frowned upon. If someone were willing to pay a high price, the item was sold at a high price.

## Saint Godric of Finchale (1069–1170)

The life story of Godric of Finchale presents an example of the growth of trade and the rags-to-riches nature of trade and commerce during the High Middle Ages. The reason historians know anything about this man and his life is because of his later rejection of the world that made him the subject of several saintly biographies.

Godric was born to a poor Anglo-Saxon family shortly after the Norman Conquest of 1066 in a small town in England. By the age of sixteen, Godric had left his home and family to seek his fortune. At first, he worked as a peddler, finding lost goods and then selling them. With his profits, Godric made a pilgrimage to Rome, partially for pious reasons but probably also for the adventure of it.

After Rome, he saved enough money to become a seafaring merchant. His enterprise expanded quickly as he exchanged goods between England, Denmark, Flanders, and Scotland. With the profits of this trade, Godric bought shares in several merchant ships. Soon he became a sea captain, sailing his own ships from port to port. Godric was such a skilled sailor that he was said to have saved several ships from shipwreck with the help of his uncanny ability to forecast the weather. With Godric's material and financial success came power, and with that power came sin. According to Godric, he committed sins of dishonesty and lust during this time on a regular basis; he was very far from being a saint.

At the turn of the twelfth century, Godric sailed to the Holy Land on a pilgrimage to Jerusalem. Along the way, he traded and maybe pirated a few ships. A crusade chronicler did describe how an Anglo-Saxon pirate named Godric rescued King Baldwin I of Jerusalem in 1102 from a Muslim army. On his return to England, Godric started to feel the hound of heaven. He was torn between living the worldly life and devoting himself to God. As a result, he gave up his career as a merchant and spent his time on pilgrimages to Rome and St. Giles in France. But to Godric even these acts of piety were not enough.

So Godric decided to get rid of all of his wealth and become a hermit. As a hermit, he moved from forest to forest in northern England. But this was still not enough. So finally, he made one last pilgrimage of penance to the holiest of cities: Jerusalem. Upon his return to England, Godric settled down on the River Wear in Finchale, England.

## Hermit and Saint

At Finchale, Godric lived a pious life as a hermit for over 60 years. His reputation for saintliness and piety spread across England and then Europe. As a result, some of the abbots and bishops of the church visited him. Some, including Thomas Becket and Pope Alexander III, who both wanted his prayers and advice, even saw him as a modern-day prophet. Godric was also admired as a poet who, at times, would set his religious verses to music. He was even said to love animals so much that he brought field mice and rabbits to his cottage to enjoy the fire. Godric lived to be 100 years old. After he died, the monks of the nearby Durham Cathedral built a monastery on the site of his cottage. Later Godric would receive sainthood.

The story of Godric's transformation is admirable, to say the least. But for historians, the information on his younger years as a merchant and sailor are the most relevant. The details of these years provide an unparalleled look into the life of an entrepreneur during the early stages of the explosion of trade and commerce during the High Middle Ages.

## The Least You Need To Know

- With the end of the ninth- and tenth-century invasions, towns developed around fortified castles.

- By the High Middle Ages, the towns had developed into large cities, which revived trade and culture.

- Although towns and cities started to enjoy more rights and privileges, women did not have many rights.

- Agricultural and technological innovations helped create a surplus of food, which created an explosion in population and commerce.

- With the growth of trade and commerce, guilds developed and helped regulate the new economy.

- The use of a money and banking system also developed with the economic boom of the High Middle Ages.

- The life of Godric of Finchale provides historians with a glimpse into the life of an entrepreneur of the High Middle Ages.

# Part 3

# The Late Middle Ages (1300–1500)

Politically, two major wars diverted two of the major kingdoms from nation building. The first was the Hundred Years' War between England and France, followed by the English Civil War or the War of the Roses, which again drained precious resources. The church had its own problems. The rationalism and scholasticism of the High Middle Ages became too heretical for the church. Religiosity in much of the population grew excessive as people sought stability in their daily lives. Controversy surrounded the authority of the popes, raising questions about the spiritual and temporal authority of the church that later emerged during the Reformation. Things only got worse during the late Middle Ages. The Great Famine weakened the constitution of the population; then the Black Death swept in on the trade routes from Asia, wiping out whole towns. Between these two events, over a third of the population of Europe was lost.

# Chapter 5

# Famine and Disease

## In This Chapter

- ◆ Climate change
- ◆ Famine and its effects
- ◆ The Black Death
- ◆ Dark days

With the late Middle Ages and the coming of the Black Death and the Great Famine, Europe experienced the kind of very bad periods it had not experienced since the early Middle Ages. The Great Famine weakened the constitution of the population; then the Black Death swept in on the trade routes from Asia, wiping out whole towns. Between the two, over a third of the population of Europe was lost.

## Real Climate Change

The mild climate that the Europeans had experienced since the first millennium fluctuated during the early fourteenth century. Of course, this did not instantly mean colder temperatures, shorter summers, and longer winters. It was an up-and-down process, almost comparable to the climate change we are experiencing today from global warming.

In general, the climate of Europe during the Middle Ages was warmer than during the Little Ice Age of Europe from 1590 to 1850. The warmest centuries of the Middle Ages compare to that of the twentieth century, while the coldest compare to the years of the early nineteenth century. From tree-ring evidence of the early Middle Ages and the chronicles of the High and Late Middle Ages, which give information about ice and snow, it is possible to guess at the temperature of the decades of the Middle Ages.

But fluctuations of rainfall are difficult to calculate for the early Middle Ages. The density of the peat during the time of the barbarian invasions suggests to those who study it that Europe was very dry during that time. And chroniclers of the High and Late Middle Ages did a good job of providing rainfall numbers, helping climatologists a great deal in making generalizations about the climate of the period.

With this information, we can pretty well explain the climate change of the Middle Ages. During the fifth century, the weather was dry and warm. Then in the eighth century it was just warm. The period of time from the seventh century to the late tenth century was especially cold. Remember also, this was the time of the ninth- and tenth-century invasions, so it was not a good time period on any level for Europeans. A warm phase followed from the early eleventh century to the start of the twelfth century.

During the twelfth century, summers were cold again in the first half but warm in the second half. This warm period coincided with the agricultural revolution in Europe. There were, of course, fluctuations of temperature and rainfall afterward until the Little Ice Age began in the sixteenth century. Those fluctuations that occurred during the fourteenth century caused problems for the population of Europe.

Signs of the change to come were evident during the late thirteenth and early fourteenth centuries. Weather patterns became increasingly unpredictable. Very good years of weather were followed by very bad ones. Heavy rains would rot crops and leach the ground for a period of several years. Then improved weather would follow for a decade or longer. Also, varying weather conditions might freeze or destroy vineyards and fields of grain for a few seasons.

The documentary evidence of the High and Late Middle Ages makes it possible to determine the weather characteristics of almost all the decades. Some decades were very wet, such as the 1090s, 1190s, 1310s, 1340s, and 1360s. Other decades were very dry, including the 1130s, 1200s, 1300s, and 1470s.

With these wild fluctuations, in rainfall especially, seedbeds were washed away, fields were submerged, grain rotted, dikes were broken, meadows grew wild because they were too wet to cut, and quarries flooded. This was not good for the people of Europe. Good land was becoming hard to find. Marginal lands that required more work to produce became impossible to work. Crop production began to drop from the High Middle Ages.

> **Notable Quote** _____
>
> "I looked, and there was a black horse! Its rider held a pair of scales in his hand, and I heard what seemed to be a voice in the midst of the four living creatures saying, 'A quart of wheat for a day's pay, and three quarts of barley for a day's pay.'"
> —*Revelations* 6:5b-6a

# The Black Horseman: Famine

The effect of the climate change was most quickly felt in the marginal lands that required more work to cultivate and whose productivity was small during the best seasons. Famine was always a danger even during the best of times, but from the early fourteenth century until the end of the Middle Ages, it occurred much more regularly. The shortage of food was not just limited to areas that experienced the severe effects of climate change. Everywhere food was in short supply.

The balance between population and agricultural surplus was threatened as the result of the population boom of the High Middle Ages. Farm sizes had been reduced as parents gave more land to more children. With climate change this led to serious consequences for the total agricultural output of Europe. With lands requiring more labor to yield a surplus, more people were needed to work the farms, but small farms meant a divided workforce. So to maintain the population for the workforce, the agricultural output needed to remain high, and that wasn't possible. The result was famine.

## The Great Famine

The famine was at its worst from 1315 to 1317. Grain prices were at an all-time high. Areas that depended on other regions for their surplus food experienced a drastic decrease in population. Some towns and regions lost from 10 to 50 percent of their population. It was the greatest famine that Europe had or would ever experience. But it was not over yet.

The agricultural system of Europe even at its best was not capable of feeding the population of Europe. As a result, fourteenth-century Europe experienced wave after wave of regional famine. Hunger was a scourge that could not be bested. Farms and villages were often deserted in its wake. Since hungry people either migrated or died, much of the land of Europe was abandoned, especially land that could no longer be worked because of the climate change. An increasing number of farms were deserted and never cultivated again.

Many people moved to towns, monasteries, or more productive regions and sought food through church charity, work, begging, or stealing. These new arrivals raised other problems, as the towns were already overcrowded and lacked planning. The new townspeople contributed little to the towns and taxed the urban food and water supply.

## The Lack of Food Pyramids

Death by starving was not the only problem associated with climate change and the resulting famine. Europeans did not understand the different properties of food, and medieval nutrition was far from adequate.

The nobles tended to eat more animal proteins and fewer vegetables. Peasants seldom had access to the animal protein and ate more vegetables and starch. In addition, animal protein was expensive and only available during the fall and winter months, when the animals were slaughtered. To keep the meat during the winter, it was salted and heavily spiced. All together these practices made for some very unhealthy diets. The food pyramid had not yet been invented but was sorely needed.

Several health problems were already associated with these diets. The noble diet of too much meat produced gout, other diseases, and vitamin deficiencies. For the peasant population, a deficiency in animal protein produced tuberculosis, dysentery, and other illnesses as well as stunted growth. The vitamin deficiency that both groups experienced also produced painful and chronic conditions like scurvy, rickets, and gallstones.

## Results of Starvation and Hunger

Starvation and hunger only raised more problems. They killed the old and weak and damaged the health of children who experienced them. The lack of a nutritious diet puts great stress on the body and creates a loss of energy. Muscles become slack, slow, and clumsy. There is a lower body temperature, anemia, a reduced blood flow, diarrhea, dehydration, and resistance to cold and disease. And these physical problems cause psychological consequences as well, which include depression and despair followed by hatred and envy.

All these factors combined to change the nature of European society of the Late Middle Ages. The number of old and sick dropped. Infant mortality rates increased while the birthrate decreased; many women died during their most fertile years. Those who survived went elsewhere to have children, which displaced generations of people. The depopulation of farms lasted not just through the famine but for several generations. European society was undergoing significant changes and was substantially weakened physically and socially because of the famines of the fourteenth century. But what came next rocked Europe even harder.

# The Pale Horseman: Plague

The *pandemics* of the sixth century through the fourteenth century divided the medieval period of European history into thirds. From 550 to 700, several outbreaks of bubonic plague occurred with little catastrophic impact. Afterward the plague disappeared until its return in the mid-fourteenth century. The effects of the fourteenth century outbreak, combined with the famine earlier in the century, had a devastating effect on the population of Europe.

**def•i•ni•tion**

**Pandemic** is an epidemic disease that spreads universally over an entire region or country.

## Fleas and Rats

The bubonic plague is thought to be a product of the bacillus, *yersinia pestis*. This bacillus has its home in the bloodstream of a specific flea, *xenopsylla cheopsis*. These fleas live in the fur of a specific rat, a black rat. This type of bacillus, flea, and rat combination thrive best in warm and moist climate.

The fleas normally stay with the rats alone, but during special times, they repeatedly bite and kill the rat with the bacillus and then jump to humans. Remember also, with the growth of towns people had trouble with sanitation, light, and space, which made a very cozy rat habitat. When the fleas jump to humans, they of course bite and transmit the bacillus. From there it starts to get very ugly.

**Notable Quote**

"I looked and there was a pale horse! Its rider's name was Death, and Hell followed him; they were given authority over a fourth of the earth to kill with … pestilence.
—*Revelation* 6:8

## The Symptoms

The bubonic plague begins with a high fever. The lymph glands of the person start to swell, then form abscesses soon afterward. The person is then subject to a number of neurological and psychological disturbances in the variety of delusions and night terrors because the nervous system is being attacked. Next, blackish-purple *buboes* that have swollen on the lymph glands bleed unceasingly. Thirty to forty percent of those infected by the plague die by day two. Fifty to eighty percent die by day seven of infection. Finally, eighty to ninety percent die by the third week of infection.

**def•i•ni•tion**

**Buboes** are lymph nodes usually in the armpit or groin that have been swollen and black-purple in color. In the bubonic plague, these buboes eventually break open and bleed.

## The Black Death in Asia

The Black Death came from the Asiatic plains, where there appears to be a reservoir of the infection among the rodents of the region to this day. From there, like the Mongol invasions, the pandemic swept east, to the south, and then to the west into Europe. In other words, the Black Death descended into China, then India, then the Middle East, then to the Crimean Peninsula, and finally to the Mediterranean world and Italy. From there it spread northward into Europe.

Both European and Islamic sources believed that the Black Death was accompanied by weather changes, such as flooding, famines, and earthquakes. During the second quarter of the fourteenth century in China, many damaging environmental disturbances occurred. These weather disasters probably destroyed rat shelters and food, which forced the rodents to seek beyond their normally restricted habitat, where they came into contact with domestic rats and humans, spreading the Black Death with them. By 1346, most of the Mediterranean world was aware that a plague was devastating the Far East. Writers of the time believed that it was caused by the corruption of the air called miasma, in which a visible mist spread over the land killing all living things.

Among the Islamic writers of the Black Death, only a few were eyewitness to it. Ibn al-Wardi was one of those eyewitnesses who also sadly died of the Black Death in Aleppo in 1349. In his account, he stated that the disease started in the "land of darkness." To al-Wardi, this was probably the region of central Asia or Mongolia. In addition, he stated that the plague had been devastating the region of Mongolia for 15 years. Counting back from the appearance of the Black Death in the Crimea in 1346, the plague reached epidemic proportions in the central steppes of Asia during the early 1330s.

## Toward the Black Sea

From the history of disease, historians know that epidemics and plagues follow trade routes. Three important trans-regional trade routes developed during the fourteenth century. The first was the overland route from Mongolia and northern China to the Black Sea region, also generally known as the Silk Road. Another was the overland and sea route from India and China through the Indian Ocean and Persian Gulf to the Middle East. The last was the sea route from China through the Indian Ocean and the Red Sea to Egypt. The Black Death appears to have been transported only on the Silk Road, as there has been no evidence of an outbreak of the plague in the Middle East or Egypt before its appearance in the Crimea.

The Silk Road served as a major artery of the international trade that was blossoming in Europe during the thirteenth and fourteenth centuries, so it was the most possible path of the Black Death into Europe. Many historical sources corroborate this and show that the plague followed this overland route from Central Asia to the Black Sea region, leaving death in its wake.

Ibn al-Wardi gathered his information about the Black Death from Islamic traders coming from the Crimea. The region of the Black Sea was a hub for the Asian trade routes and also an important commercial center for Muslims and Europeans. These merchants told al-Wardi the plague occurred in October and November of 1346 in the lands of the Golden Horde (another name for the Mongols) in the region of southern Russia and had emptied the villages and towns of people. It then came to the Crimean Peninsula and the lands of the Byzantine Empire. An Islamic official in Kaffa was reported to have counted 85,000 killed by the plague.

## From Crimea to Genoa

Historians have traced the transmission of the Black Death to Europe from a factory owned by Genoese merchants in Kaffa. The basic European source for this is an account of the transportation of the plague on Genoese galleys from the Crimea, chronicled by the merchant Gabriel de Mussi. The author was not eyewitness to this fact but obtained his information, much like Ibn al-Wardi, from colleagues returning from the Crimean region. The Golden Horde encouraged trade with the Italian city-states by creating trading posts in the Crimea that were established as early as 1266 when the Mongols gave land to the Genoese at Kaffa, which became a bustling trading port on the Black Sea.

The relations of the Mongols and the Italian merchants were not always good. In 1345, the Mongols besieged the trading port of Kaffa. During this siege, the plague appeared in the Mongolian army and spread to the Golden Horde by 1346. The leader of the Mongolian army had corpses of his plague-stricken men catapulted into the city, and the Genoese dumped the bodies back over the walls into the Black Sea. Regardless, the disease spread within the walls. In the end, the Genoese colony put up tough resistance and forced the Mongolians to raise the siege. But before the siege ended, some of the Genoese merchants had fled in their ships to Constantinople, bringing the Black Death with them.

## The Assault on Europe

The Black Death arrived in Sicily from Kaffa via Constantinople in October 1347. According to a chronicler of the time, it came via 12 Genoese vessels from Kaffa to the port of Messina in northern Sicily. The merchants of Messina exiled the ships that brought the plague from their port, which ensured that it spread farther as the Genoese sought other safe ports. As a result, the Black Death spread rapidly through-out the western Mediterranean world including North Africa, Corsica, Sardinia, the Iberian peninsula, and southern Italy.

The three major areas for the spread of the Black Death in southern Italy were Sicily, Genoa, and Venice. Three months after the plague hit Sicily; it spread to Genoa and Venice. Shortly thereafter, Pisa, which served as an entry point into central and north-ern Italy, was hit.

Florence became the first great European city to be visited by the Black Death. The Italian writer Giovanni Boccaccio described this event in great detail in the *Decameron*. During the winter of 1348, the Italians breathed a collective sigh of relief as the Black Death subsided in Italy after causing the deaths of a third of the population.

Shortly after the arrival of the Black Death in Italy, a Genoese merchant ship that had been expelled from other Mediterranean ports came to Marseilles bringing the plague with it. Quickly driven out of the city, the vessel sailed along the coast of Spain, spreading the plague as it moved from port to port. The Black Death devastated Marseilles and then started its destructive move into Europe.

The Black Death followed two destructive paths through Europe: one coming from the west to the northeast and the other moving from the south to the north. The first path went west to Bordeaux after Marseilles by August 1348. It then moved north to Avignon and Lyons and finally to Paris in June 1348, where it killed until the winter of 1349. By August 1348, it had advanced to the northern coast of France, and by the end of 1348, had crossed the English Channel. After France, the plague spread its reach outward, moving into England, Ireland, Scotland, Flanders, and Germany. Later in May 1349, the kingdoms of Scandinavia were struck as English wool ships sailed from ports in England to the port of Bergen.

The second path of the Black Death crossed the Alps and entered the region of Bavaria by June 1348 along the overland trade routes that developed so well during the High Middle Ages. The plague also swept through the Balkan peninsula into the kingdoms of Hungary and Poland.

This terrible disease hit the people of Europe with different levels of intensity, but no place was left untouched by the plague; both Europe and the Middle East shared the same fate.

## Notable Quote

"The dying Tartars (Mongols), stunned and stupefied by the immensity of the disaster brought about by the disease, and realizing that they had no hope of escape, lost interest in the siege. But they ordered corpses to be placed in catapults and lobbed into the city in hope that the intolerable stench would kill everyone inside."

—*Historia de Morbo*, Gabriele de Mussis

## The Death Toll

The suffering caused by the disease brought differing reports from the countries of Europe. Boccaccio in the *Decameron* made no reference to pain. Other witnesses of the fourteenth century reported that the sick died in three days very quietly in their sleep. It was even said that in Germany children passed away laughing and singing. In one town, the Black Death tormented people so much that they tore out their hair. In some places, people attacked each other in the streets like injured dogs.

A later eyewitness from the seventeenth century, Daniel Dafoe, related that plague boils would grow very hard and would not burst, which caused the sick so much pain that it resembled torture. To escape this torture many committed suicide. Sufferers also frequently became demented with pain and rushed to the graveyard to bury themselves. One man climbed to the top of a roof and threw tiles into the street at people passing by. Another man danced a mad grotesque dance on a roof until a soldier shot him. A third man who had been lying as if dead for four days awoke and announced the last judgment. He demanded repentance of all who listened to him and cursed those who refused to kneel before him as a prophet. These scenes only elevated the horror and fear inspired by the Black Death.

The number of dead across Europe was so vast that church cemeteries could not hold them. For example, in one city in Germany, 11 huge trenches were dug for 12,000 corpses. In Italy, extended families of as many as 70 members were completely wiped out. In Venice in 1348, 50 of the noble families died out. In Marseilles, corpses were heaped so high that the streets were impossible to walk, and in Vienna the streets were also filled with the dead and dying.

The villages and countryside were no less bad off. There, too, were not enough people to bury the dead. In many places the work of the harvest was suspended; cattle and livestock were not tended and roamed the countryside; wolves and other wild animals boldly attacked the people who remained. Ravens and vultures circled villages and countryside huts scavenging the dead, and field mice and other animals lost fear of the people and invaded their villages and homes.

## And the Number Is ...

The number of victims in the fourteenth century is estimated by some to be lower than 25 percent. Some historians believe eyewitnesses of the time greatly exaggerated the numbers, but other historians contend that number is too low. The number of victims of the plague of later outbreaks with better knowledge of the disease must be considered when looking at the death toll of 1347–1348.

In later, less devastating occurrences of the Black Death, the death toll was still high. In 1467, the city of Moscow lost 127,000 victims; Novgorod and its district, 230,000. In Venice in 1478, 300,000 died; in Milan in 1576, over 51,000 fell victim. Berlin in the same year lost a third of its people, and Rome lost 70,000 in 1591. In 1630, Milan lost over 500,000. In the French territory of Lorraine after the plague of 1637, only one percent of its people remained living. Naples lost 300,000 of its population in 1635. London lost 160,000 in 1665. Vienna in 1579 lost 123,000 people. In Marseilles in 1720, over 50,000 died. And these are not all the numbers available. Many more died during the subsequent outbreaks of the Black Death in Europe.

So with the Black Death of 1347–1348, the numbers, which aren't as specifically reported, should be taken seriously. In Germany, one of the countries that suffered least during this attack of the plague, losses were estimated at 1.2 million people. According to one fourteenth-century French physician, Guy de Chaulic, three quarters of the population of France died. Other reports put that number at one half. In Italy, half the population died. From London, it was reported that only one out of ten survived the outbreak. Historians tell us the number of deaths is said to be underestimated at a little over 100,000. In Bristol, England, only a tenth of the population survived; at Norwich, 57,000 of the 70,000 died. The clergy in England lost over 25,000 priests and bishops. In the town of Smolensk in Russia in 1386, only five people remained! And the islands of Cyprus and Iceland were supposedly completely uninhabited after the Black Death finished its devastating work.

## Immediate Responses

The people of Europe, recognizing the magnitude of the crisis, did respond to the Black Death. But these responses did little to change the course of the epidemic, and some of the responses did much more harm than good.

When the Black Death swept through France, the members of the Paris College of Physicians, which everyone saw as *the* authority in medicine, responded by declaring the plague was caused by noxious and evil vapors created by heavenly disturbances. This typically ignorant response was the norm for the doctors of medieval Europe. They could not explain the reason for the Black Death, prevent its occurrence, or help its victims.

The Black Death did much more than just decimate the population of Europe; it also changed many of the European social customs. It stopped trade and made most people scared of contact with strangers and foreigners. Many towns created laws and regulations designed to limit the spread of the plague, some of which included travel bans and primitive types of sanitation laws and quarantines.

Another response was the formation of a group known as the flagellants, religious fundamentalists who marched from town to town beating themselves with whips, singing hymns, and praying. The goal of this activity was to gain God's forgiveness for humanity's sins. If forgiveness was obtained from God, in the mind of the flagellants, the horror and destruction of the Black Death would end. But this group did not last long after the end of the Black Death of 1347–1348. Both religious and secular authorities saw the group as a threat and ended its activities.

Following the wake of the Black Death in February 1349, the surviving Christians of Strasbourg, Germany, gathered up the Jewish population of the town that numbered over 2,000 and burned them alive. This was only one example of the many different anti-Semitic atrocities committed during the Black Death. Most of these acts were the result of a combination of hundreds of years of inbred prejudice and discrimination and the mistaken belief that the Jews caused the plague by poisoning the water wells of the Christians.

The horror and suffering caused by the Black Death found another immediate graphic expression in the "dance of death" pictures and engravings. Almost every large town and city possessed one of these representations. Some have been preserved, including the most famous (or infamous) at Luebeck, Basle, Berne, Strasbourg, Minden, Paris, Dijon, and London. These graphic representations portrayed the equality of men in the face of death. This experience of equality shook the foundations of the rigid medieval society and reinforced a long-standing but seldom applied belief that all men were equal before God.

## The Long-Term Effects

The swiftness of the spread of the plague and the wholesale destruction of human life had a huge impact on European society. Not only did the Black Death provoke depression from the severe loss of life and economic disruption on an incredible scale, but it also put to question Christianity and the Christian mindset. This can be seen in the literature, devotions, and artwork afterward. In addition, the already depopulated farms and villages became even more so, and cities and towns that had developed in the High Middle Ages were devastated, as well as the new economic institutions.

The plague killed so many people that there was a shortage of labor. Fields lay fallow, and livestock roamed free. In the following decades and centuries, much of this land came to be used in other ways, such as pastureland for cattle. Of course, fallow fields did nothing to help with the ongoing famine conditions. Many people, devastated by the effects of the Black Death, wandered homeless through the countryside, while others robbed and stole.

Also with the shortage of labor, wage prices went up along with the price of all goods and services. In England, the king created the Statute of Laborers in 1351 to put a freeze on wages and prices. At the same time, labor losses created the need for the invention of labor-saving devices and technological advance. These inventions eventually appeared to lift Europe out of the preindustrial age.

Before the Black Death, all academic works of the universities were written in Latin, which served as the universal language among the educated. But after the plague, the vernacular languages gained more usage, even at universities, and Latin was replaced universally across Europe. Unlike the learning and literature, the Black Death did little to influence architectural styles. The Gothic style still reigned.

In government and the church, many experienced officials, bishops, abbots, and priests who died were replaced by people who were incompetent or untrustworthy. The economic boom of the High Middle Ages ceased; goods and services were scarce; prices were inflated; and higher prices meant social unrest. The remaining people of Europe were not happy with the state of things.

At this time, the church lost a great deal of credibility with the people since it and the prayers of the priests were powerless to stop the Black Death. In addition, priests traditionally aided the sick and administered last rites, so they died in the first wave of the plague, leaving people to administer their own spirituality and sacraments. As the church's ability to administrate faltered, fanatical religious groups formed and developed followings, such as the Flagellants, who beat themselves for the penance of Europe. And the Jews, blamed for the transmission of the disease, were persecuted and massacred.

For the remainder of the fourteenth century and into modern times, Europe suffered more, albeit smaller, plagues. A second outbreak during the fourteenth century caused a huge panic but took a much smaller death toll. But the populations of the nations of Europe would not reach their pre-plague levels until the sixteenth century.

Famine and plague were not the only factors in the decline of the fortunes of Europe during the late Middle Ages. The problem of war and economic decline also occurred during the fourteenth century.

## The Least You Need to Know

- By the fourteenth century, the climate of Europe slowly changed to shorten the growing seasons and created very unpredictable weather patterns.

- The climate change created famine across Europe, with the worst years being from 1315 to 1317.

- The famine and bad diet of Europeans created a population with weak constitutions that were very susceptible to disease.

- The Black Death spread from China along the Silk Road and reached Europe in 1348.

- The population of Europe was decimated by the spread of the plague, and so were the society and the economy.

# 16

# War and Depression

## In This Chapter

◆ The origins of the Hundred Years' War

◆ Changes in England and France

◆ Joan of Arc and the last phase of the war

◆ National identity

◆ France moves toward a nation-state

◆ The War of the Roses

The decline of Europe's fortunes during the late Middle Ages was not only influenced by the famines and plagues, but also by the problems of war and economic decline that occurred during the fourteenth century. These wars involved England and France and sometimes just peasants. The economic decline, the result of all the other previous events, was the inevitable conclusion to a bad century.

# The Hundred Years' War (1337–1453)

By the end of the fourteenth century, the rulers of both England and France had created strong national monarchies, but the goals of the English and French were in conflict. The English wanted to retain and regain the lands they had held in France under King Henry II. Of course, the kings of France took exception to this because they wanted to expand their rule over France and other regions, such as Flanders. These conflicts resulted in the Hundred Years' War, which was really a series of wars interrupted by periods of uneasy peace.

In addition to the conflict over territory in France, economic rivalry added to the differences. As you remember, the English exported a great deal of wool to Flanders, the center of textile-manufacture in northern Europe. This economic relationship benefited both the Flemish and the English. But Flanders was under the nominal control of French overlords and, when the French kings tried to assert their power in the region, uprisings occurred, which the English discreetly encouraged.

To add to these conflicts, another issue was at stake. In the past, when England tried to conquer Scotland, the French had provided aid to the Scots, and the English were very unforgiving on this point.

But in the end, the immediate cause of the conflict was a dispute over the succession of the French throne. In 1328, the king of France died without an heir. King Edward III of England had some claim to the throne through his mother, the sister of the last Capetian king. Of course, the French didn't want an English king and rejected Edward's claim based on an ancient Frankish tradition in *Salic Law* that said women could not inherit land. So the French chose Philip VI, a cousin of the late French king. Once chosen, Philip put down a revolt in Flanders and pressed his claim to the French throne. War preparations had started.

### Middle Age Myths

In the well-known movie *Braveheart,* the historical William Wallace, played by Mel Gibson, was okay with English rule until a new practice was imposed on Scotland: the right of an English overlord to sleep with any bride in his realm on her wedding night or first night. Of course, this custom affected Wallace and his new bride, so he raised a rebellion to fight his English oppressors. It makes great movie drama, but in reality "the right of the first night" never existed.

# The First Phase (1337–1380)

When the war began, the English had many advantages over the French. First, the English army was very well trained. They were also paid regularly and had acquired battle experience in the recent war with Scotland. In addition, the knights of England were used to dismounting from their horses and fighting with the infantry during battle. This created a formidable fighting force. The English also had recently developed the longbow, an invaluable weapon because it discharged steel-tipped arrows rapidly and over long distances. Finally, the English had an ally in the duke of Burgundy, who wanted to control France rather than the French kings.

The French were poorly prepared for the war. Philip VI had only recently been crowned king, and his leadership ability was in doubt. French knights wore very heavy armor and did not dismount during battle. When they did dismount, they had problems moving in their heavy armor. In addition, the French knights refused to fight with the ordinary infantry soldier because they felt they were above that sort of thing. Finally, French soldiers used crossbows, which were heavier, less efficient, and less effective than the English longbows.

As a result of these differences between the armies, the English won most of the battles early in the war. With the first battle in 1340, Edward III won a naval victory at Sluys that gave the English control of the English Channel. But the next real success did not come until 1346 at the Battle of Crécy.

In this battle, which occurred on August 26, 1346, the forces of King Edward III and the blind King John of Bohemia met the French led by King Philip VI. The English forces were outnumbered, but they gained an advantage by the lack of organization of the French and the skill of the English longbowmen, who could fire both faster and farther than the French crossbowmen. As a result, the French suffered heavy losses and were soundly defeated, but during the battle King John of Bohemia was killed. However, his service was so inspirational to the English princes that the Black Prince and later princes of Wales adopted his motto, "I serve," and emblem, three feathers.

The significance of this battle was not lost on the English; the armored knight could be beaten by a foot soldier. The beginning of the end of the feudal knight was at hand. In addition, the Battle of Crécy opened the way for the besieging of the city of Calais until it was taken in 1347. It would remain an English possession for another

> **Notable Quote**
>
> "Why are the English less brave than the French? Because they wouldn't jump into the sea in full armor, like our gallant knights."
>
> —Jester of Philip VI of France

200 years, and with Calais in English hands, the English forces could put continuous pressure on French lands.

Of course, the next year, 1348, was the year of the Black Death. Because of it, real fighting did not resume until 1356. At Poitiers, King Edward's oldest son, the Black Prince, decisively beat French forces and captured the French King John II. The French were unable to pay the ransom for King John II, and as a result, he remained imprisoned in England until his death in 1364.

# Changes in England During the War

While the war was going on, changes were occurring in England. Edward III asked Parliament repeatedly for money to fight the war. As a result, Parliament got concessions out of the king to help strengthen its political power and influence. During this period Parliament divided into two houses: the House of Lords and the House of Commons.

## The Peasants' Revolt

The famine and disease of the fourteenth century, combined with corruption and heavy taxes, led to peasant unrest in England. In 1381, this unrest found leadership with Wat Tyler and John Ball. Over 100,000 peasants marched on London, demanding to speak with King Richard II. The king was able to trick the army of peasants into disbanding; then he captured, tried, and executed Tyler and other leaders of the group. Thus the Peasants' Revolt ended as the king used his army to brutally end any more peasant armies.

England changed in other ways during this time period as well. During the late 1300s, English, or more precisely Middle English, replaced French as the official language of the royal court. In addition, English was used by writers, including Chaucer in his *Canterbury Tales* and William Langland (1330–1400) in *Piers Plowman*. Langland was a native of the region of the West Midlands but spent much of his life in London. He studied to become a member of the clergy but never entered the priesthood. Langland was most known for his poem *The Vision of Piers Plowman*, which details the theme of salvation in the popular medieval style of an allegorical dream. Of course, like many of the new works of literature of the Late Middle Ages, it was written in the vernacular.

## Dynastic Conflicts

Dynastic conflict and upheaval also took place in England. King Richard II was a bad king who was very unpopular. As a result, Henry Bolingbroke, the duke of Lancaster, led an uprising, which ended Richard's rule and enabled Bolingbroke to take power as Henry IV and establish the House of Lancaster *dynasty*. But as with other monarchs of England, Henry was forced to give in to the demands of Parliament, including allowing it to have discussions about more national issues and accepting the right of the House of Commons to make new taxes.

## def•i•ni•tion

A **dynasty** is a family of rulers whose right to rule is passed on within the family.

# Changes in France During the War

For the French, the war had brought death and destruction, and the people were not at all happy. Adding to this unhappiness was a salt tax the French king imposed on the people early in the war. In addition, the pillaging of France by bands of English and even French soldiers did not help. Finally, the miseries associated with famine and the Black Death broke the back of the French people, and their unhappiness erupted into a peasant uprising in 1358.

## The *Jacquerie*

This uprising became known as the *Jacquerie* after Jacques Bonhomme, a nickname used for all peasants. During the revolt, mobs of peasants roamed the countryside burning manor houses, nobles, and tax collectors alike. In addition, an ambitious merchant named Etienne Marcel threatened to take the French throne and led popular uprisings in Paris. Charles V (1364–1380) rallied his French armies and put the peasant uprisings down in the countryside and Paris. Charles V was brutal in his reprisals, killing over 20,000 rebels.

## The Rise of Charles the Wise

Regardless of the harshness of his response to the *Jacquerie*, most of the French considered Charles V an effective ruler, and he was known as Charles the Wise. He called meetings of the Estates General to get what he needed. And although the assembly could have taken advantage of the dire times to expand its power at the expense of the king, it didn't. Charles the Wise was able to play each of the three estates' distrust of each other to gain what he needed.

The events of the *Jacquerie* led Charles V to sign the Treaty of Bretigny in 1360. In it, the French recognized the English control over Calais and Aquitaine, and in exchange, the English king renounced any claim to the French throne. But that was not the end of the war. In 1369, it erupted again and, right before his death in 1380, Charles was forced to retreat from French territories previously won.

Charles VI (1380–1422), the successor of Charles V, was a weak monarch given to bouts of insanity. While he ruled, the dukes of Burgundy and Armagnac fought a violent and self-destructive war. As a result, the Burgundians allied themselves with the English King Henry V, son of Henry IV, and moved to renew the war with France in 1413.

## A Woman Poet?

One more very significant change happened in France during this time. Christine de Pizan (1364–1430), a gifted writer and poet, became the first woman in Europe to support herself by writing. To get to that point, Christine was educated by her father, who was a humanist scholar who left Venice for a position in the French royal court.

Once educated in the humanist tradition, Christine wrote prose and poetry on many different topics and in many literary forms, among them poems expressing her love for her husband, who had died when she was 25 years old. Christine also wrote two volumes, one for women and one for men, of advice on love and life. She detailed a history of Europe from the creation to her own time. Christine, interested in the lives of women, produced a study of the great women of history. Finally, she wrote the famous treatise *The Letter to the God of Love*, in which she criticized the conclusion of the *Romance of the Rose* by Jean de Meun.

# The Final Phase of the War (1415–1453)

By 1415, King Henry V was ready to battle again when he landed in France and met a strong army at the fields of Agincourt. The English and their Burgundian allies were ready.

The Battle of Agincourt was fought on October 25, 1415, which was St. Crispin's Day. Saint Crispin was the saint of cobblers and tanners whose feast day was rather significant to the common folk of the Middle Ages. The English forces were led by King Henry V, and the French army was led by the French noble and general d'Albert. The

French were trying to stop the English from retreating to their stronghold in Calais from the region of the Somme where they had been beaten badly.

The battle started with the English longbowmen, waiting behind a line of infantry and knights. As the French knights dismounted their horses to charge the English line, the longbowmen took deadly aim at their ranks. To make matters worse for the French knights, the field they charged across was knee deep in mud, which slowed them down considerably. Because of the weight of their armor, many got stuck in the mud. Five thousand French knights and soldiers were said to have been killed in the mud of Agincourt. Many were killed in cold blood by English longbowmen and infantry who did not respect the knight's right of ransom. The English sustained only a few losses.

With a decisive victory at the Battle of Agincourt, Henry V reconquered Normandy and forced King Charles VI of France to sign the Treaty of Troyes in 1420. Under the treaty, the French king recognized the English conquests in Normandy, and Henry V became heir to the French throne by being allowed to marry Catherine, Charles VI's daughter. Charles VI's own son, called the dauphin, was disinherited from the throne.

The king of England might have well ruled both England and France, but it wasn't meant to be. In 1422, Henry V died of dysentery, leaving an infant son who would become King Henry VI of England. Charles VI also died soon after Henry V and John, the duke of Bedford, ruled France for Henry VI. Fighting broke out again when Charles VII, son of the late King Charles VI, made an attempt to win back the throne at Rheims. But Charles was unable to rally his French forces against the English, who were besieging the city. At that crucial moment, Joan of Arc stepped onto the historical stage.

## Joan of Arc, the Maid of Orléans

Joan of Arc (1412–1431) was a young peasant girl from the small town of Domrémy, about 175 miles east of Paris. As a girl, Joan heard voices in her head that she believed were those of saints and angels. The voices became focused over time until finally she understood what the voices wanted her to do. They ordered her to lead the French army against forces at Orléans and help the dauphin claim the French crown at Rheims.

The dauphin's situation was desperate when Joan came to him and convinced him of the validity of her voices. With the dauphin's blessing, Joan inspired the French forces, who captured Orléans and ended the siege of Rheims so that the dauphin could be crowned King Charles VII of France in 1429. Afterward, Joan's voices stopped speaking to her, and she led an unsuccessful attack on Paris for King Charles VII. For the king, Joan was becoming a problem. He needed peace, and Joan wanted to completely drive the English from France. The problem soon solved itself when Joan was captured by the Burgundians, who sold her to the English.

In 1431, Joan was tried by the English on charges of witchcraft and heresy before a church court. During the trial, the examiners questioned her about her voices and her manner of dress since she dressed like a man/warrior. Despite her peasant background, Joan was able to defend her actions very successfully. But in the end she was sentenced to death by burning. Sadly, Charles VII, who owed his crown to the Maid of Orléans, as she was called, did not help her. He refused to pay her ransom even when it was given to him through collections taken by French nobles. But Joan of Arc became a symbol of French pride, and her death for the cause of the French proved to be a turning point in the war with the English.

## Why Joan?

Joan of Arc's role in the Hundred Years' War was fascinating in many different ways. It especially illustrated how war affected the ordinary folk and some new emerging identities in Europe.

Why would a peasant girl even care about the war? She, like others, cared because warfare during the Late Middle Ages had changed in many ways that involved her directly. Because the knights lost out to infantrymen and archers, peasant boys and men were drafted, trained, and sent to war. Because armies fought for longer periods of time over larger amounts of territory, they took the food and livestock of the peasants. Because commanders recognized the value of food and land during war, armies burnt fields, villages, and towns. And because unpaid soldiers attacked the people in villages and towns during periods of truce, peace was sometimes just as dangerous, if not more so, than the actual war.

Thus, since the war was fought on French territory, the French people suffered more than the English people. Even so, in both countries the new developing warfare of the Late Middle Ages added many burdens to the ordinary peasant or townsperson's household, including more taxes, conscriptions, requisitions, and terror.

Why would a peasant girl care about the king of France? It was Joan of Arc's sincere belief that France should be ruled by a French king, not an English king. Joan's belief marked the start of the growth of a national identity or consciousness among ordinary Europeans. This meant that the French were French; the English were English; the Germans were German; and so on. These types of loyalties are hard to trace and even harder to explain. But they did grow stronger in the fourteenth and fifteenth centuries and later continue to develop in modern Europe into nationalism and patriotism.

## National Consciousness

Several factors contributed to this development of the national consciousness. The importance of vernacular languages, which was still developing, was one of the factors. Another was the importance of national universities and churches. Finally, the decline in the influence of the Church in Rome was also a part of this new development.

For these reasons, people of the Late Middle Ages felt they had a common history, language, interest, and future with some of the people of Europe and not with others. Again the French were French, and the English were English. This formation of a national consciousness or identity extended into the modern Europe and was used by the monarchs of Europe to augment royal power.

## The War Is Over

After Joan's death the war dragged on. A break for the French came when the Burgundians withdrew their support from the English after signing a peace treaty with Charles VII. At that point, the French king reorganized his forces and drove the English out of Normandy and Aquitaine. Only Calais remained under English control. By 1453, the Hundred Years' War was over.

# After the War in France

When Charles VII was crowned king, he had some overwhelming problems to deal with. The English still controlled much of northern France; many towns and villages were destroyed or deserted; fields lay fallow; and wolves roamed the streets of Paris. In addition, commerce had come to a halt because many roads had fallen into disrepair. Bands of thieves called flayers wandered the countryside. Finally, poor nobles tried to get cash by charging tolls for the right to cross their estates.

So with the help of his counselors, Charles VII turned things around. First, he acquired the aid of a very able French banker to improve the handling of royal finances. With the spirit of unity created by Joan of Arc, the Estates General allowed the king to collect more taxes to hire an army without approval. Now the king of France could establish a permanent standing army without relying on nobles. With this new army, Charles VII was able to push the English out of Normandy and Aquitaine in 1453.

By the end of the Hundred Years' War, Charles had gained a lot of popularity with the French people and so used this newfound popularity to reassert royal power. He stopped nobles from trying to regain influence in the government and only sought advice from bankers and merchants. Charles used the new standing army to seek out and destroy the flayers in the countryside. He repaired neglected roads and harbors and tried to bring wastelands under cultivation. And he enforced laws that prohibited private armies and the collection of tolls by nobles.

So by the end of Charles VII's reign in 1461, the French king had acquired a strong position. The Estate General had given the king important powers of taxation, and in addition, the monarchy had limited the power of the church and nobles in France.

## A New French Nation-State

Louis XI (1461–1483), known as the Spider King because he wove a web of intrigue around Europe, continued the process of centralizing and expanding royal power that Charles VII had begun. By the end of his rule, the patchwork of rival feudal territories was a nation-state. Louis, who was well educated and shrewd, also had a lust for power and schemed in unscrupulous ways to obtain it. Although the way he did things was quite objectionable, there can be no doubt he got things done.

First, he destroyed the power of the dukes of Burgundy. He then built the best professional standing army in Europe. He chose ambitious men to serve as his advisors and imposed more control on the nobles. He strengthened the royal treasury and put the church in check. Finally, he encouraged industry and trade by improving the roads and harbors, establishing a postal system, and inviting foreign artisans to live in France.

## Charles the Bold (1467–1477)

The chief rival of Louis XI was the duke of Burgundy, Charles the Bold, who ruled the wealthy agricultural region of southern France. He also controlled the Lowlands and Flanders. But Charles was eager to acquire control over Alsace and Lorraine in eastern France. To stop this, Louis got the leaders of the Swiss Confederation and the princes of a few kingdoms of the Holy Roman Empire to fight Charles when he occupied Lorraine in 1473. This maneuver was successful, and Charles died in battle in 1477. Afterward Louis gained control of Burgundy, Artois, and Picardy, bringing all of today's France, except for Brittany, under the French king. In 1483, Charles VIII, who succeeded Louis XI as king, married Anne, the heiress to the duchy of Brittany, creating the modern nation of France.

Political stability and unity encouraged some economic progress, but this was squandered. Charles VIII, like other ambitious kings, dreamed of uniting all of Europe. His dream embroiled him and his successors in a series of wars called the Italian Wars, which lasted from 1494 to 1559 and did much to sap France's vitality.

# England After the War

Even before the Hundred Years' War ended, England was having problems. Dynastic struggles led to a 30-year war called the War of the Roses. Two families, the House of Lancaster and the House of York, were descended from the Plantagenet king, Edward III. During the war, the House of Lancaster used a red rose as its symbol, while the House of York used a white rose.

**Notable Quote**

> And here I prophesy: this brawl today
>   Grown to this faction in the Temple Garden
> Shall send, between the Red Rose and the White
> A thousand souls to death a deadly night.
> —Shakespeare, *Henry VI*

As stated earlier, Henry Bolingbroke took power from King Richard II, bringing the House of Lancaster to the throne of England. Although he and Henry V faced some social and religious discontent, they kept the throne for the House of Lancaster. However, during the reign of Henry VI, problems arose. The English had been defeated in the Hundred Years' War, and the king was showing signs of psychological instability. With the weak king, corruption grew in the English government. Factions within the government quarreled and fought for control. Royal officials were appointed to positions in exchange for their support of noble factions. The crisis deepened when Richard, Duke of York, gained the support of Parliament and Henry VI and his supporters.

## The War of the Roses

Richard died before he was crowned king, but the very ambitious earl of Warwick helped Richard's son ascend the throne as King Edward IV. Edward IV established the House of York, but his reign was filled with conflict. His backers fought nobles who still supported the House of Lancester's claim to the throne. As a result, many in the ranks of the nobility were killed.

Edward IV died in 1483, leaving two young sons as heirs. One son was named Edward V but was later declared illegitimate by Parliament. Both boys were imprisoned in the Tower of London and later secretly murdered. Many suspected the ambitious Yorkist Richard of Gloucester was behind these murders, but that did not prevent him from being crowned King Richard III. As king, he tried to restore order but had little success, with the death of the princes and factional disputes that led to more fighting.

## The Rise of the Tudors

After a time, the forces that opposed Richard found a new leader named Henry Tudor, a Lancastrian who later married Elizabeth of York. In 1485, Henry returned from exile in France, raised an army, and defeated King Richard III at the Battle of Bosworth Field. The king was killed in the battle, and Henry Tudor was named King Henry VII. He owed much of his crowning to the acceptance of Parliament.

### Age-Makers

Much of what is accepted about Richard III comes from the pen of Thomas More (1478–1535) in *The History of Richard III*. More paints an evil and unjust ruler who needed to be deposed by the just Tudors. Ironically, the actions of the son of Henry VII ended the life of More rather unjustly.

After becoming king, Henry VII set out to assure the future of the Tudor dynasty. With the death of so many nobles during the war, Henry saw a chance to increase royal power, so he worked continually to increase royal revenues, end injustice, and reestablish law and order. He also worked to restore the prestige of the throne, which had suffered much during the War of the Roses. This also enhanced royal power. Despite this, Henry VII and his successors were not absolute rulers. Parliament had done much to strengthen its power during the War of the Roses, so the Tudors avoided confrontations with Parliament that might lead to more limits on royal power.

# Economic Decline of the Late Middle Ages

The final problem Europe experienced during the fourteenth century was economic decline. And the agricultural crisis, which raised the price of goods, helped create this economic decline.

After the Black Death struck Europe, there was an increase in the wages of laborers. Although this increase would appear to be a good thing, it was not without some pain. Wage laborers were forced to trade the security of serfdom for the economic and social instability of an economic world in which there was an opportunity to both earn and lose everything. The increase of the wage laborers in the countryside who had little or no possessions led to a wider economic spectrum of the population. More differentiation of social and economic relationships grew. These new conditions eroded the old social and economic bonds of dependency and security that characterized rural society.

With the economic and social instability, prices of goods rose again, and the economy of Europe again suffered. By this time, trade and industry were also hampered by the disruption of society across Europe by both the famine and the plague.

And then to add salt to the wound of the bad economy, war broke out between England and France, the two great engines of the European economy. And, of course, in addition to the formal war, the peasant revolts didn't do much to help trade and industry. So by the end of the fourteenth century and into the fifteenth, things did not look good economically for Europe.

But all was not lost. The crisis in the price of agricultural goods and the introduction of new innovations increased the spread of commercial agriculture. Barley and hops for brewing beer got better prices than wheat and rye for bread. Other crops used to make dyes also increased in value as the wheat and rye prices declined. These changes ultimately proved to be beneficial during the Late Middle Ages, creating a commercial agricultural revolution for Europe during the late fifteenth and early sixteenth centuries.

## The Least You Need to Know

 ◆ The conflict between England and France, known as the Hundred Years' War, occurred for several reasons, including economic and political issues.

 ◆ During the first phase of the war, the English dominated the field of battle with the help of the longbow.

◆ During a lull in the war, the English and French monarchies both had to react to peasant revolts by centralizing power.

◆ In the final phase of the war, the French were able to overcome their initial inadequacies with the help of Joan of Arc and Charles VII.

◆ After the Hundred Years' War, the French kings worked to centralize the government, while the English went through a dynastic conflict called the War of the Roses.

◆ During the fourteenth century, many people developed ideas of national identity or consciousness.

# Chapter 17

# Problems with the Church

## In This Chapter

- ◆ The effect of the Black Death
- ◆ The Babylonian Captivity
- ◆ The Great Schism
- ◆ The Council of Constance
- ◆ Problems with Aristotle and Aquinas
- ◆ Occam's Razor
- ◆ Mystics and heretics

During the Middle Ages, the church used its powers for the public good. It preserved a limited peace in times of strife and war, tried to impose a code of human conduct, and acted as school headmaster, which enabled it to harness and nourish intellect. As a result it taught and provided administrators, lawyers, and doctors and encouraged and preserved architecture, literature, and art. It promoted creative work but also, at times, repressed it if it did not follow church doctrines. This repression also formed an integral part of the medieval church.

By the start of the Late Middle Ages, the Catholic Church rose to be the dominant power. But several events served to weaken this position in the lives of the people of Europe. These events included the Black Death, the Babylonian Captivity, the Great Schism, the questioning of the Scholastic movement, and the rise of mysticism and heresies. The remarkable grasp that the church had on Europe enabled Christianity to weather these storms, but the authority of the church did not survive them unscathed.

# The Losses Caused by the Black Death

The church suffered greatly, both physically and spiritually, from the Black Death. The physical loss caused an inability for it to cultivate its huge tracts of land. But the greater harm was the helplessness it faced in the disaster. Many bishops, abbots, priests, and monks were lost, which deprived the church of the control of appointing successors to those important clerical positions.

The priests, the hardest working of the clergy, died by the thousands across Europe. Afterward, according to William Langland, their positions were filled with young men not ready for parish responsibilities, who spent their time in London, enjoying the night life instead of ministering to the laity. In addition, friars and monks, who had been known for holiness and piety, became gluttons. Langland was specific about these abuses, saying that these occurred on multiple occasions only after the Black Death had passed.

In Germany and England, the church had been out of favor with the people for years. In the aftermath of the Black Death, many branches of the church in Germany and England called for the reform of abuses of the clergy. But they had no power to reform those abuses themselves because the church's power was centralized in the papacy in Rome. They were only outlying parts of a foreign organization that retained power over people in their nations, and this fact frustrated not only England and Germany but other countries of Europe as well.

For all of these reasons, very open opposition to the church developed in the years following the Black Death. This can be easily judged by comparing the murders of two important English churchmen. In 1170, if you remember, the Archbishop of Canterbury was killed after some rather hasty words by King Henry II. Although Becket was not extremely popular at the time of his death, the public outrage and horror at this sacrilegious act forced the king to submit to a humiliating penance.

In contrast, in 1381, a band of peasants seized the mild Archbishop of Canterbury Simon Sudbury and beheaded him on Tower Hill in London, with the applause of a great multitude that had come to see the event. Thus, the relationship between the church and the people had undergone a great change since the ancestors of the men who beheaded Sudbury used to make pilgrimages to see the tomb of the holy martyr and saint Thomas Becket.

# Babylonian Captivity

The authority of the church was also weakened by the Babylonian Captivity. We have seen how King Philip the Fair (1285–1314) of France tried to control the church and the papacy. In that historic episode, the French king almost captured Pope Boniface VIII who was so weakened by the struggle that he died soon after. But Philip the Fair's efforts to control the pope and the church did not end with that episode.

Benedict XI, Boniface's successor, wisely chose not to argue with Philip, but when the pope died in 1305, Philip pulled some strings to have a French cardinal elected as pope. He then had Pope Clement V move the papal palace to Avignon in southern France, which gave Philip and other succeeding French kings great influence over the church and its policies.

The pope remained in Avignon from 1305 to 1378, a period called the second Babylonian Captivity, the first being when the Jews were held captive in Babylon. During the captivity, the popes appeared to be under the control of the French kings, and people outside of France resented the Avignon papacy and its decrees. So although Philip's win over the church did much to help bring prestige to the French throne, it greatly damaged the influence and authenticity of the pope and church with the rest of Europe.

> **Notable Quote**
>
> "Avignon is indeed the mother of fornication and lust and drunkenness, full of abomination and all filthiness and seated upon the rushing waters of the Rhone, the Durance and the Sorgue. And her prelates are indeed like the scarlet woman, clothed in purple and gold and silver and precious stones, and drunk."
>
> —Benvento da Imola (1331–1380) on the Avignon Papacy

# The Great Schism

An even worse blow to the church's prestige in Europe followed the Babylonian Captivity. In 1377, Pope Gregory XI successfully returned the papacy to Rome but died the next year, leaving the people of Rome fearful that a French pope would be elected and take the papacy back to Avignon. And so the cardinals were forced to choose an Italian to be pope, Urban VI (1378–1389), who took up residence in Rome.

However, since most of the cardinals were French, once they returned to Avignon they declared the earlier election invalid. The cardinals then chose a French pope, Clement VII, who took up residence in Avignon. Now there were two popes, each calling the other an antipope.

## Picking Teams

The church quickly divided into two camps. Urban was supported by the Holy Roman Empire, the Scandinavian kingdoms, England, Hungary, and most of the Italian city-states. Clement was, of course, backed by France but also Spain, Scotland, and Sicily. The problem did not resolve itself quickly, either. When Urban died in 1389, his successors, Boniface IX (1390–1404), Innocent VII (1404–1406), and Gregory XII (1406–1415) continued the divide. Meanwhile, Clement died in 1394 and was followed by Benedict XIII (1394–1423). Neither side was willing to submit or summon a general council to resolve the crisis.

## Let's Meet Again

A minority group declared that a council was the only effective way to solve the problem. Eventually this minority group, called the conciliarists, was able to promote and secure a convening council at Pisa in 1409. This only complicated matters since they elected a third pope, Pope Alexander V (1409–1410), who was succeeded by Pope John XXIII (1410–1415). To his credit, John was receptive to another council under the urging of the Holy Roman Emperor Sigismund. As a result, the Council of Constance (1414–1418) was convened and ended the schism by accepting the resignation of Gregory XII and deposing Benedict and John. The council then elected Cardinal Oddo Colonna as Pope Martin V (1418–1431), who reestablished the papal court in Rome. He was the first sole pope in close to 40 years.

> **Notable Quote**
>
> "It is impossible for the General Council to be held without the authority of the pope. But to convene such a council in the present case the authority of the pope cannot step in because no single person is universally recognized as pope."
>
> —Conrad of Gelnhausen on the Council of Constance

## The Return of One Pope

Pope Martin V and his successors could not undo the negative PR to church prestige and power done by the Babylonian Captivity and the Great Schism. In addition, by the early fifteenth century with the strong new kings of England, Spain, and France, the church could not limit the secular power of the new developing nation-states. Many rulers continued to work with the church, but no pope was able to claim supremacy over Europe as Boniface VIII had done in his famous address *Unam Sanctam*, in which he claimed for the church spiritual and temporal authority.

---

**Illuminations**

"We learn from the gospel that in the church and in her power are two swords, the spiritual and the temporal. But the latter is used for the church, the former by her ....
The one sword, then should be under the other and the temporal authority subject to the spiritual. Furthermore we declare that it is altogether necessary for salvation for every human creature to be subject to the Roman pontiff."

—Pope Boniface VIII, *Unam Sanctam*

---

# The Revolt Against Aristotle and Aquinas

From the beginning of the appearance of Aristotle's works of philosophy in the late twelfth century, there was opposition to it, usually among Christian theologians, who could not reconcile Aristotle's philosophy with many of the tenets of Christian theology. As time progressed, this led to more bitter opposition and even condemnation of his works and ideas from 1210 to 1277.

The watershed moment was when the bishop of Paris, Stephen Tempier, condemned Aristotle. Not only was Aristotle under attack, but also Christian philosophers and theologians like Thomas Aquinas who tried to reconcile Aristotle's work with Christianity. Albert Magnus and Thomas Aquinas came under fire from outside and inside their Dominican order.

The condemnation of Aristotle and Aquinas at the University of Paris in 1277 produced a revolt against theology and philosophy based on Aristotle. Some schools, notably the University of Padua, tried to remain close to Aristotle. The Dominicans even tried to preserve the authority of Aquinas by having him canonized in 1323. But in general, a number of thinkers went off in new directions in both theology and philosophy.

## John Duns Scotus (1265–1308)

John Duns Scotus was one such theologian. He was a complex man in the mold of Augustinian and Franciscan traditions, who criticized the tendency of Aristotle to make God less divine by making him more rational and intelligent. This made God accessible to human reason, which diminished his divine status somewhat. Duns Scotus emphasized the power of the divine will that could not be analyzed by rational human thought but divine reason. He reasserted the ultimate unknowability of the divine. Reason was not the way to God; it gave no reliable information about God whatsoever.

## William of Occam (1285–1349)

Following Duns Scotus was William of Occam, whose work focused on logic and cognition. While criticizing Scotus's work, William agreed that God was transcendent and unknowable. Accordingly, only faith and revelation tell us about the divine and his will. Reason can only be used on the observable world. Occam also argued that humans are endowed with three types of knowledge: intuition, abstraction, and faith. Intuition and abstraction are for the realm of reason, while faith is outside that realm.

By insisting on the supremacy of reason in the observable world, Occam created a new authority to reason and science of the physical world. With human reason not being used to understand God, it was free to observe the world with more vigor. Occam also divided God's power into absolute and ordained powers. With the ordained powers, God operated in nature according to laws he created. Of course, God had absolute powers, meaning he could do anything, but God had made a covenant with humanity to act consistently with the ordained powers.

## Occam's Razor

Occam replaced Aristotle's realism with *nominalism*. To him, abstract categories are our only probable conclusions or what we know as concrete. Occam dumped Aristotle's four causes (final, formal, efficient, and material) for the principle of the economy of explanation. This is more widely known as Occam's Razor, stating that an explanation needs no more causes than necessary to account for the immediate behavior of the phenomena. In very layman's terms, this reads, "Keep it simple, stupid!"

# def•i•ni•tion

**Nominalism** is the theory that knowledge by intuition is the only thing that makes us individuals.

## Division and Mysticism

After Occam, theologians, philosophers, and scientists continued to reflect the division and change of religious and philosophical thinking from the late Middle Ages until the Enlightenment. Now two explanations were being offered for the world.

Voluntarism was God's will, which was unbound, limitless, and impossible to pin down. Mystic and spiritual Christianity was renewed across Europe through voluntarism. With philosophy, the door had been opened to the idea that reason was best used to find out the truths of the observable world. This cleared the path for the rational observable method of the Scientific Revolution of the sixteenth century.

> **Notable Quote** _____
>
> "A man may go into the field and say his prayer and be aware of God, or, he may be in church and be aware of God; but, if he is more aware of Him because he is in a quiet place, that is his own deficiency and not due to God, Who is alike present in all things and places, and is willing to give Himself everywhere so far as lies in Him. He knows God rightly who knows Him everywhere."
> —Meister Eckhart on the presence of God

With the revolt against Aristotle and Aquinas in full swing, a new impetus was given to theology and philosophy. Regrettably for the church, that impetus drew many of the best and brightest into the secular realm. The church was left with mystics who did not offer explanations, while the secular world drew men who wanted to observe the world and see how it worked. This divergence shaped the spiritual and scientific direction of Western thought into the modern world—even into the twenty-first century.

## The Mystics in Search of Salvation

Mystics were not entirely new in the Christian faith. Hildegard of Bingen (1098–1179) had been a prophetess of God. Even the great Thomas Aquinas, master of reason and logic, at the end of his life had turned away from study toward the divine revelation of mysticism. But with the decline of scholasticism, mystics emerged as a spiritual force during the Late Middle Ages.

The mysticism that emerged during the fourteenth and fifteenth centuries came, in part, from the influence of five people: Meister Eckhart, Saint Catherine of Siena,

Birgitta of Sweden, Lidwana of Schiedam, and Gerhard Groote. These mystics searched for God by denying themselves food, drink, sleep, and many basic comforts. They stressed worship over speculation about God, inner purity over good works, and direct contact with God over the sacraments. Most of these mystics remained orthodox, but their ideas would have great appeal to theologians and reformers of the Protestant Reformation.

# Meister Eckhart (1260–1337)

Meister Eckhart was born to a noble family in the region of Thuringia in Germany. He entered the Dominican Order at Cologne around 1280 and completed his studies at the University of Paris. Eckhart began lecturing in Paris around 1293 and later was named prior of the Dominicans in Erfurt, Germany, in 1294. He was soon appointed head of the Dominicans in Thuringia and then later Saxony and Bohemia.

Eckhart was highly respected by the church as one of the Dominican order's greatest theologians and intellectuals. As a result, he was given the title Master of Sacred Theology, from which his name Meister was derived. In addition, Eckhart received many honors at the University of Paris. But life was not all honor and medals for Eckhart. His mystical theological writings made him the first Dominican to be tried for heresy. Eckhart was charged and tried before the archbishop of Cologne and died while making an appeal to the pope over the archbishop's verdict. However, the pope was not sympathetic to Eckhart even after his years of service and condemned much of his work as heretical. This censure hurt Eckhart's reputation, causing difficulties for other theologians in assessing his mystical ideas.

Eckhart seemed to have been heading toward a kind of pantheism with his mystical writings. He called for prayer and the birth of God in the soul to overcome worldly concerns and reflect the divine light of God. Eckhart wrote over 59 sermons and many works of theology in German in defense of his mysticism. He also wrote in Latin at times, including a commentary on Peter Lombard's *Sentences* and a compendium of theology. His importance was not so much in his writings but his ideas on Christian mysticism, which influenced many other mystics and theologians of the Late Middle Ages, including Saint Catherine of Siena.

# Saint Catherine of Siena (1347–1380)

Catherine was born the daughter of a dyer in Siena, Italy. Having experienced mystical visions while young, she refused to marry as her parents desired and joined a

Dominican order of nuns and laity in 1367. Catherine spent her life in prayer and care for the sick and poor. News spread about her devout and pious nature, and disciples and followers flocked to her. This group always traveled with her on her many journeys during her lifetime.

In 1375, Catherine resolved to do what she could to help settle the struggle between the city of Florence and the Avignon pope, Gregory XI, so she traveled to Avignon where the pope resided and spoke on behalf of the Florentines. In addition, Catherine begged Gregory XI to return to Rome. Her plea strengthened the pope's resolve to leave Avignon, and in 1377, Gregory made a triumphal entry into Rome. Regrettably for the church, he died the next year and was succeeded by the erratic Pope Urban VI, whose succession marked the beginning of the Great Schism.

Meanwhile, Catherine returned to Siena but was later drawn back into church politics with the Great Schism. She gave herself entirely to this issue and wanted to restore unity to the church. As part of that desire, she dictated and sent letters to rulers, cardinals, archbishops, and other people of influence to support Urban. But the erratic behavior of the pope and confusion over the authority of the church proved difficult for her to beat, and she died in Rome without seeing the end of the split in the church.

Catherine was a profound mystic who was believed to have been the recipient of many spiritual experiences, including suffering the stigmata, the wounds of Christ. Although her wounds were invisible, Catherine and many others thought her suffering from the wounds was considerable.

Catherine's place in church history is based more on her mystical experiences than her contributions to ending the Avignon papacy and trying to end the Great Schism. Her letters reveal not just a mystic but also a woman of formidable will and determination. Her *Dialogue* is ranked as a classic of mystical Christian spirituality. Composed in four treatises, it examines the religious obligations and also challenges Christians face. She was declared a saint in the fifteenth century and was awarded the very high honor of Doctor of the Church during the twentieth century. Her mystic experiences and activism later inspired other church women, including Birgitta of Sweden and Lidwana of Schiedam.

## Birgitta, Lidwana, and Groote

Birgitta of Sweden (1302–1372) was a contemporary of Catherine of Siena who also urged the popes of Avignon to return to Rome. Also inspired by Catherine of Siena, Lidwina of Schiedam (1400–1433) challenged the authority of the priests. Once she even vomited out the bread that a priest gave her during mass because it was not consecrated properly. In addition, she then claimed to receive the bread directly from Christ himself in a miraculous vision.

Another mystic who challenged the church was Gerhard Groote (1300–1384), born a member of a wealthy family in the Netherlands. He was educated at the University of Paris and started a successful academic career by teaching in Cologne, where he enjoyed a life of luxury. But in 1374, Groote abandoned his academic pursuits to follow the spiritual life. After spending many years in a monastery, he became a deacon in the church. As deacon, Groote preached sermons on poverty and the need for church reform. As a result, he earned many enemies and his license to preach was revoked. The following year in 1384, Groote died of the plague.

Groote was highly influential because of his preaching for reform and mysticism and, as a result, became a major figure in the mystical movement of the Late Middle Ages. Before his death, his many followers formed the organization called the Brethren of the Common Life. These men and women carried on his mystical teachings of Christianity into the Late Middle Ages and early Reformation.

Many of these orthodox mystics were very individualistic in their view of the divine. But that individualism was also carried to the point of heresy by others, such as John Wycliffe and Jan Hus.

## John Wycliffe (1330–1384) and the Lollards

John Wycliffe was born in Yorkshire, England, and studied at Oxford University, receiving his doctorate in 1372. Later he taught at Balliol College at Oxford until he became regent of the college. Wycliffe was a well-known scholar at Oxford and, as a result, entered into the service of powerful government figures, including John of Gaunt and the Black Prince.

In 1375, with the protection of John of Gaunt, Wycliffe spoke out about the abuses of the Catholic Church. He called for the clergy to practice the poverty of Christ, stressed the individual's inner spiritual journey to God, and de-emphasized the importance of the sacraments. And finally, he called into question the doctrine of transubstantiation by stating it was philosophically unsound.

His questioning of the nature of the Eucharist was too much for church authorities, and a council convened at Oxford in 1381 to condemn his teachings. Later the next year, a synod met in London and also denounced his writings and teachings. People who followed the teachings of Wycliffe, called Lollards, were forced to recant their beliefs—although, oddly enough, Wycliffe died quietly and unharmed in Oxford. Later, the Council of Constance (1414–1418) ordered his writings burnt and his bones removed from holy ground.

While Wycliffe's teachings declined in popularity after his death, in part because of the peasant revolt of 1381, his ideas on a personal God had a deep effect on other scholars and theologians. The most notable people influenced by Wycliffe were Jan Hus and the Hussites in Bohemia, where he was to help give shape to their ideas.

## Jan Hus (1369–1415) and the Hussites

Jan Hus was born in Bohemia and studied at the University of Prague. Ordained a priest in 1400, he soon gained a reputation for his preaching. Hus liked the teachings of John Wycliffe and called for reform in the church from the pulpit. His criticism of church abuses led him to be denounced by the church in 1407. Following the orders of Pope Innocent VII, the archbishop of Prague also banned him from preaching in 1408.

In 1409, King Wenceslaus IV of Bohemia, who approved of Hus's jabs at church authority, appointed him rector of the University of Prague. Hus then instituted the teaching of the doctrines of Wycliffe. By 1410, the archbishop of Prague got a papal bull that ordered the destruction of all Wycliffe teachings. Hus was excommunicated by the church later that year, and in 1412 he lost his job as rector, due to the fact that Wenceslaus, who had once supported him, now needed to build bridges with the church.

Hus, feeling his life was endangered, fled to safety among members of the Czech nobility. During this time he wrote his primary work, *On the Church*, in 1413. Eventually Hus agreed to submit to a church council because he was promised safe conduct. But after arriving at the Council of Constance in 1415, he was imprisoned, condemned, and burned at the stake. Hus's death angered many people of Bohemia, so they declared him a martyr and made him a symbol of Bohemian national identity. In a few short years, the region was embroiled in the Hussite War, which lasted from 1419 to 1436.

> **Notable Quote**
>
> "The papacy is not other than the ghost of the deceased Roman Empire, sitting crowned upon the grave thereof."
>
> —Thomas Hobbes, *Leviathan*

# The Results Are In ...

During the late Middle Ages, the church suffered several setbacks to its prestige and power. First, the famines and the Black Death weakened the people's faith in the church. In addition, the Black Death did a good job of knocking off some of the best priests, who were later replaced by lackluster replacements. This, of course, further weakened the standing of the church with the people. Some started to take the matter of salvation into their own hands, rather than leave it to a bad priest or no priest at all, and began to think of salvation as an individual matter.

The Babylonian Captivity and the Great Schism also weakened the prestige and power of the church. Many people of Europe did not know which pope was legit since there were as many as three at one time. Plus, the church seemed to be more about political matters than spiritual matters, and the political strife also made some people think of salvation as an individual matter.

Finally, with the rise of Scotus and Occam, Christianity leaned more toward improvable mysticism and individualism, and many of the most intelligent minds were called out of the church. Also mysticism and individualism, by their very nature, were hard for the church to control. So again many people started to think of salvation as a personal matter. With the cards stacked, the church was going to have a tough time coming out of the Late Middle Ages.

## The Least You Need to Know

- The Black Death weakened the prestige of the church, and although some clergy called for reform, substantial changes did not happen until the sixteenth century.

- The Babylonian Captivity was a period of time during the fourteenth century when the French king controlled the papacy out of Avignon, France.

- After the Babylonian Captivity, the church experienced the Great Schism in which several men were elected and saw themselves as pope.

- By the end of the thirteenth century, theologians and philosophers had turned against the philosophy and theology of Aristotle and Thomas Aquinas.

- Duns Scotus and William Occam did much to make the distinction between the rational and the divine in philosophical and theological inquiry.

◆ The mystics and individualists of the Late Middle Ages called for more personal encounters with the divine and also reform in the church.

◆ The church's spiritual and political power and prestige were weakened by the end of the Middle Ages.

# Chapter 18

# Light at the End of the Middle Ages

## In This Chapter

- ◆ Lasting changes
- ◆ Money and banks
- ◆ Rebirth and Renaissance
- ◆ Humanism
- ◆ The early Renaissance

The fourteenth and early fifteenth centuries were a time of turbulence for medieval Europe. Much of Europe was shaken by famine, disease, war, depression, and a decline in the church. Things did not look so good. But there was some hope, and with that hope a light at the end of the tunnel.

## Change and Renewal

With the rise of national monarchies, such as England and France, at the end of the late Middle Ages, the feudal system changed. Strong kings limited the feudal warfare that had dotted most of the history of the Middle

Ages; new types of weapons and standing armies made the medieval knight obsolete; and nobles no longer had to defend their lands against invaders. To satisfy feudal obligations, they raised cash instead of providing military services. With this free time, nobles transformed their castles into luxurious palaces and bought fine clothes and jewelry to attend the king's court. In other words, the nobles got culture, and the noble warrior became a thing of the past.

With the breakdown of feudalism, life also changed for the peasants. Serfdom was on the decline in Western Europe. Many serfs sold the surplus food they were again producing and used the cash to buy their freedom. Lords rented out their estates to the serfs for money instead of servitude. In time, many serfs became tenant farmers or earned enough money to buy their own small farms.

During the middle of the fifteenth century, Europe's economy regained the spark it had lost in the fourteenth century. Population again was on the rise. Trade was revived while the towns' growing populations provided more places to sell a greater and greater surplus of agricultural goods. Demand for manufactured goods exceeded the supply the old town guilds could produce.

Entrepreneurs began to finance independent manufacturing shops, developing two new methods of creating high-quality products. Primitive factories that consisted of large buildings hired workers with various skills and produced goods in one spot. Another method was the cottage industry, where businessmen sent materials out to workers who made the goods at home. These production methods eventually replaced the craft guilds in the fifteenth and sixteenth centuries.

# The Rise of Banks

During the late Middle Ages, merchants and entrepreneurs handling large sums of cash developed banking. They learned by trial and error that the safest and quickest way to move cash was by pencil pushing and accounting entries. For example, coins were deposited at one point—Paris—and other coins of equal value were picked up at a distant location—Rome—with the presentation of a receipt of the deposit.

The city-states of Italy were at the center of this financial activity. One reason was their locations on the Mediterranean Sea; they traded with the merchants of the East and supplied Europe with those goods, so several families set up the first banks in Italy.

## The Peruzzi Family

The Peruzzi family began by making an arrangement with the pope to collect the taxes for the church in England. With the profits of this work, the Peruzzis created a network of banks in 16 cities across Europe. With those banks, they loaned money to nobles and even kings, including the kings of Naples and England. But business has always been a risky venture, and their enterprise went belly up when the king of Naples repudiated his debt and the Hundred Years' War bankrupted the English treasury.

## The Medici Family

The Medici family of Florence also tried the banking business, establishing independent banks throughout Europe. Learning from the mistakes of the Peruzzis, they set up a system to prevent any collapse. In this system, the manager of each bank branch was responsible for any loans he made and could not expect the debts that his bank incurred to be taken by another branch or parent bank. So if one bank failed, the whole system did not collapse. The plan worked, and the Medici family became very wealthy. With that wealth, they dominated the government of Florence, won control of the church, and married into the royals of Europe.

## Jacques Coeur (1395–1456)

The French and Germans were also into banking. In France, Jacques Coeur, the son of a fur merchant, became one of the more prominent bankers. When his father died, Coeur expanded the fur business he inherited into a company that dealt with all types of goods in which to make a profit. The company established warehouses, developed mines, and traded with the East.

By 1437, the king of France had taken notice of Coeur and asked him to organize the royal mint. Two years later, the king appointed Coeur to treasurer-steward of the royal household. With that power, Coeur loaned money to rulers, nobles, and popes in return for arranged marriages and high church positions for his children. With this activity came accusations from various French nobles against Coeur. As a result, the wealthy banker was put into prison and tortured, and all his wealth and property was confiscated. He was to be executed, but the pope intervened on his behalf. Later Coeur escaped prison and fled to an island in the Aegean Sea, where he died in poverty in 1456.

## The Fuggers

In Germany, Jacob Fugger (1459–1525) established the leading German bank. Fugger was born in Augsburg and first studied to become a monk, but that life didn't suit him, so he left the monastery to work in the textile industry.

In textiles, Fugger rose to the top and accumulated enough money to become a moneylender. He loaned huge sums of cash to popes and even the Holy Roman Emperor, Maximilian I. Fugger's son, called Jacob the Rich, loaned money to bribe the electors of the Holy Roman Empire who chose Emperor Charles V. In payment for the loans, the Fuggers gained access to the gold and silver mines of Hungary and Spain, and with that new asset, spread bank branches across the chief cities of Europe. By the seventeenth century, they retired from banking, but not before the Fugger family was elevated to nobility by the Holy Roman Emperor.

### Age-Makers

Jacob Burckhardt was a famous nineteenth-century historian who produced the famous Renaissance study titled *Civilization of the Renaissance in Italy* in 1867. According to Burkhardt, the Renaissance marked the birth of the modern world. In addition, the rediscovery of the learning of antiquity helped Europeans expand their medieval perspective. In reality, Burkhardt overstated his argument and didn't give the late Middle Ages their due, but sadly his view has stuck with most people to this day.

# Rebirth

With stronger national monarchies, a breakdown of feudalism, a renewal of trade and industry, and the rise of banking, it was a perfect time for a new cultural movement in Europe. When it began in Italy in the middle of the fourteenth century, it slowly gave new life to the late Middle Ages. The movement was called the Renaissance.

The term *Renaissance*, French for "rebirth," was first coined during the sixteenth century by the Italians who thought that the Greco-Roman civilization was reborn in Italy after the long and dark Middle Ages. To many, this view stuck although it had been overstated. Today most historians consider the Renaissance an era of transition between the Middle Ages and the modern age.

There was one fundamental difference between the Middle Ages and Renaissance Europe: religion. During the Renaissance, Christianity remained important, but more *secular* values were introduced into European society. In the Middle Ages, salvation in heaven was stressed, while in the Renaissance *humanism* was stressed. This combination of Christianity and humanism is most evident in the words and works of art of the Renaissance. The Renaissance, which began in Italy in the late Middle Ages, soon spread to France, England, and Germany. For this history, we will concentrate on the early Renaissance of late-Middle Age Italy.

## def•i•ni•tion

**Humanism** is a system of thought with man at the center. In other words, man is the sum of all things. **Secular** defines things that are worldly or temporal and definitely not religious in nature.

# The Importance of Geography for Italy

Geography gave the Italian city-states an advantage over the rest of Europe, as Italy jutted out into the Mediterranean Sea and became a natural pipeline of trade goods and ideas from the Middle East into Europe. During the Middle Ages, the Italian city-states prospered from trade as they brought the luxury goods of the Middle East and Asia to Europe. By the fourteenth century, three city-states became leaders: Venice, Florence, and Milan. These powerful cities ruled large areas of the Italian peninsula beyond their city limits.

For several reasons, Italy was never very united, which for the Renaissance was a benefit. Feudalism had little impact on Italy during the Middle Ages, partially due to the survival of trade, which allowed a money economy to continue. In addition, Italy did not develop strong centralized monarchies and states like France and England. The Holy Roman Emperors had tried to rule the region but had given up by the fourteenth century, and Italy had been divided into several states. Another obstacle to unity was the fierce competition between the city-states and the papacy in Rome, which ruled over a large territory called the Papal States. But all these rival centers of power and money made the Italian Peninsula the seedbed of the Renaissance because the competition allowed for the civilization to prosper and advance.

# Ah, Venice!

According to legend, people fleeing Attila the Hun's invasion during the fifth century founded the city of Venice, which is built on a group of islands at the north end of the Adriatic Sea not far from the Alps. Since it is located on the sea, the economy of the city was tied to it. With the Crusades of the High Middle Ages, the city's power grew as it provided ships for crusaders heading for the Holy Land. By the late Middle Ages, it had grown to be one of the most wealthy cities in Europe as the Venetian merchant ships carried luxury goods from around the world to all ports of Europe. At the top of its game, Venice could boast over 3,000 merchant ships operated by over 30,000 sailors, making it the dominant commercial center in the Mediterranean.

The Venetian government also had a commercial flavor. In 1297, the leading merchants of the city took charge of the government and created the Golden Book, a listing of names of the most influential families of the city. Afterward, only people in the book were eligible to serve on the Great Council, which appointed all public officials and enacted all laws. Every year, the Great Council met and elected from its members the Council of Ten to serve as administrators of the city. The Great Council also elected one of its members to be the doge or duke of Venice, a ceremonial position as head of the city that held little real power.

Venice owned all the merchant ships that sailed from the city, leasing them to merchants on a voyage-by-voyage basis. The city also collected taxes on all goods brought into Venice. With this revenue, Venice built warships to protect its ships from the various pirates of the Mediterranean. Venice also controlled the mountain passes of the Alps and collected tolls from merchants who came to trade. So with the huge wealth from trade, the leading families of Venice had disposable income to compete with each other, which meant they could build better palaces and commission the work of great artists.

# The City of Flowers

Florence, the city of flowers, is located in north-central Italy. It received its independence in the mid-thirteenth century from the kingdom of Tuscany. During most of its history, Florence was a center for a struggle between the popes and the Holy Roman Emperors. With that struggle, a deep division was created between the Guelfs, who supported the pope, and the Ghibellines, who liked the Holy Roman Emperor (remember, Dante was a Guelf). Other struggles included workers fighting the wealthy and nobles fighting the bourgeoisie. Despite all this turmoil, Florence did prosper, mainly because of the wool industry. Sheep were raised in the hill country of central Italy, and as a result, Florence became a center of wool processing.

During most of the Renaissance, Florence's political power was in the hands of the few wealthy wool merchants, and like the wealthy families of Venice, these merchants were constantly competing with one another. They built the grandest houses in the city and the country and tried to beautify the city in significant ways, usually with their name attached. Most of them thought that people who prospered should show their appreciation for success by building churches to glorify God. To carry out this plan, they hired talented artists and paid them well to produce their best work.

**Notable Quote**

"Our city of Florence, daughter and creation of Rome, is rising and destined to achieve great things."

—Giovanni Villiani (1363)

Four social groups divided the people of Renaissance Florence. The nobles owned much of the land and lived in splendid castles on large estates outside the city walls. They behaved according to the rules of chivalry and disdained the new rich merchants of Florence.

The wealthy merchants formed a class called the fat people. They sought to protect their wealth by controlling the government. In addition, they tried to enhance their social status by marrying into nobility. To curry favor with the public of Florence, these merchants became great patrons of the arts.

The middle class was made up of shopkeepers and professionals, who were called the little people, and workers made up the final, lower class. Over 30,000 workers, most of whom lived under the domination of the wool merchants, worked long hours for little wages and were dependent on their employers for most aspects of life. Workers who violated rules could have their wages withheld or be discharged from their jobs. Of course, as difficult as their lives seemed to be, these urban workers had it better than the rural peasants in the countryside.

## The Rise of the Medici Family

During the fifteenth century, when the neighboring city-states posed a growing threat to Florence, influential people of the government came to the realization that they needed a strong leader and picked Cosimo de Medici, a wealthy banker. By 1434, he had consolidated power in his own hands while maintaining the appearance of the republican form of government. Cosimo then appointed his relatives to important positions in the government so he could control it. He also commissioned works of art to beautify the city and encouraged builders to construct churches. In 1438, he established a school for the study of the philosophy of Plato and invited scholars to join this elite school where they lived in wonderful villas near the city. The only requirement was that they had to dine with him once a week.

Cosimo died in 1468. His son Piero (1464–1469) and great-grandson Lorenzo (1469–1492) continued his policies of government. The Medici created a stable state by exiling the people who did not share their views and encouraging other city-states of Italy to join them in shifting alliances to maintain the balance of power. Under Lorenzo's leadership, the economy of Florence expanded. Despite the fact that the workers were poorly paid, they were protected from the fluctuations in the economy around them. As a result, Florence became the most important city-state in Italy and one of most beautiful cities in Europe.

# Savonarola (1452–1495)

After Lorenzo's death, a popular uprising, led by a fiery Dominican priest named Girolamo Savonarola, forced the Medici to leave Florence. Starting in 1491, when he had been elected prior to the convent of San Marco, Savonarola preached sermons condemning the worldliness of the papacy and the secularism of the Renaissance. These sermons attracted many because he called for the return to the simple faith of the early Christians and warned of the spiritual corruption caused by wealth and power.

When Savonarola assumed leadership of Florence after the fall of the Medici, he wrote up a constitution based on that of Venice. He also reorganized the collection of taxes and tried to reform the system of justice in the city. He wanted to change pleasure-loving Florence into the example of a good, pious Christian city. To do that, Savonarola exiled many scholars and artists and encouraged people to gather up what he considered immoral books and art and burn them.

This was all a bit much for the pope, who was in fact a patron of the arts himself. And in 1495, Pope Alexander VI ordered Savonarola to stop preaching and threatened to put Florence under interdict. Savonarola was not scared of the pope in the slightest and issued a call for general counsel to depose the pope. By this time, the town of Florence had turned against Savonarola. He was proclaimed a heretic and burned at the stake—probably close to where some of the books were burnt (a very ironic historical moment).

After Savonarola's demise, the Medici were asked to return to Florence as leaders. But the city had lost its edge and never again regained its position of power. In 1494, Charles VIII of France invaded Italy, and for the next 50 years the kings of France and Spain grappled for control of Italy. Regardless of this political disorder, the Renaissance continued to flourish in Florence.

# Military Milan

The city-state of Milan near the center of the broad plain of Lombardy dominated the Po River valley by the late Middle Ages. Situated on a major trade route connecting Genoa to northern Europe, Milan developed greater military than economic importance. With its location and military, a strong leader was needed to rule the city-state, and as a result, Milan became a monarchy under a succession of dukes.

The Visconti family ruled as the dukes of Milan from 1317 to 1447. At their height, they controlled a majority of northern Italy. When the last Visconti duke passed away, the people of Milan tried to establish a republic, but the republic failed to hold the military of Milan in check. So in 1450, Franceso Sforza, a mercenary soldier of the Milanese army, seized control of the government. He and his successors ruled Milan until France and Spain invaded northern Italy in the late Middle Ages.

# Humanist Scholarship

With the coming of the Renaissance, people's attitudes changed, especially in the better-educated middle class. Many wanted to understand the nature of how things worked. They were interested in life in this world, not the next. Individual achievement started to gain ground. This interest in learning and the importance of the individual were reflected in education as well as art. Scholars of the Renaissance rejected much about the Middle Ages. They wanted to dig deeper into the philosophy of the ancient Greeks and Romans. With the works of antiquity, they found an individual spirit very similar to their own.

During the late fifteenth century, many Greek scholars had left Constantinople when it was conquered by the Ottoman Turks in 1453. Some took refuge in the Italian city-states, bringing with them the knowledge of Greek antiquity. With the arrival of so many Greeks, many remarked that Athens had migrated to Florence. But it wasn't just Florence—the Greeks were spread over the Italian peninsula, creating an interest in the learning of antiquity.

The Renaissance called for humanism or *studia humanitatis*, a system of learning that included the subjects of grammar, rhetoric, poetry, and history. The scholars who studied these subjects became known as humanists. Renaissance humanists thought that all humans had potential for achievement in the arts, literature, politics, or life. To achieve this, everyone must be allowed human dignity since humans are God's most valuable creation.

# Petrarch (1304–1374) and Laura

Petrarch, one of the first of the new humanist writers, was an important transitional figure who bridged the divide between the Middle Ages and the Renaissance. Petrarch was born near Florence, the son of a Florentine notary. His father and family had been exiled from Florence by the Guelphs in 1311 and moved to Avignon. Petrarch excelled at school and pursued his studies at Montpellier before going to Bologna. Later he returned to Avignon and fathered two illegitimate children.

In 1336, Petrarch journeyed to Italy and then Rome. He found Rome a better spot than Avignon because it encouraged the renewal of classical traditions in poetry. In 1341, Petrarch was awarded the crown of poet laureate of Rome. But Rome was not his only home. He enjoyed the patronage of merchants and nobles from Milan, Venice, and Padua. Petrarch lived in Venice from 1362 to 1367, and it was there that his friend Boccaccio presented him a translation of Homer's poem, *The Iliad*, in Latin. From 1367 forward, Petrarch spent time in both Padua and Argua. When he died in Argua in 1374, legend has it that he was found with his head resting on a manuscript of the Roman poet Virgil.

Petrarch's colleagues considered him one of the greatest scholars of the time. He was definitely one of the first humanists and arguably the best Italian poet since Dante. But he was also a brilliant classical scholar. He translated a text of the Roman Livy during his early twenties that earned him the name the Father of Humanism.

Petrarch, like many Renaissance intellectuals, had two personalities. While he was comfortable in the monastery, he also loved to travel to new places. While he liked the idea of self-denial, he loved the pleasures of the world. While he liked to learn, he sometimes believed that too much worldly knowledge might prevent him from entering heaven.

Petrarch became famous during his lifetime for the love poems he wrote in vernacular Italian collected in the *Canzoniere*. The poems honored Laura, a kindly woman whom he loved and admired. This love was a chaste or platonic love for a woman he saw a handful of times (like Dante's situation, both were married). The poems consisted of 14 lines, rhymed according to a certain pattern. Poets later called poems written in this style Petrarchan sonnets, and William Shakespeare would even later adopt this style.

Of course, Petrarch, being a classicist, combined his love of Laura with philosophy to produce *My Secret Book*. In this book, he has a dialogue with his beloved Saint

Augustine in the presence of Truth over the nature of happiness and love of Laura. In the end, Augustine tells Petrarch that happiness is a state of mind. Petrarch can be happy if he is willing to part with his love for the kindly woman Laura. But in the end, that is a price for happiness Petrarch will not pay.

> **Notable Quote**
>
> "After the darkness has been dispelled, our grandsons will be able to walk back into the pure radiance of the past."
>
> —Petrarch

# The Early Renaissance

The humanist scholars who followed Petrarch agreed with him that there was a need to study classical literature but also saw a need for an active life. To fulfill human potential, they thought people needed to excel in many areas of life including politics, art, material possessions, and the appreciation of beauty. This developed into the ideal of the "Renaissance man," a well-rounded and cultured individual who was comfortable with all expression of the human spirit. This ideal was best expressed in the work *The Book of the Courtier*, by Baldassare Castiglione (1478–1529). It details the ideal courtier: intelligent, charming, honorable, and skilled in sports, all with little effort. In addition, the ideal courtier must have knowledge of the classics, appreciate the arts, and know what is beautiful. It was a tall order even by today's standards.

With Castiglione's ideals in focus, the goals of Renaissance education were set, at least for the upper classes. Universities continued to keep their medieval structures and curriculums, but it was now more fashionable for the sons of nobles to attend universities. There, they would learn what they needed to display in polite society. In addition, noble sons learned to read and write Latin and Greek and also to speak well and know about the authors of antiquity.

## History Lessons

During the early Renaissance, scholars begin to develop new methods of analyzing the past. They started to examine historical documents in the light of new scholarship. This textual criticism was introduced by two high-ranking church officials: Lorenzo Valla (1407–1457) and Nicholas of Cusa (1400–1464). In this type of study, scholars analyzed a written document to determine its consistency, a technique that led to some interesting results.

One example involved the church. The Roman Catholic Church had long claimed that the Roman Emperor Constantine had given control of Italy to Pope Sylvester I when the Roman capital moved to Constantinople. It was called the Donation of Constantine. Valla and Nicholas both proved that the document was, in fact, a forgery that was written 400 years after the death of Constantine. This spirit of inquiry inspired later historians to question accepted notions. The church, of course, did not like this type of talk at the time.

## Women in the Renaissance

For most women, life in the late Middle Ages and the early Renaissance remained the same: bad. Expected to be only wives and mothers, they were subject to their parents before marriage and their husbands afterward. Peasant women worked right beside their husbands in the fields. In the cities, women had to run the household and also help with the husband's work. Women who didn't marry had to live in the houses of their male relatives or enter convents to become nuns, and only a few wealthy women were able to break the traditional mold.

## Painting During the Early Renaissance

The arts changed dramatically during the fifteenth century. In the spirit of humanism, artists tried to create lifelike people, dressed in contemporary clothes and set in a background of Italian scenery. These artists also experimented with new artistic techniques and materials. They created formulas to guide their work in showing the human body in correct proportions. In addition, the early Renaissance artists set standards for judging other works of art. They created techniques for shading and perspective in paintings that gave a 3-D look very different from the flat 2-D look of the Middle Ages. And in the quest for accuracy, they observed flora and studied animals with exacting detail.

> **Notable Quote** _____
>
> "The painter is lord of all types of people and of all things."
> —Leonardo da Vinci

Although the guilds had dominated the artwork of the Middle Ages, the Renaissance artists had more freedom, signed their works, and enjoyed fame and glory. Master artists were assigned commissions by patrons. They then painted or carved the most important features of the work and let students complete the rest. With this type of apprenticing, aspiring artists learned the techniques of their masters and then perhaps would go on to produce their own works. The competition among the wealthy to acquire the services of the best artists made artists feel entitled to special treatment.

## The Big Six

Several important artists of the early Renaissance paved the way for the artists of the High Renaissance. They were Giotto (1266–1337), Massacio (1401–1428), Botticelli (1444–1510), Ghiberti (1378–1455), Brunelleschi (1377–1446), and Donatello (1386–1466). The first three artists were known for their paintings while the last three were known for sculpture and architecture, although all of them dabbled in several different art forms.

Giotto, the first important painter of the early Renaissance, broke away from the rigid forms of medieval art and inspired later artists to study the natural world so they could paint it accurately. Masaccio or "Messy Tom" mastered the technique of perspectives and light and shadow foreshadowed by Giotto. Botticelli, influenced by mysticism, tried to blend the teachings and philosophy of Christianity and Plato on the canvas. One of his more famous examples is the *Birth of Venus*.

In architecture and sculpture, early Renaissance artists attempted to achieve symmetry and harmony in buildings while providing great detail to give a sense of perfection to their sculptures. Ghiberti was famous for his bronze sculptures, including the doors to the Church of Saint John the Baptist in Florence. Brunelleschi, who competed with Ghiberti, was most famed for his great octagon dome of the cathedral in Florence inspired by the dome of Rome. It rises 133 feet above the supporting walls of the cathedral. Finally there was Donatello, the greatest sculptor of the early Renaissance. His most famous work, the statue of *David*, was commissioned by Cosimo de Medici.

## The Elevator Stops Here

The artists of the early Renaissance broke from the rigid art of the Middle Ages as they used perspective and represented humans and animals in a natural way. The artists of the High Renaissance went beyond these advances to create works that evoke an emotional response from the viewer. The best known of these artists included Leonardo da Vinci, Michaelangelo, Raphael, and Titian. Each was thought to be divinely inspired, and wealthy patrons flocked to them to acquire their services. But the beginning of the High Renaissance marks the end of the Middle Ages and the beginning of the modern history of Europe, which is where we stop in this text.

By the end of the Middle Ages in 1500, the independence of the Italian city-states had disappeared as the nation-states of France and Spain emerged to take control of the peninsula. But the excitement of the Renaissance could no longer be contained in Italy. It spread to northern Europe through war, trade, and the invention of the printing press by Johannes Gutenberg. The Northern European Renaissance had a more religious tone represented in the works of Desiderius Erasmus (1466–1536), who wrote the *Praise of Folly*, a work very critical of the Catholic Church, and Thomas More (1478–1535), an English philosopher and writer who wrote *Utopia*. Also the artwork of the Northern Renaissance retained a distinctive perspective by remaining more medieval than classical in focus, with the oil painting of Jan and Hubert van Eyck and Pieter Brueghel being the most notable.

## The Least You Need to Know

- ◆ During the late Middle Ages, several lasting changes began to occur, including the development of strong national monarchies, the decline of feudalism, and the revival of trade and industry.

- ◆ Also during the fourteenth and fifteenth centuries, the practice of banking developed, which helped Europe with its commercial development.

- ◆ The Renaissance or rebirth of Europe started in Italy because of its geographic location close to trade routes and on the site of the center of the old Greco-Roman civilization.

- ◆ The Renaissance renewed interest in the classical traditions of Greece and Rome and a humanistic perspective that found its way into all the different humanities, including art and literature.

- ◆ The Renaissance would eventually spread from the Italian peninsula into northern Europe, ushering in the modern age.

# Chapter 19

# A Thousand Points of Light

## In This Chapter

The early Renaissance of the Italian city-states was not the only bright light of the late Middle Ages. As previously detailed, the national monarchies of England and France strengthened a great deal after the wars of the fourteenth and fifteenth centuries, and other nations also developed. But also an event extinguished one of the oldest continuous lights of Europe, Constantinople and the Byzantine Empire.

## Smaller Lights Grow Stronger

Several smaller kingdoms of Europe began to develop at a rapid pace during the later Middle Ages to become some of the leading nations of modern Europe. These were the Swiss Confederation, the kingdoms of Poland and Hungary, and Russia.

# The Swiss

When we last left the Swiss Confederation, they had asserted their power by defeating the Hapsburgs of Austria represented by Duke Leopold III in 1386. But all was not well with the Swiss. In the fifteenth century, a dispute between the townspeople of Zurich and the peasants of Schwyz got ugly. The Hapsburgs tried to invade again with the help of an alliance with the people of Zurich, but it was not enough; the armies of the other Swiss cantons defeated the combined armies of Zurich and Austria. Zurich then renounced its alliance with the Austrians and rejoined the confederation. The fighting of the Swiss so impressed Louis XI of France that he tried to have them fight for him. This arrangement remains a tradition to this day with the Swiss Guards who protect the Vatican.

Although the Swiss were small, they did carry a big influential stick in the events of Europe. In 1476, they defeated the ambitious Charles the Bold, the Duke of Burgundy. This reduced his power greatly, allowing France to annex the region. Unfortunately for the Swiss, the victory produced tension between the cantons, especially when they tried to divide the spoils of the war. This put a spotlight on the cantons' main problem: they had no strong central government to enforce decisions. As a result, disputes often arose between the large urban cantons and the small rural cantons.

Early in the sixteenth century, the Swiss Confederation pursued a policy of expansionism. France had become involved in the Italian Wars of northern Italy under Charles VIII. The Swiss wanted to control the Alpine passes that led into Italy and so attacked the French in 1512 and 1513. The French very easily beat the Swiss, so the Swiss decided to put their plans for expansion on the back burner.

The Swiss Confederation was very different from the other developing nations of Europe. Without a strong central government, the confederation was a union of many states with a weak *federal* government. Each of the cantons continued to preserve its own culture by choosing its language and religion. Another amazing fact about the small confederation was that it was able to keep its independence and progressive government while storms of upheavals blew Europe into the modern age.

## def•i•ni•tion

A **federal** government is one that balances power between the states and the national or central government.

# The Polish

When we left the Polish, several rulers had strengthened the monarchy. Wladislaw I (1320–1333) developed alliances with Hungary and Lithuania that ensured peace. His successor, Casimir III, also worked to establish a strong central government. Casimir's daughter, Queen Jadwiga, ascended to the throne after the death of her father. She married Jagello, the grand-duke of Lithuania, in 1384. This marriage merged both Poland and Lithuania into one of the largest kingdoms in Europe. In 1410, the kingdom gained more territory when Jagello defeated the Germanic Teutonic Knights in the Battle of Tannenberg. With that win, Poland gained western and eastern Prussia, although they were ruled by the Teutonic Knights, who were vassals of the kings of Poland.

The monarchs who followed Jadwiga and Jagello ruled a united Poland for 200 years until 1572. Although it was united, Poland faced continuous threats from Russia and lesser Polish nobles. Because of this, the monarchs of Poland were not able to continue helping the economy and centralizing power.

In 1493, the first national diet or parliament was established. It consisted of an upper house, which included clergy, nobles, and royal officials, and a lower house of townspeople. The lower house had little power over the upper house. The nobles of the upper house also controlled the army and held the best positions in the royal bureaucracy. Of course, they guarded their position and made laws that reduced peasants to serfs. This policy was used to exploit peasant labor on their lands. But an unseen negative effect of their laws was that it crippled the economy of towns so the middle class could not develop fully.

Despite some of the obvious problems, the 200 years of rule by the Jagellonian dynasty has been called the Golden Age of Poland. During this time Poland produced its most famous scientist, Nicolaus Copernicus (1473–1543), who advanced a theory that changed many beliefs held in astronomy. Copernicus held that the Earth and other planets revolved around the sun, not that the sun and other planets revolved around the Earth. Also during the sixteenth century, the royal Polish court was a center of Renaissance culture.

# Hungary

When we left Hungary, Louis the Great had developed a strong monarchy by bringing the feudal nobles under royal control. Thus things in the kingdom of Hungary looked good. But after the death of Louis, the monarchy suffered a decline. Sigismund

(1387–1447) was not only king of Hungary but was also the Holy Roman Emperor and king of Bohemia. So he was unable to reign in the nobles of Hungary because he spent so much time in the Germanic regions.

During the late Middle Ages, the kingdom of Hungary crusaded against the Ottoman Turks who were advancing into Europe. With Osman (1290–1326), the founder of the Ottoman dynasty, the Turks conquered most of the Middle East and moved into Europe. Their advance stopped in 1437 when John Hunyadi, a Hungarian noble, defeated them in battle. For the next few years, John repeatedly battled with the Turks and even ended the siege of Belgrade. After John's death in 1456, his son Mathais (1458–1490) was elected king of Hungary partially because of his father's popularity.

King Mathais was not a very able administrator, but he was a great warrior. He created a standing army called the Magyar Hussars, one of the best-disciplined armies of Europe during its time, and beat the Czechs, forcing them from northern Hungary. Mathais also beat the Hapsburgs, forcing them to leave western Hungary, and was able to annex Moravia, Lusitia, and Silesia. Finally, in 1485, Mathais besieged Vienna and forced the Holy Roman Emperor to give him Austria and other territories.

By the time of King Mathais's death in 1490, Hungary had become one of the dominant powers of central Europe. Sadly, his successors were ineffective, both as administrators and military tacticians, and were forced to give up the lands Mathais had gained. They were also unable to control the nobles, and during this time serfdom became entrenched in Hungary although it was in the decline everywhere else in Europe. Mathais's successors also had to face the Turks, who advanced into the country and seized Belgrade. By the middle of the sixteenth century, the Turks had conquered central Hungary and created their own government. Despite that fact, the kingdom of Hungary was making its way out of the Middle Ages.

## The Russians

When we left the Russians, the kingdom of Kiev was in decline. By the thirteenth century, Russia had been overrun and conquered by the Mongols. Under Genghis Khan (1155–1227), the Mongols had conquered a good portion of Asia and the Middle East and were working their way into Europe through Russia and Hungary. They swept into regions with overwhelming numbers and mounted warriors, achieving the conquest of Russia in stages. By 1240, they had captured and destroyed the city of Kiev, and for the next 250 years, the Mongols ruled Russia.

To capture Russia, the Golden Horde, or Tartars as they were called, annihilated any resistance by using terror techniques. But once they conquered the country, they were relatively tolerant rulers, allowing the Russians to rule themselves as long as they paid an annual tribute in money and men to the Mongol army. But the story does not end there, as the Mongols conquered all the city-states of the principality except one, the city-state of Moscow.

Moscow remained free by cooperating with the invading Mongol armies. By 1350, their cooperation was paying huge dividends, and Moscow was the most powerful city-state in the region of Russia. Of course, the yoke of outside rule had to be thrown off eventually, and the Muscovite forces defeated the Mongols and claimed independence in 1380.

Gradually the principality of Moscow acquired more territory from the Mongols. It also freed other Russian city-states from Mongol rule, who then gratefully accepted the supremacy of Moscow. Finally, in 1480, Ivan III, also known as the Great, pushed the last of the Mongols from Russian territories.

**Notable Quote**

"[The czar] is on earth the sole emperor of the Christians, the leader of the Apostolic church which stands no longer in Rome or Constantinople, but in the blessed city of Moscow. She alone shines in the whole world brighter than the sun ....
Two Romes have fallen, but the third stands."
—Letter from Philotheus of Pskov to Czar Basil III

To acquire the name "the Great" as Ivan III did, there had to be some accomplishments, and in his case there were several. Ivan III was, of course, an Eastern Orthodox Christian, which still imparted a strong relationship with the Byzantine Empire regardless of its state or lack of state. (The Ottoman Turks conquered Constantinople in 1453.)

In 1472, Ivan III married Sophia, the niece of the last Byzantine Emperor, which made Russia, to some, an extension of the Roman imperial tradition. Ivan III and all subsequent rulers took the title czar, meaning "caesar," in reference to the Roman imperial rulers. If the Byzantine Empire was an extension of the old Roman Empire, then Russia was now, through Ivan III's marriage, also by extension becoming the third Rome. That mentality influenced the Russian state and its political philosophy until the early twentieth century, when a revolution toppled the czar.

# The End of Constantinople

Not everything was getting better for Europe in the late Middle Ages. The Byzantine Empire and its capital, Constantinople, had been a source of light that had shone since Roman antiquity, but that light was extinguished with the rise of the Ottoman Turks, who also for a time threatened to extinguish other lights in Europe.

The Ottomans emerged during the thirteenth century from the region in the northwest Anatolian peninsula. Under the Ottoman leader Osman, they created a sizeable empire in the fourteenth century, taking territory from the declining Seljuk Empire. Osman's leadership marked the beginning of the Ottoman dynasty; following his lead, Ottoman rulers took the title of *sultan*.

Ottoman ambitions quickly became even more militaristic. They mastered the use of gunpowder with muskets and cannons and soon dominated the territories of the Bosporus and Dardanelles and threatened the Byzantine Empire, which by that point was on its way out. This domination was solidified and expanded with the defeat of the Serbs at the Battle of Kosovo in 1389. By 1400, the Ottomans had conquered the region of Bulgaria and were ready for the big show: the siege and conquest of Constantinople.

The Ottoman ruler Mehmed II (1451–1481) initiated the attack on Constantinople. After several attempts in 1453, the Ottoman Turks conquered Constantinople and killed the Byzantine emperor in the battle for the city. The last remains of the Byzantine Empire were gone from the pages of history. Constantinople was then named Istanbul and became the capital of the new and expanding Ottoman Empire. And the Ottomans did not stop with Constantinople. From 1514 to 1517, the Sultan Selim I (1512–1520) led several successful campaigns into the regions of Mesopotamia, Egypt, and Arabia, leading to Turkish control of Jerusalem, Mecca, and Medina. Later, Selim I led Ottoman forces into North Africa, conquering much of the region. This led to Selim I being declared *caliph* and the new defender of Islam.

## def•i•ni•tion

A **sultan** is the military and political head of the Seljuk and Ottoman Turks. A **caliph** is a spiritual and temporal successor of Mohammad as leader of the Muslims.

With expansion into the Middle East and North Africa complete, Suleiman I (1520–1566) pushed into Europe, advancing up the Danube River and seizing the city of Belgrade. In 1526, Turkish forces defeated the Hungarians in the Battle of Mohacs. This allowed the Ottoman armies to conquer Hungary and expand into the borders of Austria. All hope appeared to be lost from a Christian perspective as the Islamic Ottoman Turks conquered Eastern Europe and moved in to put Vienna under siege. But at Vienna in 1529, Suleiman I and his armies were finally stopped. The siege failed with the help of a combined military effort of the Holy Roman Emperor and several German princes. At this point, Ottoman expansion northward into Europe ceased.

> **Notable Quote**
>
> "The soldiers fell on the citizens with anger and great wrath …. Now they killed so as to frighten all the city, and to terrorize and enslave all by the slaughter."
>
> —Greek observer of the fall of Constantinople

# Larger Lights

Beyond the developments in the Swiss Confederation, Poland, Hungary, and Russia, two larger nations, Spain and Portugal, were making some very big moves that helped lift Europe out of the Middle Ages into the modern age.

## Spain

When we left Spain, the three Christian kingdoms were busy taking back the Iberian peninsula from the Muslims. By the mid-fifteenth century, the Muslims were expelled, and the peninsula was divided among the three Christian kingdoms: Aragon in the northeast, Castile in the center, and Portugal bordering the Atlantic. In 1469, Ferdinand, king of Aragon, married Queen Isabella of Castile, uniting most of Spain. But the royal power was weak, so Ferdinand and Isabella began to centralize and consolidate authority.

In centralizing power, they allied themselves with the towns against the nobles of Spain by giving the towns charters that gave the townspeople rights. The monarchs also gave lesser nobles positions in the royal court and exempted them from some taxes, and destroyed the castles of nobles who did not fall into line. In addition, Ferdinand and Isabella seized large amounts of treasure and appointed officials they could trust to positions of responsibility. Finally, they took the property of the crusader orders that were not under their control and created a standing army. In all these actions, they seldom consulted the Cortés of the kingdoms.

Ferdinand and Isabella helped strengthen the economy by creating a uniform system of weights and measures and replacing the money with newly minted coins with their faces on them. They improved the roads and harbors, built bridges, and organized trade fairs that attracted merchants from all over Europe. In addition, they encouraged learning by exempting printers from taxes, creating a new university, and sponsoring translations of classical writings of antiquity into Spanish.

Queen Isabella also decided that to become a stronger nation, they must enforce religious as well as political unity. To do this, the monarchs became major allies of the church, avoiding the typical confrontation between church and state by merging their interests. They persuaded the pontiff to allow them to appoint bishops and abbots and introduced the Inquisition to Spain.

The Inquisition, established in the early thirteenth century, was a church court that suppressed heresies. People accused of heresy were guilty until proven innocent. They were not even allowed to question their accusers. Sometimes torture was involved in the confession process: most found guilty of heresy were burned at the stake. Using the church to increase religious unity also meant that Ferdinand and Isabella were able to increase royal power. Most were scared of the Inquisition and quickly professed their loyalty to the church and the crown. The Inquisition especially targeted two groups: Muslims and Jews. Both groups were used to tolerant rulers in Spain, but things had changed. Christians often assaulted them and forced some to convert. Even then the Inquisition sometimes tried converted Muslims and Jews for suspicion of clinging to their former religions.

In 1492, Spanish Jews were given a choice: convert to Christianity or leave the country and their property behind. As a result, tens of thousands of Spanish Jews went into exile. These Jews, called *Sephardim*, went to North Africa and the Middle East to enjoy religious toleration under the Ottoman Turks. Later in 1502, the Islamic population of Spain was given no choice; they had to accept Christian baptism. Historians think that over 100,000 Muslims and Jews left Spain as the result of the Inquisition and persecution.

# Portugal

The monarchs of Portugal struggled to centralize power and maintain independence from Castile. Portugal was able to keep that independence under the leadership of John I, who established the Aviz dynasty and set Portugal on a course of expansion that would make it a premier power of Europe during the late Middle Ages and into early modern Europe.

In 1386, King John I signed the Treaty of Windsor with England, helping to gather support against the Spanish threat. John also continued to push against the Moors, taking territory in North Africa. His youngest son, Henry (1394–1460), also known as Prince Henry the Navigator, followed his father's example. Henry was driven by both religious and economic motives to look outside the country's borders. He crusaded against Islam by taking Arab towns along the coast of North Africa where he hoped to create a Christian kingdom. Because of Portugal's lack of resources, his policy of overseas expansion seemed an excellent idea.

> **Illuminations**
>
> The Treaty of Windsor, signed in 1386 between England and Portugal, is still in effect to this day. That makes the political alliance between England and Portugal the oldest in Europe.

# Exploration and the End of the Middle Ages

With the centralizing of power in Spain and Portugal, both nations were in a position to increase commerce and trade with the East. But the Italian city-states had that market pretty well cornered. So Portugal and then Spain began to look for other ways to get to the goods of the East.

Portugal was the first nation to make attempts at exploration, in 1420, by probing the western coast of Africa with several expeditions. Why did Portugal do this and not some other nation of Europe? The debate will continue about the specific cultural, social, and geographic reasons for Portugal's taking the plunge, but one individual factor was Prince Henry the Navigator, who took a strong interest in exploration and sponsored the expeditions.

As the expeditions continued, new sources of gold were discovered in the region in Africa justifiably called the Gold Coast. In 1488, Bartholomeu Dias rounded the Cape of Good Hope. Vasco da Gama went even farther, rounding the cape and sailing to India before returning to Portugal with a cargo hold filled with spices. For his labors, Vasco da Gama made over 1,000 percent in profits, making him a rich man and generating a lot of interest with Portuguese traders in the spice trade.

Rather than compete with Portuguese interests in the east, Spain decided to explore westward. The voyages of Christopher Columbus were the beginning of this exploration. In 1492, Columbus, the Italian sailing for Isabella and Ferdinand, sailed the ocean blue, specifically westward over the Atlantic Ocean in hopes of finding of a direct route to Asia. By October 1492, Columbus reached his destination—well, not quite. He thought he had reached Asia and proceeded to call the inhabitants Indians, but in reality Columbus had reached the Caribbean Islands off of North America. After three more voyages in which he discovered all the major islands of the Caribbean and Honduras, he still believed he had reached Asia, but it was America he was exploring.

The Catholic Church saw a possible conflict on the horizon between two Catholic nations, Portugal and Spain, who from all appearances had conflicting claims of territory in Asia. So in 1494, with the help of the church, the two nations signed the Treaty of Tordesillas in hopes of averting a war. This treaty created an imaginary line north and south through the Atlantic Ocean and South America. The unexplored territories east of the line belonged to Portugal, while the unexplored territories west of the line belonged to Spain. Later, this treaty proved much more advantageous to Spain because they acquired the majority of the rights to America, while Portugal only acquired rights to the trade route around Africa. Spain was set up to be the next leading European trading empire.

## Racing Across the Americas

Christopher Columbus's legacy has been questioned as of this age, but during his time, Columbus was an inspiration. Many explorers followed in his wake, representing several different nations of Europe. John Cabot, who represented England, explored the area of New England during the early sixteenth century. The Portuguese captain Pedro Cabral led an expedition to explore parts of South America around the same time. And finally, Amerigo Vespucci, who used America in his letters to describe the voyages, explored even more of South America for Spanish interests.

After these and other expeditions were made, explorers reached one general conclusion: the land they were exploring was not Asia but a New World that Europeans had not seen before.

## The Spanish Empire

This New World that explorers were discovering belonged, at least according to the Treaty of Tordesillas, to Spain. So Spain now had an instant empire. For Europeans in general, an empire was something to control and exploit for the benefit of the mother country. So Spain sent men called *conquistadors* to subdue or conquer the natives of their empire, and these men brought with them weapons of success that the native Americans had not seen: muskets, horses, and epidemic diseases.

> **Notable Quote** _____
>
> "They are credulous and aware that there is a god in heaven and convinced that
> we come from there. And they repeat very quickly any prayer we tell them and
> make the sign of the cross. So your Highness should resolve to make them Christians."
> —Christopher Columbus in letter to Queen Isabella and King Ferdinand in 1492

## The Impact of Exploration

These explorations brought several new benefits to Spain, Portugal, and the other
European nations. Gold and silver, found in the New World, flowed to Spain, making
it one of the richest and most powerful nations of Europe. Portugal benefited from its
explorations as it became the chief entry point of spices into Europe, displacing the
Venetians from that rich and important role. All of Europe acquired new agricultural
products—potatoes, corn, tobacco, and coffee—which became staple and luxury crops
for Europeans in the modern period. This trading exchange is sometimes referred to
as the *Columbia Exchange*. Finally a new competition developed among the sixteenth-
century European nation-states, a competition for trade.

## def•i•ni•tion _____

The **Columbia Exchange** was an exchange of goods, plants, animals, and also
diseases that happened after Columbus's initial discovery between Europe and the
Americas. The agricultural production of staples including potatoes and corn were
introduced to Europe, while wheat production was initiated in the Americas. Animals
such as the horse, sheep, goats, and cattle were brought to the Americas, while Europe
received the turkey and squirrel. Diseases were also included, with the Europeans
spreading smallpox, typhus, influenza, and measles among the Native Americans.

In the end, what was the global impact of European exploration? First and foremost,
earlier interregional connections were solidified to create a truly global economy.
With the emergence of the interregional connections, regional trade networks were
disrupted and declined in importance. This development allowed for a shift in trade
dominance, with Europe being the center of the global market. Naturally, with the
shift in trade was a shift in political power, and the European nations emerged to
become *the* global political powers for the next 400 years.

# Last Remarks

With the early Renaissance in Italy, the development of the nation-states of Europe, and the beginning of European exploration, the Middle Ages drew to a close by 1500, which marked the start of modern European history.

Things had changed a great deal since the fall of Rome in 476 when the Middle Ages began. Germanic tribes formed kingdoms that eventually became nations. Those nations had ups and downs but, by 1500, commerce was thriving across Europe, cities were growing, and population was booming. More people were getting educated in schools and universities. Books were being published cheaply and quickly by the new printing presses of Europe.

The power of the church was weakened considerably, having once ruled an international Christendom but now only a small kingdom around Rome. England, France, Spain, Russia, Hungary, Portugal, and the Swiss Confederation had stable, centralized governments that were developing into nationhood. European vessels had explored the Americas, Africa, and the Indian subcontinent.

So the people of Europe had done more than survive the downs of the late Middle Ages; they had survived and built a Europe that by 1500 was encountering a new world. Later they would come to dominate that new world and export Western civilization to it.

Many have viewed this time as a dark period, but, after this close look at the Middle Ages, I hope you see it wasn't that dark at all. In fact, there are some uncomfortable similarities between the so-called Dark Ages and the modern world, including a gap between the rich and the poor, violent acts done in the name of God, gangs of barbarians threatening the peace, poverty and displacement created by war, arguments over the authority of church and state, people looking for riches in the wrong places, and diseases without cures. With realization that the modern world is not as well off as first thought, I hope you might be spurred to action to end some of its problems.

In addition, I hope you see that the Middle Ages was an important part of the slow and steady progression of Western civilization through time. It did have some bad moments, but it continued to move forward nonetheless. The Western civilization that we enjoy now is built on the firm foundations of the Middle Ages. There would be no Copernicus without Occam, no Shakespeare without Petrarch, no Leonardo without Giotto, and no Luther without Hus. Yes, we do have a strong sense of being modern, but we still depend on many medieval ways and habits of thought. That is never more evident than during big events like the marriage of Princess Diana or the death of Pope John Paul II, when the ceremony triggers the familiar thing that we can't place but we don't question. Have no doubt; the Middle Ages are still with us today.

## The Least You Need to Know

♦ The Swiss Confederation, Hungary, Russia, and Poland centralized power as nation-states with the help of strong monarchs.

♦ The Ottoman Turks ended the thousand-year reign of the Byzantine Empire in 1453 when they took the capital of Constantinople.

♦ Spain and Portugal also sought to centralize power as nation-states with the help of strong monarchs and, in Spain's case, the church.

♦ Portugal was the first European nation to begin exploration beyond Europe, with Spain following close behind.

♦ European exploration established Europe as the dominant world power for the next 400 years.

♦ The Middle Ages ended in 1500 but still influence the twenty-first century.

# Glossary

This is a selective list of words you might run into when you're exploring the Middle Ages. It's not comprehensive by any means, but is a good beginning to understanding the jargon of the Middle Ages.

**abbey**   A monastic community governed by an abbot or abbess.

**Albigensianism**   Another word for the heresy of Catharism in the region of southern France.

**anti-clericalism**   Opposition to the clergy of the church.

**apprentice**   A young man training in a craft or trade.

**Arians**   Early Christian heretics who conceived of the Trinity as three separate and unequal divine beings.

**artisan**   A craftsperson who skillfully makes products such as weapons and jewelry.

**bailiff**   The chief administrative officer of a manor.

**barbarian**   A term originating from Greece for those who did not speak Greek.

**bishop**   The chief priest of a district or diocese.

**burgess**   A citizen of a town or city.

**caliph**   A spiritual and temporal successor of Muhammad as leader of the Muslims.

**canon law** The law of the church.

**capitulary** Laws and regulations enacted by Charlemagne that were to be observed throughout the Carolingian Empire.

**cardinal** A church position that entitled its holder to participate in papal elections.

**cathedral** The principle church of a bishop, usually located in the city that was the center of his district or diocese.

**cathedral schools** Schools attached to cathedrals.

**catholic** A term that means "universal."

**chansons de geste** A vernacular literature in the High Middle Ages that consisted of heroic epics focusing on the deeds of warriors.

**charter** A document that records a gift, grant, sale, or other transaction.

**Christendom** A Christian realm or *imperium Christianum*.

**church** A place of worship.

**clergy** Church leaders.

*comitatus* A barbarian war band led by a war chief to whom the men owed allegiance.

**common law** A system of law that developed in England based on court decisions and customs.

**compurgation** Proof of innocence established through oath swearing.

**conciliar movement** A medieval movement to make councils the supreme authority of the church.

**cortés** Representative assemblies of the kingdoms of the Iberian peninsula.

**council** A meeting of church officials.

**courtly love** A term coined to describe romantic love between women and men in the Middle Ages.

**crusader states** The four kingdoms established after the successful First Crusade.

*curia* Latin for court, this term was used for the highest courts.

*Curia Regis* The king's high court or council in England.

**custom** A practice that has legal force because of a long tradition.

**dauphin**   The title given to the heir to the French throne.

**deacon**   A rank just below a priest in the church clerical hierarchy.

**demesne**   The part of a manor under the direct control of the lord and worked by the serfs.

**diet**   An assembly in the German states.

**diocese**   The area under the jurisdiction of church bishop.

**double monastery**   Monasteries that housed both women and men.

**dualism**   The belief that the universe is composed of two opposing forces, good and evil.

**ecclesiastical**   Related to church structure.

**Estates General**   The representative assembly of France.

**Eucharist**   The church sacrament that commemorates the Last Supper of Jesus.

**excommunication**   Removal from communion with the church.

**fable**   A genre of literature, allegories in which characters were presented as animals.

**fallow**   Uncultivated land.

**family church**   A church or monastery founded by a family and treated as family property.

**feudalism**   Political and social system that developed during the Middle Ages.

**fief**   A grant of land made to a vassal.

**flying buttress**   A buttress that stands apart from the roof it supports and connects to the main supporting wall by arches.

**free peasant**   As distinct from a serf or slave, a peasant who could move, work, marry, and make his or her own life decisions.

**friar**   A member of the Dominican or Franciscan orders.

**gloss**   A comment on a text written in its margins.

**Gothic**   An architectural style developed during the High Middle Ages.

**guild**   A business association connected with a particular trade or craft.

**hagiography**   The writing about a saint's life.

**heretic**   A person who diverges from established belief of his or her religion.

**Holy Roman Empire**   Emperors in northern Italy and Germany after the divide of the Carolingian Empire.

**humanism**   An intellectual movement based on the study of the humanities including grammar, rhetoric, poetry, moral philosophy, and history.

**icon**   An image of a saint or divine figure.

**indulgence**   A release from all or part of punishment for sin by the Catholic Church.

**infidel**   A nonbeliever.

**inquisitor**   A church official given the power by the church to punish heretics.

**interdict**   A decree by the pope that stopped priests from giving the sacraments of the church to the people of a region or nation.

**itinerant judge**   A judge who moved through the countryside carrying the power of the king's justice.

**journeyman**   A young man who finished an apprenticeship but did not own a shop as an independent master.

**knight**   A man trained and armed to fight on horseback.

**laity**   Church members.

**lay investiture**   The practice by which secular rulers both chose nominees to church offices and gave them the symbols of their office.

**legate**   An ambassador of the church who had the power to act on the pope's behalf.

**lord**   A man who had power over others, such as a manorial lord, a feudal lord, or a king or prince.

**magnate**   A wealthy and influential aristocrat.

**manorialism**   The economic arrangement in which serfs supported the landowning lord of a manor.

**master**   A male head of a household or of a guild shop.

**military order**   An order that developed during the Crusades in which the skills of soldiering were mixed with monastic vows.

***missi dominici***   Envoys used by Charlemagne to enforce his laws in the Carolingian Empire.

**monastic order**   A collection of monastic houses linked by a common monastic rule or formal structures of administration and governance.

**monastic rules**   A guide for monastic living.

**monastic school**   A school sponsored by a monastery.

**mystery play**   A kind of drama mounted by the church and later guilds that recounted stories from the Bible.

**mystery religions**   Ancient religions and cults that promise a mystical revelation.

**mysticism**   Direct contact between humanity and divinity.

**Neoplatonism**   An elaboration of Plato's theory of forms that taught that one infinite and unknowable God can only be approached through mystical experience.

**oblation**   A gift.

**ordeal**   A form of trial derived from barbarian law that relied on the divine to determine guilt.

**orthodox**   Correct opinion as judged by a religious authority.

**pagan**   An irreligious person.

**papacy**   The office of the pope.

**papal bull**   A document ratified by the papal seal.

*papal curia*   The court and bureaucracy of the pope.

**parish**   The smallest geographical unit in the church; the basic unit of public worship.

**Parlement**   A judicial body that administered royal justice in France.

**Parliament**   A representative assembly in England composed of lords and representatives from the shire knights and burgesses.

**pontificate**   The office of the pope or a time period of the rule of a pope.

**pope**   The bishop of Rome and leader of the Roman Catholic Church.

**prelate**   A high-ranking church officer.

**primogeniture**   Preference of inheritance to the first-born son.

**prince**   The son of a king or the chief ruler of a region.

**priory**   A monastic community governed by a prior or prioress.

*quadrivium*   The study of mathematics, music, astronomy, and geometry.

**rationalism**   A system of thought based on the belief that reason is the source of knowledge.

**regular clergy**   Members of a monastic order: monks or nuns.

**relic**   Bones or other objects connected to the saints.

**romance**   A literary genre of heroic stories in historical or legendary ages.

**Romanesque**   An architectural style of the Middle Ages characterized by rounded arches and stone vault roofs supported by thick walls and columns.

**sacrament**   Christian rites.

**saint**   A holy person.

**schism**   A religious division.

**scholasticism**   A medieval philosophical and theological system that sought to reconcile faith and reason.

**scriptorium**   The place where monks and nuns copied manuscripts.

**secular**   Worldly, nonreligious.

**secular clergy**   Clergy that serve the pastoral needs of the laity: priests, bishops, and archbishops.

**see**   The diocese of a bishop.

**serf**   A peasant bound to the land of a lord.

**sheriff**   An English officer who served as a link between the county and the royal administration.

**simony**   The sale and purchase of church offices.

**slave**   A person wholly at the disposal of his owner.

**sovereignty**   A governmental authority not limited by competing jurisdictions.

**steward**   A manorial officer.

**strip**   A long and narrow area of land within an open field.

**synod**   A meeting of church officers from one region or realm.

**three-field system**   An agricultural system in which peasants rotated crops between three fields.

**tithe**   The obligation of Christians to offer one tenth of all produce and income to the church.

**toll**   A charge to use a road or bridge.

*trivium*   The study of grammar, rhetoric, and logic.

**urban charter**   A document that granted a town or city rights of self-government.

**usury**   Loaning money at interest.

**vassal**   A man who served a lord in a military capacity.

**vernacular language**   The native spoken language of a region or country.

**Vulgate Bible**   A Latin version of the Bible translated by St. Jerome (c. 340–420).

**wergeld**   Compensation paid for offenses to the victim or family of the victim.

# Timeline of the Middle Ages

The purpose of this timeline is to help the reader keep the many historically relevant events of late antiquity and the Middle Ages in order.

324–337: Constantine reigns as emperor of the Roman Empire

325: The Council of Nicaea convenes to solidify Christian doctrine

330: The beginning of Constantinople, capital of the Eastern Roman Empire

341–420: The life of Saint Jerome, theologian and creator of the Latin Vulgate Bible

354–430: The life of Saint Augustine, theologian and author of the *City of God*

400s: The Angles, Saxons, and Jutes migrate to Britain

406: The Vandals cross the Roman borders into Gaul

410: King Alaric and the Visigoths sack Rome

429: The Vandals migrate into North Africa

431: The Franks cross the Roman borders into Gaul

452: Attila leads the Huns into Italy

476: The last Roman emperor is deposed; the official date for the end of the Roman Empire

568: The Lombards invade the Italian peninsula

570–632: The life of Muhammad, prophet of Islam

587: The Visigoths migrate into the Iberian peninsula and convert to Catholic Christianity

625: The death of East Anglian King Raewald buried at Sutton Hoo

711–719: The Muslims conquer the Iberian peninsula

714–741: The rule of Charles Martel as mayor of the palace of the Frankish Merovingian kings

732: Charles Martel and Frankish forces defeat the Muslims at the Battle of Tours

800: The Frankish king Charlemagne crowned Holy Roman Emperor by Pope

871–899: The rule of Alfred the Great as king of Angle Land (England)

987–996: The rule of Hugh Capet as king of France; the beginning of the Capetian dynasty

1054: The Schism of the Catholic and Orthodox Churches

1066: William the Conqueror leads Norman invasion of England; the beginning of the Anglo-Norman line of kings in England

1073: The reign of Pope Gregory VII over the Catholic Church

1077: Holy Roman Emperor Henry IV does penance at Canossa for pope over investiture controversy

1095–1099: The First Crusade

1170: The murder of Thomas Becket by knights of King Henry II

1189–1199: The rule of King Richard the Lionhearted of England

1189–1192: The Third Crusade

1192–1194: King Richard the Lionhearted taken captive upon returning from the Third Crusade

1199: The end of the ill-fated romance between Abelard and Heloise

1202–1204: The Fourth Crusade

1204: The sack of Constantinople by crusading knights

1212: The ill-fated Children's Crusade

1215: King John signs the Magna Carta, granting rights to the English nobility

1215: The Fourth Lateran Council convenes

1217–1221: The Fifth Crusade

1225–1274: The life of Saint Thomas Aquinas, greatest of medieval scholastics

1226–1270: The rule of King Louis IX of France

1228–1229: The Sixth Crusade

1245–1254: The Seventh Crusade

1265: Simon de Montfort's Parliament convenes in England

1265–1321: The life of Dante Alighieri, author of the *Divine Comedy*

1278: The Eighth Crusade

1294–1303: The reign of Pope Boniface VIII over the Catholic Church

1295: The Model Parliament convenes in England

1302: Pope Boniface VIII issues the papal bull *Unam Sanctum*

1304–1374: The life of Petrarch, author who coined term "Dark Ages"

1309–1377: The Babylonian Captivity in the Catholic Church

1315–1322: The Great Famine in Europe

1320s: Gunpowder first used in warfare

1337: The start of the Hundred Years' War between France and England

1346: English forces defeat the French at the Battle of Crécy

1347–1349: The scourge of the Black Death

1348: The Order of the Garter created in England

1356: English forces defeat the French at the Battle of Poitiers and also capture King John of France

1358: Jacquerie revolt in France

1378–1415: The Great Schism in the Catholic Church

1378: Ciompi Revolt in Florence, Italy

1381: Peasants' Revolt breaks out in England

1382: John Wycliffe's Bible is published in English

1413–1422: The rule of King Henry V of England

1415: English forces defeat the French at the Battle of Agincourt

1415: The Council of Constance executes John Hus for heresy

1417: The Council of Constance ends the Great Schism

1429: The dauphin is crowned King Charles VII of France

1431: Joan of Arc is burned at the stake as a heretic

1453: The English lose all territory in France save Calais

1453: Constantinople falls to the Turks; the end of the Byzantine Empire

1455–1485: The dynastic War of the Roses in England between the noble houses of York and Lancaster

1455: The Gutenburg Bible is published

1461–1483: The rule of King Louis XI of France

1469: Marriage of King Ferdinand and Queen Isabella unites kingdoms of Aragon and Castile in Iberian peninsula

1485: Henry VII becomes king of England; the start of the Tudor dynasty

1492: Christopher Columbus, sponsored by Spain, discovers the Americas

1492: The conquest of Granada by Spanish forces

1498: Vasco da Gama, sponsored by Portugal, sails to the Indian subcontinent

# Appendix C

# Further Resources

## General Works

Backman, Clifford R. *The Worlds of Medieval Europe.*

Bennett, Judith and C. Warren Hollister. *Medieval Europe: A Short History.*

Cantor, Norman. *The Civilization of the Middle Ages.*

———. *Inventing the Middle Ages.*

Dawson, Christopher. *Medieval Essays.*

———. *Religion and the Rise of Western Culture.*

Evans, G.R., ed. *Fifty Key Medieval Thinkers.*

Frankforter, A. Daniel. *The Medieval Millennium: An Introduction.*

Loyn, H.R., ed. *The Middle Ages: A Concise Encyclopædia.*

Peters, Edward. *Europe and the Middle Ages.*

Southern, R.W. *The Making of the Middle Ages.*

# Late Antiquity and Early Medieval Europe

Angold, Michael. *Byzantium: The Bridge from Antiquity to the Middle Ages.*

Barnes, T.D. *The New Empire of Diocletian and Constantine.*

Bloch, Marc. *Feudal Society.*

Brown, Peter. *Augustine of Hippo: A Biography.*

———. *The Rise of Western Christendom.*

Campbell, James, ed. *The Anglo-Saxons.*

Collins, Roger. *Charlemagne.*

———. *Early Medieval Europe, 300–1000.*

Daniel, Norman. *The Arabs and Medieval Europe.*

Enright, Michael. *Lady with a Mead Cup.*

———. *The Sutton Hoo Sceptre and the Roots of Celtic Kingship Theory.*

Fletcher, Richard. *The Barbarian Conversion: From Paganism to Christianity.*

———. *The Cross and the Crescent.*

Geary, Patrick. *Before France and Germany.*

Green, D.H. *Language and History in the Early Germanic World.*

Herrin, Judith. *The Formation of Christendom.*

Holum, Kenneth. *Theodosian Empresses: Women and Imperial Dominion in Late Antiquity.*

Hourani, Albert H. *A History of the Arab Peoples.*

MacMullen, Ramsay. *Christianizing the Roman Empire, A.D. 100–400.*

Mayr-Harting, Henry. *The Coming of Christianity to Anglo-Saxon England.*

McKitterick, Rosamond, ed. *The Uses of Literacy in Early Medieval Europe.*

Nees, Lawrence. *Early Medieval Art.*

Nelson, Janet. *The Frankish World.*

Noble, Thomas F.X. *The Republic of St. Peter: The Birth of the Papal State 680–825.*

Randsborg, Klars. *The First Millennium A.D. in Europe and the Mediterranean: An Archaeological Essay.*

Reuter, Timothy. *Germany in the Early Middle Ages.*

Stark, Rodney. *Cities of God.*

———. *The Rise of Christianity.*

Wilken, Robert. *The Christians as the Romans Saw Them.*

# The High Middle Ages

Baldwin, John. *The Scholastic Culture of the Middle Ages, 100–1300.*

Barlow, Frank. *Thomas Becket.*

Bouchard, Constance Brittain. *Strong of Body, Brave and Noble: Chivalry and Society in Medieval France.*

Clanchy, M.T. *Abelard: A Medieval Life.*

Duby, George. *France in the Middle Ages, 987–1460.*

Grant, Edward. *The Foundations of Modern Science in the Middle Ages.*

Holt, James C. *Magna Carta.*

Le Goff, Jacques. *Intellectuals in the Middle Ages.*

Pounds, N.J.G. *An Economic History of Medieval Europe.*

Ridder-Symoens, Hilde de, ed. *Universities in the Middle Ages.*

Riley-Smith, Johnathan, ed. *The Oxford Illustrated History of the Crusades.*

Runciman, Steven. *A History of the Crusades.*

Schimmelpfennig, Bernard. *The Papacy.*

Shinners, John, ed. *Medieval Popular Religion, 1000–1500.*

# The Late Middle Ages

Black, Anthony. *Political Thought in Europe, 1250–1450.*

Bloch, Marc. *The Royal Touch.*

Burns, J.H. *Lordship, Kingship, and Empire: The Idea of Monarchy 1400–1525.*

Curry, Anne. *The Hundred Years' War.*

Hay, Denys. *Europe in the Fourteenth and Fifteenth Centuries.*

Jordan, William. *The Great Famine: Northern Europe in the Early Fourteenth Century.*

Marenbon, John. *Later Medieval Philosophy.*

Nicholas, David. *The Transformation of Europe, 1300–1600.*

Pernoud, Régine. *Joan of Arc: By Herself and Her Witnesses.*

Phillips, J.R.S. *The Medieval Expansion of Europe.*

Weir, Alison. *Lancaster and York.*

Ziegler, Phillip. *The Black Death.*

# The Middle Ages in the Movies

The following movies depict the Middle Ages. This list is not exhaustive, to say the least, but it does represent some of the more interesting films about the Middle Ages. Once you have a good background of the Middle Ages, watch at your own risk!

*The Abyss* (1988), Director: Andre Delvaux

*The Adventures of Marco Polo* (1938), Director: Archie Mayo

*The Adventures of Robin Hood* (1938), Director: Michael Curtiz

*The Advocate* (1993), Director: Lesley Magahey

*The Agony and the Ecstasy* (1965), Director: Carol Reed

*Alexander Nevsky* (1937), Director: Sergei Eisenstein

*Alfred the Great* (1969), Director: Clive Donner

*The Anchoress* (1993), Director: Chris Newby

*Andrei Rublev* (1969), Director: Andrei Tarkovsky

*Arabian Nights* (2000), Director: Steve Barron

*The Bandit of Sherwood Forest* (1946), Director: George Sherman and Henry Levin

*Becket* (1964), Director: Peter Glenville

*The Black Arrow* (1948), Director: Gordon Douglas

*The Black Cauldron* (1985), Director: Ted Berman and Richard Rich

*The Black Shield of Falworth* (1954), Director: Rudoph Mate

*Braveheart* (1995), Director: Mel Gibson

*Brother Sun, Sister Moon* (1973), Director: Franco Zeffirelli

*Cadfael* (1994), Director: Graham Theakston

*The Court Jester* (1956), Director: Melvin Frank and Norman Panama

*The Crusades* (1935), Director: Cecil B. DeMille

*Dangerous Beauty* (1998), Director: Marshall Herskovitz

*Diane* (1956), Director: David Miller

*Doctor Faustus* (1967), Director: Richard Burton and Nevill Coghill

*Don Quixote* (2000), Director: Peter Yates

*Dragonheart* (1996), Director: Rob Cohen

*Dragonslayer* (1981), Director: Matthew Robbins

*Edward II* (1991), Director: Derek Jarman

*El Cid* (1961), Director: Anthony Mann

*Erik the Viking* (1989), Director: Terry Jones

*Excalibur* (1981), Director: John Boorman

*First Knight* (1995), Director: Jerry Zucker

*The Flame and the Arrow* (1950), Director: Jacques Tourneur

*Flesh and Blood* (1985), Director: Paul Verhoeven

*The Four Diamonds* (1995), Director: Peter Werner

*Galileo* (1975), Director: Joseph Losey

*Galgameth* (1996), Director: Sean McNamara

*Hamlet* (US, 1990), Director: Franco Zeffirelli

*Henry V* (1989), Director: Kenneth Branagh

*Hildegard* (1994), Director: James Runcie

*If I Were King* (1938), Director: Frank Lloyd

*Ivanhoe* (1952), Director: Richard Thorpe

*Jabberwocky* (1977), Director: Terry Gilliam

*Joan of Arc* (1948), Director: Victor Fleming

*A Kid in King Arthur's Court* (1995), Director: Michael Gottlieb

*King Arthur* (2004), Director: Antoine Fuqua

*Kingdom of Heaven (2005)*, Director: Ridley Scott

*King Lear* (1971), Director: Peter Brook

*King Richard and the Crusaders* (1954), Director: David Butler

*A Knight's Tale* (2001), Director: Brian Helgeland

*Knights of the Round Table* (1953), Director: Richard Thorpe

*Lady Godiva* (1955), Director: Arthur Lubin

*Ladyhawke* (US, 1985). Director: Clive Donner

*Lion in Winter* (1968), Director: Anthony Harvey

*Lionheart* (1987), Director: Franklin Schaffner

*The Long Ships* (1964), Director: Jack Cardiff

*Lord of the Rings: The Fellowship of the Ring* (2001), Director: Peter Jackson

*Lord of the Rings: The Two Towers* (2002), Director: Peter Jackson

*Lord of the Rings: The Return of the King* (2003), Director: Peter Jackson

*Macbeth* (1971), Director: Roman Polanski

*Macbeth* (1948), Director: Orson Welles

*Mary of Scotland* (1936), Director: John Ford

*The Masque of the Red Death* (1964), Director: Roger Corman

*Men of Sherwood Forest* (1954), Director: Val Guest

*Messenger: The Story of Joan of Arc* (1999), Director: Luc Besson

*Monty Python and the Holy Grail* (1975), Director: Terry Gilliam

*The Name of the Rose* (1986), Director: Jean-Jacques Annaud

*The Navigator* (1988), Director: Vincent Ward

*The Norseman* (1978), Director: Charles B. Pierce

*Othello* (1995), Director: Oliver Parker

*The Passion of Joan of Arc* (1928), Director: Carl Theodor Dreyer

*The Prince and the Pauper* (1962), Director: Don Chaffey

*Prince of Thieves* (1948), Director: Howard Bretherton

*The Princess Bride* (1987), Director: Rob Reiner

*Prince Valiant* (1954), Director: Henry Hathaway

*The Private Life of Henry VIII* (1933), Director: Alexander Korda

*The Private Lives of Elizabeth and Essex* (1939), Director: Michael Curtiz

*Quest for Camelot* (1998), Director: Frederik Du Chau

*The Return of Martin Guerre* (1982), Director: Daniel Vigne

*Richard III* (1995), Director: Richard Loncraine

*Robin and Marian* (1976), Director: Richard Lester

*Robin Hood: Men in Tights* (1993), Director: Mel Brooks

*Robin Hood: Prince of Thieves* (1991), Director: Kevin Reynolds

*Saint Joan* (1957), Director: Otto Preminger

*The Seventh Seal* (1957), Director: Ingmar Bergman

*Stealing Heaven* (1988), Director: Clive Donner

*The Story of Robin Hood and His Merrie Men* (1952), Director: Ken Annakin

*The Sword and the Rose* (1953), Director: Ken Annakin

*The Sword in the Stone* (1963), Director: Wolfgang Reitherman

*Sword of Lancelot* (1963), Director: Cornell Wilde

*Sword of Sherwood Forest* (1961), Director: Terence Fisher

*The Sword of the Valiant* (1983), Director: Stephen Weeks

*The 13th Warrior* (1999), Director: John McTiernan

*Timeline* (2003), Director: Richard Donner

*Titus* (1999), Director: Julie Taymor

*The Trial of Joan of Arc* (1962), Director: Robert Bresson

*Tristan and Isolde* (US, 2006), Director: Kevin Reynolds

*The Vikings* (1958), Director: Richard Fleischer

*The Virgin Spring* (1960), Director: Ingmar Bergman

*A Walk with Love and Death* (1969), Director: John Huston

*The War Lord* (1965), Director: Franklin Schaffner

*Willow* (1988), Director: Ron Howard

# Index